Going Multiplayer

A Complete Guide: From Design to Post-release

Paolo Abela

Apress®

Going Multiplayer: A Complete Guide: From Design to Post-release

Paolo Abela
Calle Pelayo, Las Palmas, Spain

ISBN-13 (pbk): 979-8-8688-2030-4   ISBN-13 (electronic): 979-8-8688-2031-1
https://doi.org/10.1007/979-8-8688-2031-1

Copyright © 2025 by Paolo Abela

This work is subject to copyright. All rights are reserved by the Publisher, whether the whole or part of the material is concerned, specifically the rights of translation, reprinting, reuse of illustrations, recitation, broadcasting, reproduction on microfilms or in any other physical way, and transmission or information storage and retrieval, electronic adaptation, computer software, or by similar or dissimilar methodology now known or hereafter developed.

Trademarked names, logos, and images may appear in this book. Rather than use a trademark symbol with every occurrence of a trademarked name, logo, or image we use the names, logos, and images only in an editorial fashion and to the benefit of the trademark owner, with no intention of infringement of the trademark.

The use in this publication of trade names, trademarks, service marks, and similar terms, even if they are not identified as such, is not to be taken as an expression of opinion as to whether or not they are subject to proprietary rights.

While the advice and information in this book are believed to be true and accurate at the date of publication, neither the authors nor the editors nor the publisher can accept any legal responsibility for any errors or omissions that may be made. The publisher makes no warranty, express or implied, with respect to the material contained herein.

Managing Director, Apress Media LLC: Welmoed Spahr
Acquisitions Editor: Spandana Chatterjee
Editorial Assistant: Gryffin Winkler

Cover designed by eStudioCalamar

Cover image designed by Freepik (www.freepik.com)

Distributed to the book trade worldwide by Springer Science+Business Media New York, 1 New York Plaza, New York, NY 10004. Phone 1-800-SPRINGER, fax (201) 348-4505, e-mail orders-ny@springer-sbm.com, or visit www.springeronline.com. Apress Media, LLC is a Delaware LLC and the sole member (owner) is Springer Science + Business Media Finance Inc (SSBM Finance Inc). SSBM Finance Inc is a **Delaware** corporation.

For information on translations, please e-mail booktranslations@springernature.com; for reprint, paperback, or audio rights, please e-mail bookpermissions@springernature.com.

Apress titles may be purchased in bulk for academic, corporate, or promotional use. eBook versions and licenses are also available for most titles. For more information, reference our Print and eBook Bulk Sales web page at http://www.apress.com/bulk-sales.

Any source code or other supplementary material referenced by the author in this book is available to readers on GitHub. For more detailed information, please visit https://www.apress.com/gp/services/source-code.

If disposing of this product, please recycle the paper

To my grandparents, Vito and Rosa, who supported me when nobody else would.

To my mum, Concetta, for never giving up.

To my father, Gaetano, for introducing me to the world of computers.

To my teachers Anna Papadia and Nicola Luigi Guglielmo Di Nanna, for leading me to this path.

And to Margherita Roncone, whose Assassin's Spaghetti and moral support fueled the Saturdays spent writing this book.

Table of Contents

About the Author xi

About the Technical Reviewer xiii

Acknowledgments xv

Preface xvii

Chapter 1: Why Is It So Hard to Make a Multiplayer Game? 1
   Single-Player vs. Multiplayer Games 1
   Limitations of a Multiplayer Game 2
      Fast-Paced Player Movement 2
      Physics-Based Interactions 3
      Time Manipulation 3
   Differences in Architecture 4
      The "Core Game Loop" 4
      The "Metagame" 6
   The Lifecycle of Games 9
      Lifecycle of a Single-Player Fame 10
      Lifecycle of a Multiplayer Game 11
   Playtesting 12
      Playtesting a Single-Player Game 12
      Playtesting a Multiplayer Game 13
   Conclusion 14

Chapter 2: How the Internet Works 15
   What Is Communication? 15
   Communication Frameworks 18
      The OSI Model 18

TABLE OF CONTENTS

  The TCP/IP Model 20
 Network Addresses 22
  What Is an IP Address? 22
  Public and Private IP Addresses 24
  Network Address Translation (NAT) 25
  Reserved IP Addresses 26
 Routing and Its Consequences 26
  Delivery Schemes 27
 Network Ports 28
  Port Numbers 28
 Transport Protocols 30
  Transmission Control Protocol 30
  User Datagram Protocol 33
 Network Architectures 34
  What Is a Server? 35
  What Is a Client? 35
  Client–Server Architecture 36
  Peer-to-Peer Architecture (P2P) 37
  Conclusion 38

Chapter 3: Developing a Multiplayer Game 39
 When Should I Add Multiplayer? 39
  What Does Multiplayer-Centric Mean? 40
 Async vs. Sync Multiplayer 41
  Async Multiplayer 41
  Sync Multiplayer 41
 Authority Models 42
  Server-Authoritative 42
  Client-Authoritative 44
  Distributed Authority 45
  Choosing the Right Authoritative Model 47

TABLE OF CONTENTS

Netcode Frameworks 48
   Picking the Right Netcode Framework 49
   Existing vs. Custom Netcode Frameworks 50
Synchronization of Game State and Events 51
   Network Tick Rate 51
   Networked Variables 53
   Remote Procedure Calls (RPCs) 58
   Network Messages 61
Best Practices for Multiplayer Codebases 62
   Prefixes 62
   Role-Specific Code 63
Lag Compensation Techniques 65
   Client-Side Prediction with Server Reconciliation 65
   Client Authority 67
   Deterministic Lockstep 67
Playtesting Techniques 73
   Running Multiple Instances of the Game 73
   Host Mode 76
   Meta-Configuration Files 76
Conclusion 78

Chapter 4: Going Global 79

Connecting Players in Different Scenarios 79
   Local Multiplayer 79
   LAN Multiplayer 81
   Online Multiplayer 85
Security and Anti-cheating Strategies 91
   Why Do Players Cheat? 92
   How Do Players Cheat? 93
   How to Prevent Cheats and Deal with Hackers 95
Live Service Games 114

TABLE OF CONTENTS

    Remote Configuration 115

    Game Analytics 117

  Conclusion 122

Chapter 5: Monetization 123

  Why Is Monetization Important? 123

  Revenue Models 123

    Premium 124

    Free-to-Play 126

    Freemium 136

    Subscription 137

    Licensing 138

    Secondary Markets 139

    Summary 140

  Should I Make a Demo? 140

  Distribution 141

    Physical Distribution 142

    Digital Distribution 142

    Direct to Consumer ("D2C") 144

  Pricing 144

    Regional Pricing 145

    Discounts 146

  Conclusion 147

Chapter 6: Optimizing Your Multiplayer Game 149

  Why Is Optimization Important? 149

  Server Density 150

  Optimizing Servers 150

    Pick a Lightweight Operating System 150

    Remove Media Files 151

    Remove Client-Only Scene Objects 153

Limit the Framerate	154
Run in Headless Mode	155
Use the Smallest Data Type Possible	156
Synchronizing Only What Is Needed	157
Store Data in Non-conventional Ways	159
Delta Updates	161
Conclusion	161

Chapter 7: Common Multiplayer Features 163

Bots	163
Bots' Logic Always Runs on the Server to Reduce Latency	163
Bots Should Be Able to Do What Players Can Do	164
Bots Need Different Skill Levels	165
Treat Bots as Remote Players	170
Bots Need to Be Credible	170
Reconnection	170
Accepting Late Joiners and Reconnecting	171
Synchronizing for Reconnection	171
Restoring Player Characters	173
Replays	174
Recorded Replays	174
Simulated Replays	174
Spectator Mode	185
Spectating Through Direct Connection	185
Spectating Through Delayed Streaming	186
Party Matchmaking	187
Conclusion	189

TABLE OF CONTENTS

Chapter 8: User-Generated Content 191
Why Is UGC Important? 191
Empowering Players 192
Balancing UGC 196
Testing UGC 199
Moderation 200
Not Safe for Work ("NSFW") 200
Offensive Content 202
Copyrighted Content 204
UGC Content at Scale 205
Storage and Delivery 205
Synchronizing Local and Global Content 207
Conclusion 207

Epilogue 209

Index 211

About the Author

Paolo Abela is an Italian studio founder, game developer, and consultant specialized in multiplayer games. Since 2013, he has run multiple studios and worked hands-on on multiplayer games such as "Ariokan," "Overknights," and "Eggscape" at scale. He also helps Indie and AA teams make and ship multiplayer games and likes to spread knowledge through conference talks and LinkedIn posts for those who come after.

About the Technical Reviewer

Simon Jackson is a long-time software engineer and architect with many years of game development experience as well as the author of several game development titles. He loves to both create game projects as well as lend a hand to help educate others, whether it's via a blog, vlog, user group, or major speaking event.

His primary focus at the moment is with the Reality Toolkit project, which is aimed at building a cross-platform Mixed Reality framework to enable both VR and AR developers to build efficient solutions in Unity and then build/distribute them to as many platforms as possible. He is also a board member of the MonoGame Foundation, aiming to secure and promote open source game development for all developers.

Acknowledgments

I want to express my gratitude to all the people who, directly or indirectly, helped me in writing this book.

A big "thank you" to Spandana Chatterjee for the opportunity, Deepa Shirley Tryphosa Chellappa for the clear guidelines and regularly checking in, and to all the people at Apress for making this book real.

Thanks to all the teams who made the amazing games mentioned in this book, including my colleagues at Fatum Games, and to all the fellow players who support the industry.

Preface

Video games are one of humanity's favorite hobbies. Most of us love to play them, alone or with friends, to escape from reality, embrace new challenges, and create bonds that last for years. As game developers, it's our responsibility to create these awesome and life-changing experiences that can bring light even in someone's darkest day.

The last 12 years in the gaming industry taught me a lot about how commercial games are made: as a two times studio founder, I experienced firsthand what it means to make games from design to commercialization and what emotional, technical, and business challenges a team of people has to go through to release something worth playing. Being a consultant too, I've had the chance to tap into projects that span over different game genres, team sizes, and cultures. Finally, the experience gained by working on multiplayer and onboarding tools at Unity made me aware of what's needed to make tools that multiply the capabilities and speed of a team.

The purpose of this book is to pave the way for those who come after: I hope that, by reading it, you'll be able to make the right choices and avoid many of the mistakes me and my clients made during our game development journeys. The chapters ahead are a practical guide to the several business, design, and technical aspects of developing multiplayer games: follow them at your own peril (of being successful).

Coding knowledge is not required to understand most of the book, but knowing C# will help you get more value from the examples in the most technical chapters. It doesn't matter whether you're a solo founder that wears multiple hats in your studio, a creative director, or a hyper-specialized developer: this book covers many aspects of the production and commercialization process of videogames, so I'm confident you'll find something valuable in it for you or someone else in your team. In fact, I strongly encourage you to discuss your findings with your colleagues: it might have a huge impact on your roadmap, strategy, and future.

CHAPTER 1

Why Is It So Hard to Make a Multiplayer Game?

Making games is hard. Making multiplayer games is 10x–100x harder. This chapter explains why, diving into the differences between making a *single-player* game vs. making a *multiplayer* one. First, you'll learn about the lifecycle of both types of games. Then, I'll show you the differences in playtesting. Finally, we'll talk about the architectural differences between those types of games, and you'll learn why developing "just the game" is not enough. At the end of this chapter, you should have a clear understanding of why *multiplayer* games require way more resources (and luck) to become successful.

Single-Player vs. Multiplayer Games

First of all, we need to give a clear definition to *single player* and *multiplayer*: A **single-player** game is a game whose **core game loop** can be played by only one human player. A **multiplayer** game is a game whose **core game loop** can be played only by two or more human players.

And what is a **core game loop**? A core game loop is a repeated set of (hopefully) fun activities that stay fun even if you repeat them with some variations.

A core game loop takes players through all major pieces of the system, encouraging them to continue playing, and for an RPG, it might be something like "Get a quest, go to a new area, face some random encounters, complete the quest, gain rewards, upgrade character, repeat." For a puzzle game, it'd be "come across a puzzle, solve it, go to a new area, repeat."

So "***Solitaire***" is an example of a *single-player* game. "***Chess***" is an example of a *multiplayer* game. Games can have different game modes, each one with its own core game loop, so they can be both *single-player* and *multiplayer*.

CHAPTER 1   WHY IS IT SO HARD TO MAKE A MULTIPLAYER GAME?

Due to their nature, *multiplayer* games usually require an internet connection to connect several players with each other, and this is where most of the challenges we'll talk about in Chapter 3 come from.

Limitations of a Multiplayer Game

When designing mechanics for a multiplayer game, we need to consider that there are some constraints imposed by the time information takes to travel from one device to another over the internet ("latency") and by the techniques used to make that information travel.

Fast-Paced Player Movement

Imagine this: a single-player game can easily handle 1000 non-playing characters (NPCs) walking around and doing actions in front of the player, because everything happens on a single device and information doesn't have to travel across the internet. But what if those 1000 characters were other players all around the world? Then every single one of them would need to get information about what the others are doing and send their own information around.

In fast-paced games like shooters or fighting games, precise positioning is critical for a satisfying user experience, and even a small delay of 50 milliseconds becomes noticeable as movement between players becomes laggy or unresponsive. As a consequence, the proper implementation of features like parkour, wall-running, and bunny-hopping (especially on slippery surfaces) is a true challenge in multiplayer, and you should think twice before making the game revolve around them.

As we'll see with more details in Chapter 2, information takes time to travel (especially if we want it to travel reliably), and this is why a single match of a real-time multiplayer game usually has only up to ten players.

> **Note**   Massively Multiplayer Online (MMO) games and battle royale games manage to fit hundreds of players in a single map, but they implement several game-specific optimizations and technologies made exactly for this use case. We'll talk more about this in Chapter 3.

Physics-Based Interactions

Physics-based games are games in which the laws of physics play a major part in how the player interacts with other game elements (i.e., racing games fall under this category, card games don't).

And who is in charge of simulating the laws of physics in a game's digital world? It's one code library called "physics engine" (i.e., Unity's PhysX or Unreal's Chaos). Now, the problem with physics engines in multiplayer games is that these engines are (usually) designed to be deterministic per simulation, as they represent information using 32-bit floating-point numbers since they are faster on modern CPUs. This means that running the same input on two different machines with different hardware will yield different results: in other words, physics will work "a little differently" on different machines. While a little deviation in the physics state of the world is negligible in single-player games, in a multiplayer game, this has a catastrophic snowball effect that eventually makes the whole world simulation desync.

That's why ragdolls, vehicles, and destructible environments are rarely seen in multiplayer games.

Note It is possible to use physics-based interactions if the physics engine is deterministic, or server-authoritative physics with periodic state synchronization. We'll talk more about this in Chapter 3.

Time Manipulation

Time traveling is a fascinating yet dangerous concept in science fiction. You've probably heard stories or watched movies about people ending up erasing themselves from existence by mistake, or dooming the world.

When it comes to multiplayer games, where we already have to deal with the limits of physics and delays in traveling information, time manipulation must be handled with even more care. A good option is to use local time dilation effects in gameplay moments where players can't send any input, for example, when the player deals the final blow at the end of a boss battle and the match ends.

CHAPTER 1 WHY IS IT SO HARD TO MAKE A MULTIPLAYER GAME?

Differences in Architecture

All games, whether multiplayer or not, are made up of two parts: the "Core game loop" and the "Metagame." Multiplayer games also have an additional part called "Backend services."

The "Core Game Loop"

As mentioned earlier, the "core game Loop" is the fundamental minute-to-minute gameplay players go through when playing the game. It's "where all the action happens": where you fight other champions in "League of Legends,"[1] where you play cards in "Ariokan,"[2] and where you catch Pokémons in "Pokémon."[3]

It's called "core game loop" because players repeat a specific set of actions over and over until the match (or "play session") ends, even though the details of these actions can vary.

As you can see in Figure 1-1, the core game loop a classic role-playing game (RPG) would look like:

1. Get a quest by a non-playing character
2. Go to the area where the quest takes place
3. Complete the objectives of the quest
4. Go back to who gave you the quest
5. Redeem the rewards
6. Use the reward to improve your character
7. Repeat

---

[1] A multiplayer online battle arena (MOBA) game in which two teams of five players battle in player-vs.-player combat, each team occupying and defending their half of the map. Each of the ten players controls a character, known as a "champion," with unique abilities and playstyles.

[2] The online collectible card game where players can create new balanced cards at any time to break the status quo of the Metagame.

[3] A role-playing game based around building a small team of monsters to battle other monsters in a quest to become the best.

4

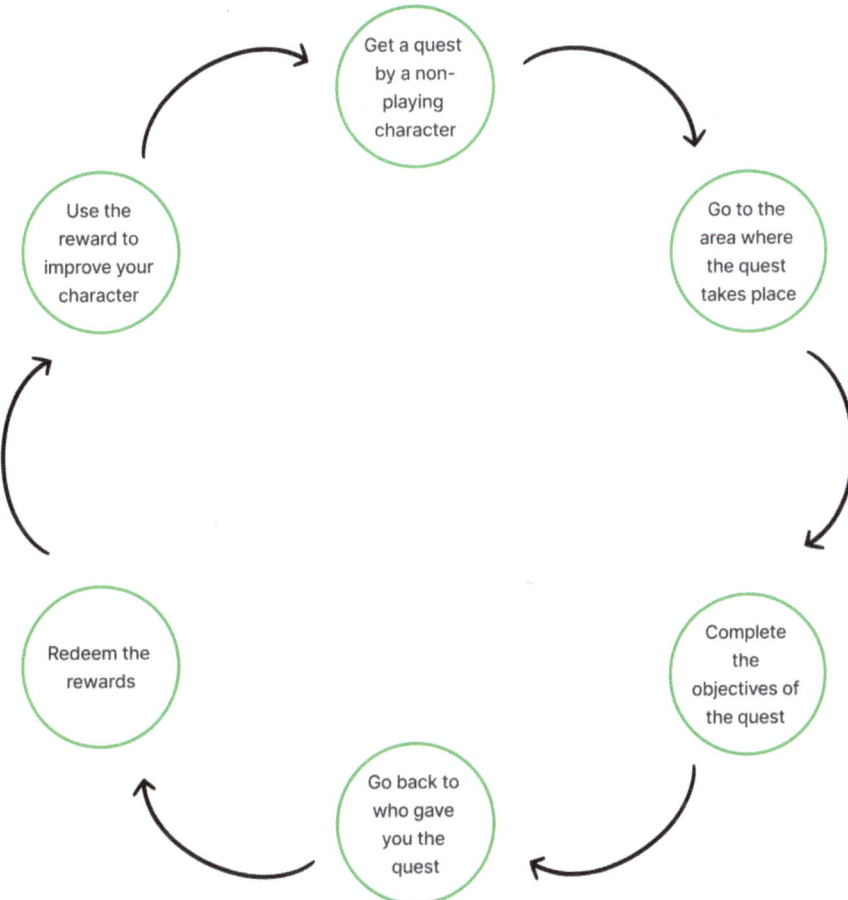

Figure 1-1. *Example of core game loop of a role-playing game (RPG)*

Even if the details of each quest are different to ensure the player doesn't get bored, the loop above repeats endlessly and drives the player from the beginning to the end of the game.

That's why the game loop is the most important part: there's no game without a core game loop, and there's no successful game without a core game loop that stays fun and rewarding even if you repeat it a thousand times.

The main difference between the core game loop of a single-player game and the one of a multiplayer game is in its technical implementation: the one of a multiplayer game needs to respect the constraints imposed by the time information takes to travel from one device to another over the internet ("latency"), and needs to implement the logic needed to validate player's actions through an authoritative source which determines if what the player wants to do is allowed given the current game state.

That's why there's no point in making the "single-player version" of a game first if the goal is to make it multiplayer: the very foundation of the game will need to change to accommodate the needs of multiplayer, and this means wasting months rewriting the entire codebase. Set up the multiplayer foundation first, then work on the core game loop.

The "Metagame"

The "Metagame" is the part that builds on top of the core game loop to give players a sense of progression, keep them engaged outside of the core game loop, and let them access the core loop. For example, in a card game like Ariokan the Metagame is where players spend currency acquired at the end of a game loop to unlock new cards to improve their decks. In a tower defense game, it's where you unlock new units that you can deploy in your next match. In League of Legends, it's where you unlock new characters or choose what cosmetics to bring to your next match. Many games also have a "leveling system" that lets players level up and unlock new features or perks with the rewards they earn after each match.

As you can see from the examples above, the Metagame is what really contributes to creating a sense of progression in the overall scheme of the game and gives players a reason to come back for more. This is even more important in competitive multiplayer games, where global leaderboards and ranked systems exist to incentivize players to get better at the game and spend time playing it, which eventually leads to a stronger, self-growing community and increased revenue.

Considering that Metagame consists of pretty much everything that is outside of the core game loop, development and design teams use that term to refer to all menus and features players have access to between matches.

Note In competitive games, players use the term "Metagame" (or "Meta") to refer to "the best strategies and approaches to play the game." For example, in *Magic: The Gathering*, "Meta decks" are "the strongest decks available given the existing rules and cards."

The "Backend Services"

"Backend services" are the set of online services that power all Metagame features of online games, and store, retrieve and alter player's data online.

These are web applications running on a machine (a "server"), usually in the Cloud, that interact with the game through Application Programming Interfaces (APIs).

To understand this concept better, let's make a practical example: imagine a player wants to unlock a cosmetic using in-game currency. This is what happens

1. Player opens the in-game shop.
2. Player selects the cosmetic they want.
3. Player clicks "unlock" in the UI.
4. The game sends an "unlock cosmetic" request, containing enough info to recognize the player and the cosmetic, to a backend service.
5. The service verifies that the player has enough currency to unlock the cosmetic.
    a. If the player has enough currency, the service updates the data of the player in a database, removing the currency and adding the cosmetic, and sends back a "success" response to the game.
    b. If the player doesn't have enough currency, the service sends back an "error" response to the game.
6. The game receives a response from the service and displays it to the player.

As you can see, the backend service plays a crucial role in validating player's requests. If the checks regarding player's currency were performed locally, a malicious player could use a hacked version of the game's build to skip them and unlock whatever they wanted, cheating the system.

In single-player games, cheating is usually not a problem as it causes no economic damage to the studio behind the game, but in multiplayer games, which usually use a revenue model that relies on in-app purchases, it can cause a sensible loss of revenue. That's why multiplayer games, and even single-player games that store relevant data or unlockable items for players online, need backend services to function.

CHAPTER 1   WHY IS IT SO HARD TO MAKE A MULTIPLAYER GAME?

Backend services support all features of the Metagame, including the ones related to matching players with each other and initializing servers when enough players want to play, so they need to be able to support tens of thousands of concurrent players making requests every second. Making a service like that is an incredibly time-consuming and resource-intensive challenge even for large, experienced teams:

> *In the U.S., [...] large publishers are spending an average of $21.6 million to build and maintain their backend tech. [...] The average number of employees working predominantly in internal tech is 52. It takes about 36 months for companies to build their own internal tech.*
>
> —Dean Takahashi on Metaplay's report, VentureBeat, May 24, 2024[4]

Luckily, nowadays there are many companies offering battle-tested and affordable backend services for games. For example, you can use Epic Games' "Epic Online Services," and Unity technologies' "Unity Gaming Services" as backend services for your game.

The specific services to use depend on your game's specific features, your project's goals, and target platforms, and it is very important to make the right choice from the beginning: switching infrastructure mid-project is an extremely time-consuming and risky operation, and the more active players you have, the harder it gets to prioritize.

A few questions that can help you figure out your use cases when it comes to backend services are:

- How will you host your games?
    - Peer-To-Peer?
    - Dedicated servers?
    - Distributed authority?
- How will your players find each other?
    - Direction connection with NAT punchthrough?
    - Matchmaker?
    - Lobbies with join codes?

---

[4] https://venturebeat.com/games/mobile-game-publishers-spend-21m-on-backend-tech-metaplay/

- How will you store players/game data?
    - Relational database?
    - NoSQL database?
    - Content delivery network?
    - Binary cloud saves?
- Do you want to be able to change the balancing of the game without releasing new updates?
- What information do you want to collect at runtime?
    - Retention metrics?
    - Behavioral metrics?
    - Feature or content-related metrics?
- Does the API layer need to be active 24/7, or can I leverage serverless tech?

In the following chapters of this book, I'll try to cover as many of those questions as possible.

The Lifecycle of Games

Like every other product, games have a lifecycle too: they're developed, pre-released (optional), released, and abandoned. *Single player* and *multiplayer* games go through some of these stages in completely different ways.

As you can see in Figure 1-2, revenue from direct sales to new players, or in-app purchases from existing ones, is influenced by the current stage of the lifecycle of the game.

CHAPTER 1   WHY IS IT SO HARD TO MAKE A MULTIPLAYER GAME?

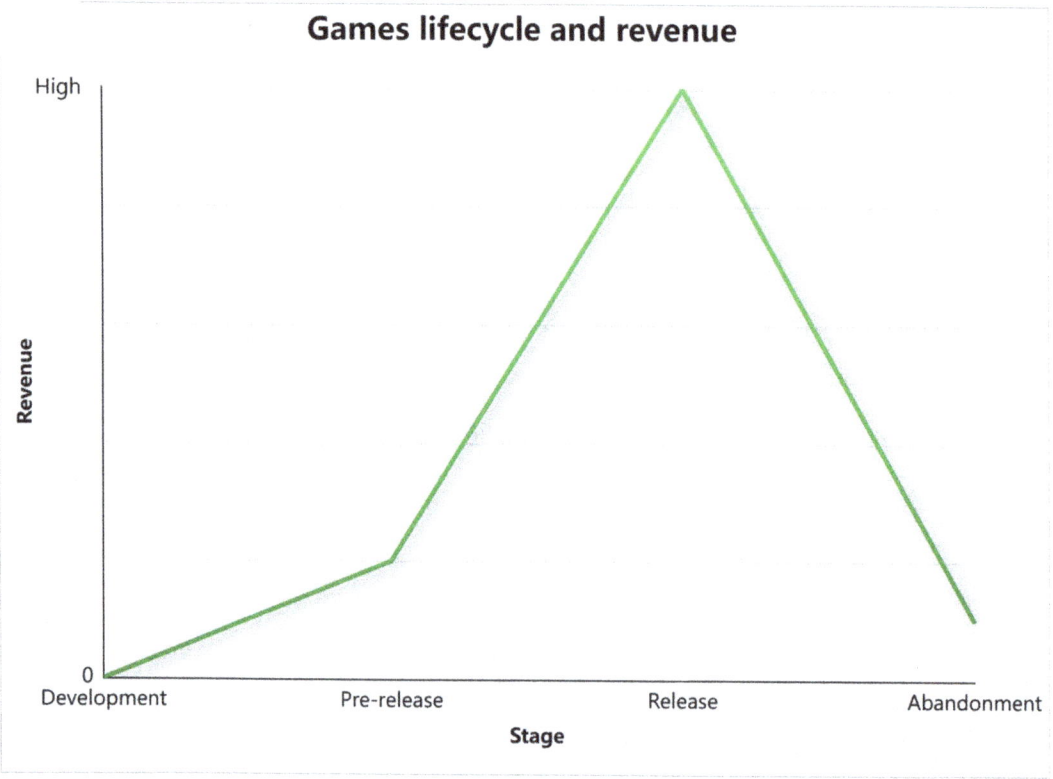

Figure 1-2. *Indicative chart that shows how revenue correlates to the current stage of the lifecycle of the game. Most games depend on a successful release to generate considerable revenue*

All games go through this, but **how** and **how long** each game goes through this is what determines if a game was successful or not.

Lifecycle of a Single-Player Fame

Most *single-player* games use a "**Premium**" revenue model, which means that they have a price tag that players pay in order to get a copy of the game, so their lifecycle is usually straightforward: you work on the game, release it, and try to sell enough copies to make a profit. Table 1-1 shows more details about the stages of the lifecycle of a single-player game.

Table 1-1. Lifecycle stages of a premium single-player game

Stage	Who plays	Main revenue source
Development	Gaming studio's team	/
Pre-release (optional)	Early adopters comfortable with unfinished games	Preorders
Release	Broader public	Sales
Abandonment	Engaged players replaying the game	/

As you can see, once a premium *single-player* game is released, there's no way to get more revenue from it. For this reason, some *single-player* games adopt a more hybrid approach, adding in-game content that can be purchased through **In-App Purchases** (*"IAP"*). An alternative is to add *"**Downloadable Content**"* (*"**DLC**"*), which are Premium updates that add more content to the game (i.e., new levels, characters, items).

Lifecycle of a Multiplayer Game

When it comes to multiplayer games, the lifecycle is similar but different: for a multiplayer game, the public release is a new beginning, not the end of the cycle. This is particularly true in the case of the so-called "Games as a Service" ("GaaS") or "Live-service game", a term used to group all games that release new content updates and host seasonal events after their public release.

These games require a continuous investment of resources by the development team that must support them and constantly make new content to appeal to players, but, when done right, can retain players for a very long time.

There's also an additional aspect that is crucial for multiplayer titles: they need concurrent players that can play with each other. This means that a multiplayer title must build interest early to nail the launch and attract as many players as possible upon release (often referred to as "Day 1") or, as we'll see in Chapters 5 and 7, use bots to "fake it until they make it." Moreover, to lower the entry barriers for players that would like to try it, multiplayer games tend to adopt a free-to-play revenue model, which allows players to invite their friends easily as they don't have to buy a copy of the game first.

Considering how important Day 1 is, a team can't risk getting there unprepared. That's why multiplayer titles often undergo longer pre-release testing cycles (Alpha and Beta phases) where players provide feedback about core mechanics while the team collects usage, retention, and performance metrics. Games that skip those testing phases usually end up with their server infrastructure and online systems blowing up under the massive influx of players on Day 1, with players leaving immediately without ever giving the game a second chance.

Table 1-2 shows more details about the stages of the lifecycle of a multiplayer game.

Table 1-2. Lifecycle stages of a free-to-play multiplayer game

Stage	Who plays	Main revenue source
Development	Gaming studio's team	/
Alpha pre-release (optional)	Early adopters comfortable with unfinished games	/
Beta pre-release (optional)	Early adopters comfortable with unfinished games	Sales & IAP
Release	Broader public	Sales & IAP
Live service	Broader public	In-App purchases
Abandonment	Engaged players replaying the game	In-App purchases

Playtesting

Playtesting is the act of trying out a build of the game to understand what can be improved, detect bugs, and check that the game is as engaging as it should.

Playtesting a Single-Player Game

Playtesting a single-player game is simple:

1. Make a build
2. Give it to your players
3. Let them play whenever they want while they record their screen and voice
4. Get feedback (directly from players and from the recordings)

Sounds easy peasy lemon squeezy, right? It is. When it comes to testing, single-player games have the advantage of needing only one person and no dependencies on external systems or servers.

Playtesting a Multiplayer Game

But what about testing a multiplayer game that connects players through a dedicated online device with no local player? (also known as "dedicated server")

1. Make a build for the server, stripping out all unneeded assets (audio, textures, UI, etc.) to make it fit the server's limited resources.

2. Upload the build to the server, and make sure to use a progressive update system to avoid kicking out players from existing matches.

3. Change the "latest game build version" in some public API so players that are on older builds are forced to update when the game starts.

4. Make a build for the players, using the same codebase (commit) to avoid structural desyncs, and including all assets you removed from the server build.

5. Give the build to players.

6. Organize a playtest session so they can connect all together at the same time to play with each other while they record their screen and voice.

7. Get feedback.

For multiplayer games, the process is much more complicated as it requires you to coordinate your testers and prepare multiple builds for different platforms.

That's why you need to approach testing differently in this case: you can simulate other players through bots while developing, organize specific playtesting sessions at a certain date and time when you have an alpha version of the game, and set up a permanent online environment called "Public Beta Environments" (also referred to as a "Staging Environment") that let selected players ("Beta Testers") access unreleased features autonomously.

To avoid a mix of work-in-progress and ready features, the Staging Environment needs to be maintained and updated separately from the "Live" (or "Production") Environment, which is the one all players have access to, and from the "Development" Environment where only developers and testers of the gaming studio run experiments and test features before releasing them to other environments.

Conclusion

As you've learnt in this chapter, multiplayer games are a way more difficult challenge compared to single-player games: making a fun and interesting core game loop is not enough; you also need to develop an engaging metagame experience and adopt a set of backend services that can support both.

You also need to take into account latency and other limiting factors when designing your game mechanics, carefully think about your playtesting strategy, and how you'll support the game in the long run after the first release.

If this sounds like a lot of work, it's because it is: making games is hard, but making multiplayer games is harder. However, with the right team, knowledge, and scope, it is doable.

In the next chapter, you'll learn more about how information travels on the internet and how different devices operate when they need to communicate with each other.

Later in the book, you'll learn how to leverage this knowledge to properly design and implement features in your multiplayer game.

CHAPTER 2

How the Internet Works

In Chapter 1, we acknowledged that multiplayer games need to connect multiple players at the same time to fulfill their purpose. We also understood that players' devices often exchange data, request, and responses with Backend Services, which run on "server" machines, physically far from the player's device.

This chapter is about how information travels on the internet, and how different devices operate when they need to communicate with each other. At the end of this chapter, you should have a clear understanding of the different roles a device can take when it needs to interact with other devices, and how these interactions happen.

What Is Communication?

Before diving into the details of how devices communicate, let's clarify how communication works at a higher level: first, a communication process is a process that allows the exchange of information between two or more entities.

We can represent this process using the Shannon–Weaver model described in the paper "A Mathematical Theory of Communication," published in 1948, which defines communication as five elements covering specific roles, as shown in Figure 2-1 and described in Table 2-1.

CHAPTER 2 HOW THE INTERNET WORKS

Table 2-1. *Elements of Shannon–Weaver model for communication, in a face-to-face conversation between 2 people*

Element	Description	Example
Source	Human/automated entity that wants to send a message	Person 1
Transmitter	Human/automated element capable of transforming the message and transferring it through the channel in the form of a signal	Person 1's Mouth
Channel	Physical medium that allows the transfer of the signal	Air (for sound waves)
Receiver	Human/automated that receives the signal through the channel and converts it into a message understandable by the recipient	Person 2's Ear
Destination	Human/automated system that receives the message and interprets it	Person 2

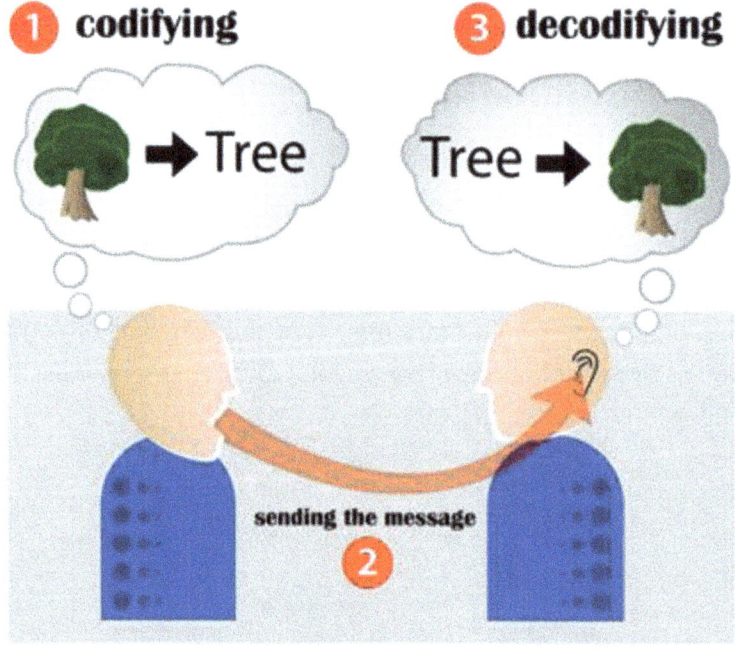

Figure 2-1. *Example of human communication using Shannon–Weaver's model. Source: https://en.wikipedia.org/wiki/Shannon%E2%80%93Weaver_model#/media/File:Encoding_communication.jpg*

To carry out communication correctly, it is also necessary to define in advance a communication protocol that describes all the rules required for proper communication, for example:

1. How to start and end communication

    a. That is, saying "Hello?" and "Bye" at the beginning and end of a phone call

2. How to recognize one message from another

    a. That is, the silence after a spoken sentence

3. How to recognize communication errors

    a. That is, telling each other that there's "interference" or "noise" during a phone call

4. The communication code (or "Encoding")

    a. That is, what human language to use (English, Italian, Spanish, etc.) to interpret the signal

As humans, we have interiorized most of these protocols in our day-to-day communication. For example, we know that we can speak after the person we're calling answers the phone and says "Hello?". We also know that we can use a specific language to communicate with people who used that language to communicate with us in the past.

As you can imagine, the encoding is one of the most important parts of a communication protocol: it's a technique that allows data to be represented by means of a set of more elementary symbols or data of any nature (graphic, luminous, acoustic).

These symbols (i.e., letters) form sequences (i.e., words) that are in a one-to-one relationship with the elements that represent the information. For example, people who know English associate the word "tree" with a natural object that has a trunk, branches, and leaves. People who speak Italian encode the same information with the word "albero," which for an English speaker means nothing. That's why both the source and destination of a communication need to know the encoding before starting the communication if they want to understand each other.

Rare forms of encoding are capable of overcoming language barriers: images and music can transmit information and evoke emotions without spelling a single word. That's why we can appreciate paintings from all over the world and feel a turbulent mix of emotive states while listening to The Four Seasons of Antonio Vivaldi.

CHAPTER 2 HOW THE INTERNET WORKS

Machines, lacking human intelligence, need to follow protocols strictly to properly communicate. They also need to represent information in a consistent way: that's why computers (or electronic devices in general) store information in the form of sequences of binary digits, or "bits." Each bit can have a value of "0" or "1," determined by the voltage on a circuit of the device. This simple binary representation is the fundamental of every single piece of information stored in our devices: images, videos, text, and so on all boil down to a series of "0" and "1."

Once information is stored in this format, devices use communication frameworks to send them around.

Communication Frameworks

Communication frameworks are a set of rules that describe how devices communicate with each other during each step of the communication. The two frameworks all game developers making multiplayer games should know about are the OSI model and the TCP/IP one.

The OSI Model

The OSI model ("*Open Systems Interconnection*") is a reference model for the exchange of information between two devices, commonly referred to as "Hosts" in the world of networked devices. Nowadays, it is mostly theoretical, but still worth knowing for troubleshooting.

It is divided into seven layers: four lower layers and three upper layers, as shown in Table 2-2.

Table 2-2. *Layers of the OSI model*

Layer	Description	Examples and features
Application (Upper)	Provides users with the means to access networks, acting as an interface between the information system and the real world	HTTP, FTP, DNS, SMTP, apps (i.e., Google Chrome)
Presentation (Upper)	Handles the syntax and semantics of the information to be transferred, and allows communication between different standards by serializing data structures into flat byte-strings	Encoding, Encryption, and Decryption, Compression
Session (Upper)	Defines how a session between end-user applications is opened, closed, and managed, and how requests and responses are handled between applications	Authentication, Authorization, Reconnection, RPCs
Transport (Low)	Breaks down and reconstructs the "segments" that make up a message, detecting any failures on the network	TCP/UDP
Network (Low)	Provides the logical medium on which variable-length data sequences are transferred from a source to a destination in the form of "packets" via one or more networks, also maintaining Quality-of-Service ("QoS") functions	IPv4/IPv6, IPsec, QoS
Data Link (Low)	Defines the structure of messages sent over the physical layer, dividing them into "frames," and adds ways to detect/correct problems that may occur in the physical layer	MAC; VLAN; Encapsulation into frames, flow control
Physical (Low)	Defines the characteristics of the "signals," the devices necessary to connect two or more hosts through the transmission medium, and physically carries bits between two devices	Wi-Fi, Ethernet Cable, Repeaters, Bluetooth

As game developers, most of our work happens at the upper layers of this model, but knowing how Transport and Network-level protocols work is essential both to troubleshoot most connection and transmission errors of modern online games, and to optimize their online features.

CHAPTER 2 HOW THE INTERNET WORKS

The TCP/IP Model

The TCP/IP (*"Transmission Control Protocol/Internet Protocol"*) model is one of the most used models for digital network communications, and the de-facto global standard.

It's a more concise version of the OSI one: as you can see from Figure 2-2, the application layer of TCP/IP maps to the top three layers of OSI, performing the same functions, and the network interface layer of TCP/IP includes the bottom two layers of OSI.

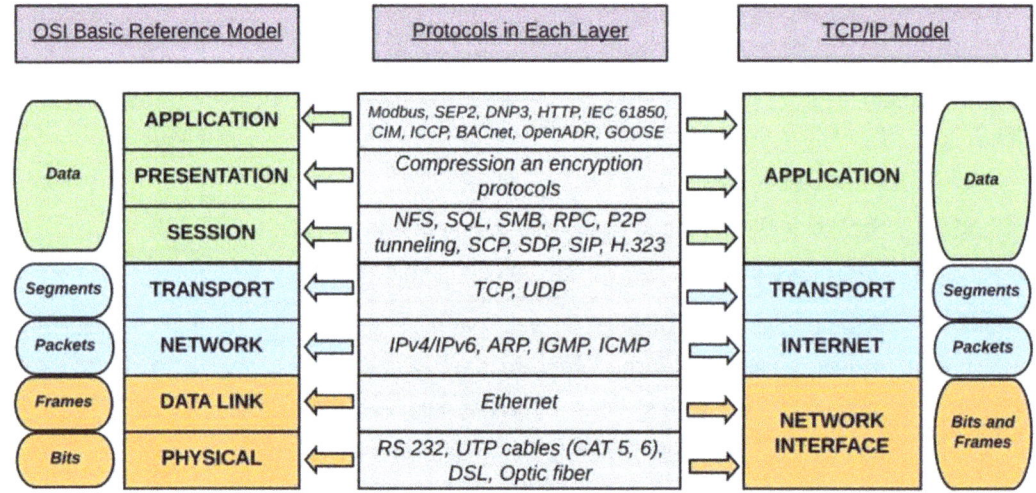

Figure 2-2. *How the layers of the OSI model map to the ones of TCP/IP. Source:* `https://stackoverflow.com/a/54785276`

As users, we interact with TCP/IP-based software every time we use an online application to send a video, visit a website, or play with our friends.

Table 2-3 shows a real-world situation: imagine you want to search for something on Google.

Table 2-3. The roles of OSI and TCP/IP models during a Google search

Action	OSI and TCP/IP layers
You open your web browser (i.e., Google Chrome), type what you want in the search bar (i.e., "Pizza") and press "Search"	Application/application
The browser generates an HTTPS[1] request that includes your search text, which is encrypted	Presentation/application
The browser establishes a secure session between itself and the server via the TLS ("Transport Layer Security") handshake, which manages session setup and teardown	Session/application
The HTTPS request is broken into segments by TCP ("Transport control protocol")	Transport/transport
Your computer's IP stack assigns source and destination IP addresses (i.e., your IP and the Google server's IP), to route data through the internet	Network/Internet
The data is framed into Ethernet frames (or Wi-Fi frames if wireless) and includes physical addresses like MAC addresses.	Data Link/network Interface
The raw bits (0s and 1s) of your request are transmitted as electrical signals across physical media	Physical/network interface

Note Don't worry if you're unfamiliar with many of the terms in the table. After all, the internet is a very complex system. In the upcoming sections of this chapter, you'll read more about the terms and concepts you really need to know as a game developer working on a multiplayer game.

The process is reversed on the other side: frames are reconstructed from the received bits, then sent to the right host, unencrypted, and finally read by the application running on Google's server, which is now able to respond with the results of your search.

---

[1] Hypertext Transfer Protocol Secure (HTTPS), a protocol used to securely encrypt and transmit information between a user's web browser and the website they are interacting with

But how do messages find the right recipient in the vast and turbulent sea of the internet? What allows hosts far away from each other to have a communication process? The answer is: network addresses and protocols.

Network Addresses

To communicate with somebody else, you need to know where to find them. For example, you need to know what phone number to call, or the email address you want to send an email to.

That's the same for machines on the internet: to find each other, they use an Internet Protocol Address ("IP Address").

What Is an IP Address?

An IP address is a human-readable numerical label that identifies a specific network interface that uses the Internet Protocol for communication and is connected to a computer network. The IP address is what allows routers, the devices that forward data packets across hosts, to identify a specific host, and the network it is part of. It's like saying "Madame Anna lives at the 5th floor of Papadia Street 77, 12345, Rome, Italy." If you think about it, to deliver a package to Madame Anna is not enough to know just the name or the city she lives in: the courier needs to know which doorbell to ring within a specific building.

As of 2025, the 2 versions of the Internet Protocol that are commonly used globally are IPv4 and IPv6. The former has been around since 1983, uses a 4-bytes sequence to represent an IP address (i.e., 192.168.1.200), and is what people usually refer to when talking about IP addresses.

To distinguish between the "network" and "host" parts of an address, we use the CIDR ("Classless Inter-Domain Routing") notation to write the address. This notation adds a "/<number>" suffix, called "subnet mask," that indicates the number of bits representing the network part of the address. For example, the "/24" in the IPv4 address "192.168.1.100/24" indicates that the first 24 bits from the left of the address represent the network part ("192.168.1"), and the last 8 bits represent a specific host within the network ("100").

Caution The first and last addresses of a network can't be assigned to any individual host. The first address is used to identify the network itself and is essential for routing packets correctly; the last address is reserved for broadcasting messages to all hosts on that network.

When troubleshooting, you can use the `ipconfig` command in your computer's terminal / shell / command prompt tool, to check what your IP address and subnet masks are. Here's how to do it in Windows 11:

1. Open the command prompt

    a. Method 1

        i. Press the `<Windows key>` + R to make the *Run* window show up

        ii. Type `cmd` in it

        iii. Click "Ok"

    b. Method 2:

        i. Press the `<Windows key>`

        ii. Type `Command prompt` in the search bar

        iii. Press Enter.

2. In the Command Prompt window that showed up, type `ipconfig`

3. Press Enter

Figure 2-3 shows the output of running the `ipconfig` command on the Command Prompt of my Windows 11 machine.

CHAPTER 2   HOW THE INTERNET WORKS

```
C:\WINDOWS\system32\cmd.
Wireless LAN adapter Wi-Fi:

   Connection-specific DNS Suffix  . :
   IPv6 Address. . . . . . . . . . . : 2a0c:5a80:3b0a:c900:f078:35eb:f11a:14ab
   Temporary IPv6 Address. . . . . . : 2a0c:5a80:3b0a:c900:a4f7:8b58:8a:507
   Link-local IPv6 Address . . . . . : fe80::569c:31ff:184e:fb12%6
   IPv4 Address. . . . . . . . . . . : 192.168.1.130
   Subnet Mask . . . . . . . . . . . : 255.255.255.0
   Default Gateway . . . . . . . . . : fe80::1%6
                                       192.168.1.1
```

Figure 2-3. *Output of an* `ipconfig` *command. Note the 192.168.1.130 IPv4 address and the subnet mask whose 24 bits are set to 1, resulting in the value "255" for the first three bytes)*

With 4 bytes there can only be 2^32 IP address (~4.3 billion), which sounded a lot in the early days of the internet but eventually became too few for today's needs, when there are billions of hosts connected to the internet.

That's why IPv6, which uses 16-bytes IP addresses, and techniques like NAT ("Network Address Translation"), CIDR ("Classless Inter-Domain Routing"), were introduced over time to slow down the rapid exhaustion of IPv4 addresses while maintaining IPv4 operative.

Note an IP address is tied to a network interface, not to a device: this means that a Wi-Fi receiver and an Ethernet adapter, which are two different types of network interface, will have different addresses even if they are part of the same computer and connected to the same network.

Public and Private IP Addresses

A public IP address is unique and visible to everyone. When you sign a contract with an Internet Service Provider ("ISPs"), they give you a network, a router to access it, and a public address associated with the network. The public IP address is used to establish a connection to the internet and communicate outside of your own network. Without it, you can't go online, because hosts outside of your network won't know how to find you.

Giving an IPv4 address to every device became unsustainable soon, also because it proved to be a security risk, and that's why in 1996 the Internet Engineering Task Force (IETF) introduced the idea of "Address Allocation for Private Internets" in RFC[2] 1918. That document outlined specific IP address ranges to be used exclusively for internal network purposes and not routable on the global internet:

- Class A: 10.0.0.0 to 10.255.255.255
- Class B: 172.16.0.0 to 172.31.255.255
- Class C: 192.168.0.0 to 192.168.255.255

Since these addresses are not routable on the internet by routers as a result of the RFC's implementation, they do not conflict with public IP addresses, and therefore, routers can assign them to hosts connected to them in their internal ("local") network. If you have ever had to configure a router or troubleshoot connectivity issues, you probably came across a Class C address before.

However, this created a new problem to solve: how can a host with a private IP address send packets over the internet?

Network Address Translation (NAT)

Network address translation (NAT) enables multiple hosts to share a single public IP address. With NAT, hosts on a private network can communicate with hosts on a public network even if the former lack a unique public IP address.

Usually, NAT is implemented on a router: when a host on the private network sends a packet to a host on the public network, the router captures the packet and replaces the source IP address with its own public IP address, then sends the packet to the destination host. When the destination host replies to the router, the router captures the incoming packet and replaces the public IP address with the original source IP address, then sends the packet to the original source host.

---

[2] A Request for Comments (RFC): a publication in a series from the principal technical development and standards-setting bodies of the Internet. Engineers and computer scientists submit them for peer review to propose ideas, or to describe how the Internet and Internet-connected systems work.

For us game developers, NAT is particularly problematic because it prevents us from connecting directly to other players as it hides their public IP address. In Chapter 4, we'll talk more about "NAT punchthrough," a technique that, under specific circumstances, allows us to connect with hosts hidden by routers that use NAT.

Reserved IP Addresses

Some IP addresses are reserved for special purposes. The relevant ones for game developers are displayed in Table 2-4.

Table 2-4. *IPv4 reserved addresses relevant for game developers*

Address	Description
0.0.0.0/8	"No address" placeholder. In the context of servers, it means "any IPv4 address on the local machine." If a host has two IP addresses, 192.168.1.3 and 10.1.2.3, it will be reachable at both if it also has a server listening on 0.0.0.0
127.0.0.0/8	Also known as "localhost" or "loopback address." Allows to establish IP connections to the same device used by the end-user to test the TCP/IP protocol implementation. This address virtually short-circuits the lower layers, nullifying the chance of manifesting problems related to them, allowing the higher layers (IP and above) to be tested properly
169.254.0.0/16	If a host has an IP address starting with 169.254, something is wrong with its network interface. It means that the host couldn't obtain a valid IP address from the router's DHCP[3] server, and it will be unable to connect to the Internet

Routing and Its Consequences

A router that knows the IP address of the destination host can send packets to it through the process of "routing": depending on several parameters such as the firewall protection rules enabled on the router, the routing algorithm, the status of the network, and Quality of Service requirements, the router chooses the "best next router" that will have to handle the packets, and sends them to it. The process repeats until the packets

---

[3] Dynamic Host Configuration Protocol (DHCP): a protocol that assigns IP addresses and other communication parameters automatically to devices connected to the network. Usually implemented on routers.

eventually reach the destination, or die trying by exhausting their "time to live" ("TTL"): a counter that is part of IP packets and that determines how many "hops" (= devices) the packet can go through before being discarded.

I won't dive into the details of routing protocols because the chance that you'll have to deal with them on your day-to-day as a game developer is basically zero, but I need to point out an extremely important consequence of routing, which is the root cause of all problems when it comes to multiplayer: no matter how efficient routers are, it takes time to deliver packages over the Internet because routers are physically distant from each other, so the electrical signal that physically represents packets on the medium has to travel for kilometers every time it goes from an hop to the other. On top of that, routers take some milliseconds to perform calculations every time they process a packet. This all adds up and causes communication over the Internet to have a Round-Trip Time ("RTT"), the time it takes to send a message and receive a response back, of tens of milliseconds at best.

Based on this, you can deduce that communication in Local Area Networks ("LAN") is way faster as packets don't have to deal with NAT and Internet routing, which is why it's way easier to achieve smooth, low-latency gameplay in LAN.

Delivery Schemes

There are different ways to deliver packets, and each has its own use cases in multiplayer games too. Table 2-5 shows the different delivery schemes and examples of their use cases.

Table 2-5. Delivery schemes and examples

Scheme	Description	Example
Unicast	Delivers a message to a single host. Each destination address identifies a single receiver, univocally	Sending a private chat message to someone
Multicast	Delivers a message to a group of hosts. A single transmission routes the message simultaneously to many recipients, but not all the available ones	Sending a chat message to players of your team
Broadcast	Delivers a message to every host in the group	Sending a chat message to all players, including opponents

Network Ports

Since a host can have multiple applications running on it simultaneously, knowing only the IP address is not enough to interact with a specific application. That's why IP packets also include a source and target "port number."

A port is like an open door on the host, and is a way for different applications or services to communicate with each other over a network as it identifies a specific service or application.

Port Numbers

As displayed in Table 2-6, a port number is a 16-bit number in the 0 to 65535 range, used to identify specific processes or services on a machine.

Table 2-6. Port types and examples

Name	Range	Description	Examples
Well-known ports	0–1023	Reserved for specific services and protocols	HTTP (80) HTTPS (443) FTP (21)
Registered ports	1024–49151	Assigned to specific services or applications as destination ports, not as standardized as well-known ports	Varies by application
Dynamic/ Ephemeral ports	49152–65535	Used for temporary or client-side connections as source ports	When a computer communicates with a web server, it may use a dynamic port for the outgoing request

The combination of an IP address and port number uniquely identifies a specific service on a host. For example, the full identifier of a secure web server service in a local area network could be *192.168.1.150:443*, indicating that HTTPS traffic (port 443) should be directed to this server's IP.

Ports are part of the transport layer (Layer 4) of the OSI model, where transport protocols like TCP ("Transmission Control Protocol") and UDP ("User Datagram Protocol") use ports to route data to the correct service or application.

When a host sends data to another one, it generates IP packets that include the IP address of the destination, the port of the requested service on that host, and the protocol to use to ensure the correct rules for communication. The combination of these three elements is called "Socket." The packet also includes its own IP address (which NAT will replace if the hosts are not in the same local network), a dynamic port that represents the local application requesting the service, so the other host knows how to reply to the request.

For example, imagine *Host A* with IP *192.168.1.150* wants to send an HTTPS request to *Host B*, whose IP is *192.168.1.220* and that is listening for incoming requests[4] on its own socket bound to HTTPS' port (443). The communication would work like this:

1. Host A picks an ephemeral port (55555)

2. Host A creates a socket using its own IP and port (*192.168.1.150:55555*) to listen for the reply Host B will send after Host A's request.

3. Host A connects to the socket Host B is listening onto, which has destination address and port *192.168.1.220:443*.

4. Host A sends the request over the socket, specifying *192.168.1.150:55555* as the source address and port.

5. Host B sees the incoming request from *192.168.1.150:55555*, so it sends replies to the socket Host A opened, using 443 as a source port and *192.168.1.150:55555* as the destination address and port.

6. Host A receives the response and processes it, closing the socket.

---

[4] Hosts that provide a service ("Servers") need to be actively listening for incoming requests, otherwise no one will be able to connect to them. That's why they usually start listening upon startup.

Transport Protocols

Some applications need data segments[5] to be received in a precise order to be processed correctly. Others can tolerate a small loss of data without impacting functionality. That's why two different transport protocols exist to address these use cases: TCP ("Transmission Control Protocol") and UDP ("User Datagram Protocol").

As game developers, it's extremely important that we know what transport protocols are and which ones to use to implement specific networked features, because using the wrong one heavily impacts the user experience in a negative way.

Transmission Control Protocol

TCP is a transport protocol that ensures the ordered delivery of all segments (if possible). It defines how hosts acknowledge the receipt of a segment, how they retransmit the ones that got lost along the way, and how a communication session is established, handled, and closed.

TCP requires a bigger overhead (20-60 bytes) to encapsulate information, consuming more bandwidth and CPU time as it has to check that all segments made it to the destination, and retransmit the lost ones.

To initialize a TCP Socket, the source and destination hosts exchange a few messages in a process known as "three-way handshake":

1. The source host sends a synchronization message ("SYN") to initialize a TCP session, synchronizing the starting number of segments that it wants to send, so that both hosts can keep track of how many of those segments get to the destination.

2. The destination host responds to the SYN message with an acknowledgement (SYN-ACK) message that confirms the SYN information.

3. The source host responds to the SYN-ACK with an acknowledge message (ACK) and at this point the two hosts establish a reliable connection over which to perform the actual data transfer.

---

[5] Remember: as lower OSI layer further encapsulates the data coming from the upper layers, data has different names depending on the layer that is handling it. Segments is how we call data at layer 4. When in doubt, go back to Table 2-2.

CHAPTER 2   HOW THE INTERNET WORKS

From that point onward, when a host receives a segment from a TCP socket, it sends back an acknowledgment message. When a host sends a segment, TCP starts a countdown: if no acknowledgment is received by the destination host before the countdown ends, the segment is considered lost and is re-sent.

TCP also assigns a sequence number to every segment sent, so they can be reordered by the destination host to reconstruct the original message. Figure 2-4 shows the structure of a TCP segment.

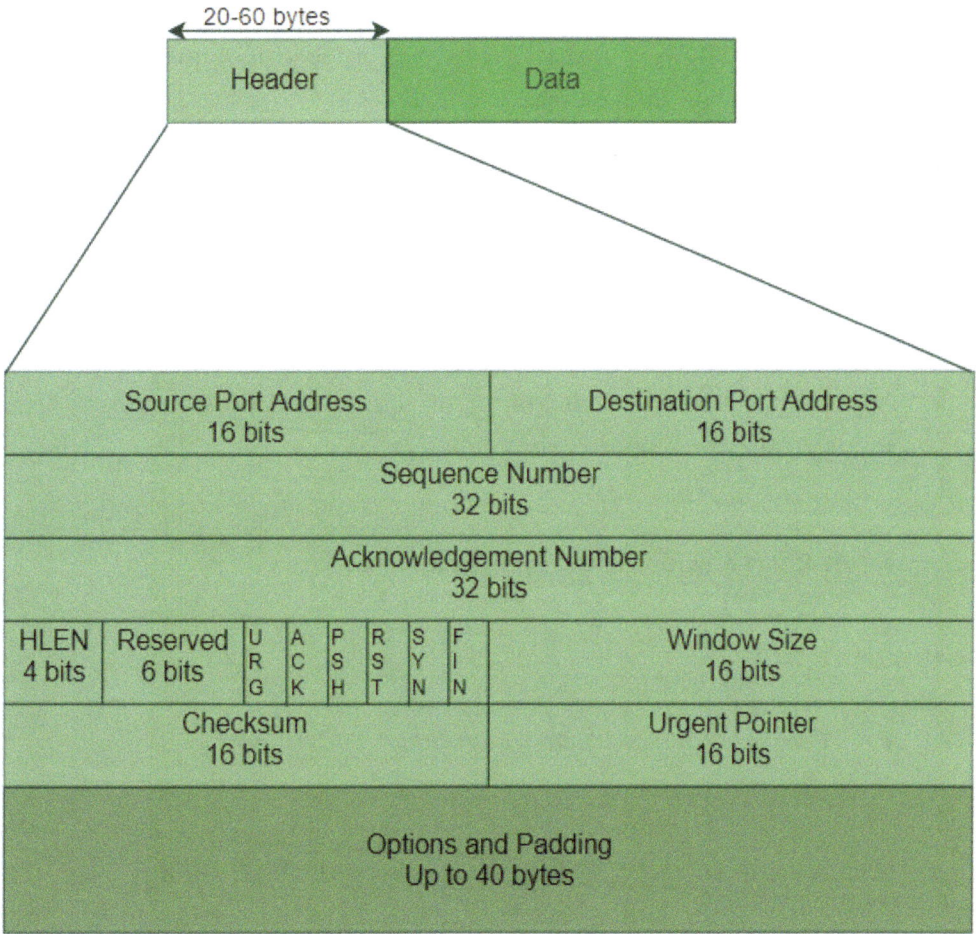

Figure 2-4. Structure of the header of a TCP segment. Source: https://www.geeksforgeeks.org/tcp-3-way-handshake-process/

CHAPTER 2   HOW THE INTERNET WORKS

And for the curious ones, here's a full breakdown of all the mandatory fields of the TCP header:

- Source Port Address (16 bits): the port address of the application in the sender host that sends the data segment.

- Destination Port Address (16 bits): the port address of the application in the receiving host that will receive the data segment.

- Sequence Number (32 bits): the number of the first byte sent in that segment. Used by the destination host to reorder segments and reassemble the original message.

- Acknowledgement Number (32 bits): the next byte number that the receiver expects to receive. Used to acknowledge that the previous bytes were received successfully.

- Header Length (HLEN, 4 bits): the length of the TCP header divided by 4. That is, if the header is 24 bytes, the value of this field will be "6."

- Control flags (6 bits): 6 1-bit control bits that control the lifecycle and status of the connection. Their function is

    - URG: Determines if the Urgent pointer is required (see below)
    - ACK: Acknowledgement number is valid
    - PSH: Request for push
    - RST: Reset the connection
    - SYN: Synchronize sequence numbers
    - FIN: Terminate the connection

- Window size (16 bits): how many bytes can be buffered during a connection. After sending that many bytes, the host must wait for a window update and acknowledgment from the receiver before it can start sending more bytes.

- Checksum (16 bits): holds a checksum for error control.

- Urgent pointer (16 bits): (used only when the value of the URG flag is 1) points to data that needs to reach the receiver's process as soon as possible. The value of this field is added to the sequence number to identify the last urgent byte.

Most gameplay-related functionalities are built on top of TCP: player inputs, events, and state changes need to be delivered reliably and in the exact order for a game to run properly. Imagine what a disaster it would be if the segment that contains the "player C spawned" or "your health is now 100" information would be lost! However, this makes TCP unfit for sending packets that can't afford the retransmission and acknowledgment delay, and that's where UDP comes to the rescue.

User Datagram Protocol

UDP is faster than TCP, as it tolerates data loss at the expense of reliability. It only uses 8 bytes to encapsulate information, and does not ensure neither the delivery nor the order of delivered segments (which are called "datagrams" in UDP's world). Being a connectionless protocol, it doesn't even care that the receiver is there to receive the datagram. It's the digital equivalent of a courier that throws a package at your door and goes away without asking you to sign for the parcel.

This makes UDP the best choice for features like voice chats, which would be completely unusable if every single sound had to be retransmitted, and for multicast and broadcast transmissions.

> *I would tell you a joke about UDP, but you probably wouldn't get it.*
>
> —Thomas_HF on r/ProgrammerHumor (Reddit)[6]

---

[6] https://www.reddit.com/r/ProgrammerHumor/comments/33ctkq/i_would_tell_you_a_joke_about_udp_but_you/

Figure 2-5 shows the structure of a UDP datagram.

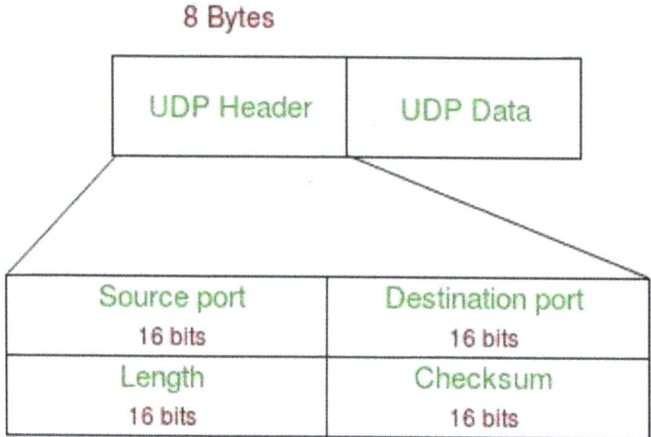

Figure 2-5. *Structure of the header of a UDP datagram. Source:* `https://www.geeksforgeeks.org/user-datagram-protocol-udp/`

And here's a breakdown of the header's fields:

- Source Port (16 bits): the port address of the application in the sender host that is sending the datagram.

- Destination Port (16 bits): the port address of the application in the receiving host that is receiving the data segment.

- Length (16 bits): size (in bytes) of the datagram, including the header/data.

- Checksum (16 bits): used to check for errors in the header/data. Optional in IPv4, mandatory in most cases in IPv6.

Network Architectures

Now that we've gone through the low-level details of how communication between two hosts works, it's time to understand the two different roles a host can have within a network, and the related responsibilities: "Client" and "Server."

What Is a Server?

A server is a passive host that provides a service on the network. It is "passive" because it listens for incoming connections from other hosts that want to use the server. Due to their nature, servers tend to be powerful devices with no human user controlling them: this is often the case for high-performance game and web servers. These machines can be shared among different organizations that can access a fraction of their physical resources (RAM, CPU, and GPU) simultaneously, or be dedicated to a single organization. In the latter case, the server is called a "Dedicated server." Since the server is the one providing the service, it usually has privileged access to protected systems like databases, where user information (i.e., player's accounts and inventories) is stored, and for this reason, it must be protected from unauthorized access and attacks of hackers, crackers, and malicious users. That's why the servers are usually protected by firewalls and access control lists, which determine what traffic can reach the server and what resources (i.e., ports or applications) can be used.

To save costs and exploit the full potential of the physical resources of a server, these machines usually run in "headless mode," which means that they never perform any rendering or look for user input, saving processing power that can be used to perform faster calculations. This is very common in game servers, as players play from their own client device.

What Is a Client?

A client is an active host that wants to use a service provided by a server. It is "active" because it actively tries to connect to servers. Clients are usually controlled by a user, and their physical resources can vary a lot. In games, we mostly think of three different categories of client devices:

- Computers: Mid/high-end devices with highly variable hardware, but predictable screen sizes
- Consoles: Mid-end devices with predictable hardware and screen sizes
- Mobile devices: Low/mid-end devices with highly variable hardware and screen sizes

CHAPTER 2 HOW THE INTERNET WORKS

Clients usually run multiple applications at a time, requesting multiple services from different servers, and rarely have direct access to critical systems like databases.

Client–Server Architecture

A client–server architecture is one of the two common ways to organize the hosts of a network. As shown in Figure 2-6, the roles of a client and of a server in a client–server architecture are assigned to different hosts, and for security reasons, the server is usually physically inaccessible to the same users that own one or more clients. As the server is the only provider and all communication goes through it, the capabilities of the network decrease when the number of clients requesting the service increases.

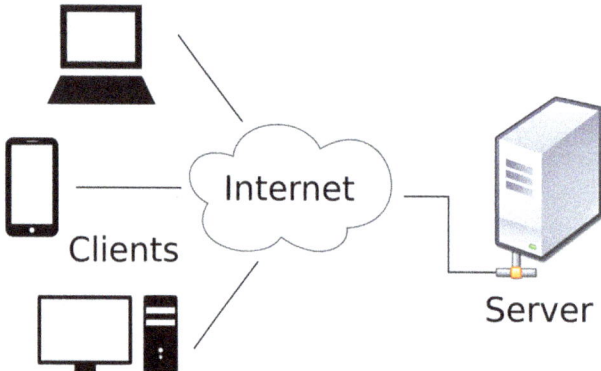

Figure 2-6. *Representation of a client-server architecture. Source:* `https://en.wikipedia.org/wiki/Client%E2%80%93server_model#/media/File:Client-server-model.svg`

Most multiplayer games use a client-server architecture, even though in some specific circumstances the server can be one of the clients. We'll talk about the specifics of this and the correlated security risks in Chapter 4.

CHAPTER 2 HOW THE INTERNET WORKS

Peer-to-Peer Architecture (P2P)

In a P2P architecture, every host (called "node") acts as both a server and a client simultaneously, sharing data with other nodes in the same network. Contrary to the client-server architecture, when the number of nodes in a P2P network increases, the resource-sharing capabilities of the network increase too, as shown in Figure 2-7. P2P is a very common architecture used by file-sharing applications built on top of the BitTorrent protocol: the more nodes owning and uploading a copy of the requested file are part of the network, the faster the other nodes can download the file from multiple sources.

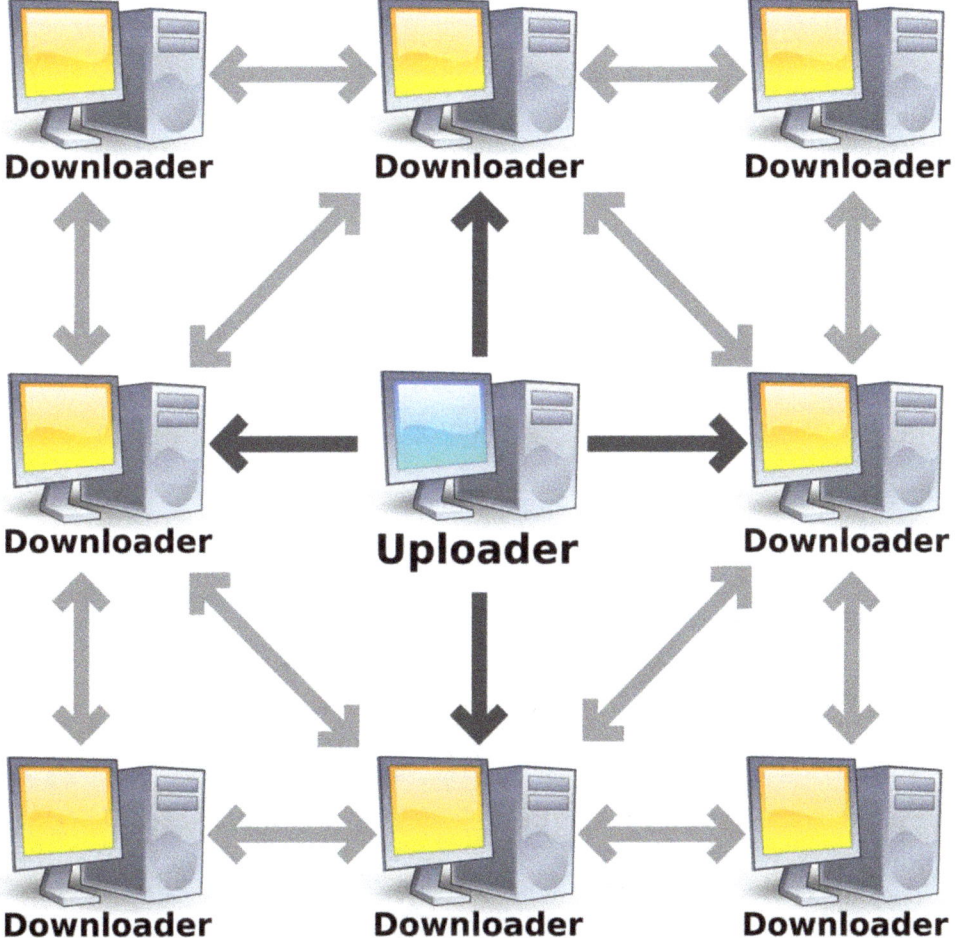

Figure 2-7. *Representation of a peer-to-peer architecture. Source:* https://en.wikipedia.org/wiki/BitTorrent#/media/File:BitTorrent_network.svg

Conclusion

As you've learnt in this chapter, hosts are identified by a logical address called "IP address" and follow standardized protocols to communicate with each other, both in local networks and over the Internet. Depending on the role they have, hosts can provide services or request them by generating requests that are then encapsulated using the protocols defined at each layer of the TCP/IP and OSI model, routed on the physical mediums in the form of signals, and reconstructed and interpreted by the receiving host. You've also learnt that it takes time for information to travel from one device to another, that some protocols allow for fast communication at the expense of reliability, and that hosts can be organized in networks using different architectures.

In the next chapter, you'll learn more about how to structure a multiplayer game, choosing between authority models, netcode frameworks, and synchronization techniques. You'll also learn about lag-compensation techniques and testing workflows.

CHAPTER 3

Developing a Multiplayer Game

In Chapter 2, you learnt how information travels on the internet, and how different devices operate when they need to communicate with each other.

In this chapter, you'll learn how to structure a multiplayer game, choosing between authority models and netcode frameworks. You'll learn about data synchronization, lag-compensation techniques, good practices to apply in your game's codebase, testing workflows that will make your life easier, and how to prevent cheating. At the end of the chapter, you'll be able to understand what the right architectural choices for the type of game you're working on are, and how to ensure your players have a smooth, enjoyable, and fair experience.

When Should I Add Multiplayer?

There's a common misconception in the world of game development: many think that multiplayer is an "add-on" and that you can implement multiplayer "later." As you've read in Chapter 1, reality is different: multiplayer is the foundation of the entire game loop, and introducing it later means that you must rewrite most of your codebase. This is one of the main reasons why these studios often fail to make a successful multiplayer game on time and on budget.

Many studio leads who have made successful single-player games fall into this trap too, focusing too much on making "the single player version first" and then trying to add multiplayer "later." Unless your gameplay has 0 multiplayer features in it, you need to write such features in a way that they work in a networked environment, where things can (and will) go wrong, latency exists, and state needs to be validated to avoid cheating.

© Paolo Abela 2025
P. Abela, *Going Multiplayer*, https://doi.org/10.1007/979-8-8688-2031-1_3

For example, imagine working on a post-apocalyptic survival game where players can:

1. Do missions to gather resources
2. Recruit other survivors to build a team
3. Build and customize their own outpost

Let's say your team spends 1 year working on a single-player campaign mode. You finish the vertical slice, and after a week, your publisher comes and says: "We need to make these multiplayer."

Now the team has to spend all their time rewriting the game so that:

1. Data of missions is synchronized and managed to avoid cheating.
2. NPC survivors can be replaced by real players whose movements and actions need to travel on the Internet in a reliable and optimized way.
3. Outposts can be attacked and built by multiple players, who need to be able to find and target such outposts somehow.

That's months of work if you're lucky. If you have five engineers working on your game at a $10K gross salary for these months, it means you just wasted $50K/month adjusting something that you could've done right since the beginning if you had made your game multiplayer-centric since day 1 of the Production phase.

What Does Multiplayer-Centric Mean?

"Multiplayer-centric" means that all features are designed and implemented so they work in a networked environment, even if the game is run in a simulated single-player mode ("host mode"). The main objection I hear when I tell this to studios is "we don't want players to go against each other from day 1, because the playerbase will be small at the beginning."

The point is multiplayer-centric doesn't mean that you should have Player vs. Players ("PvP") game modes enabled from day 1.

If you want to make your game "singleplayer" in a networked environment, just run it in host mode: start a local server, and connect a local client to it. This allows you to inject artificial network lag for testing and, in the meantime, will force you to write your features so they work in a "multiplayer" environment from the beginning, preventing tech debt.

Async vs. Sync Multiplayer

Before we start diving into the technical details on how to make a multiplayer game, it's important to distinguish between the two main types of multiplayer features: "Asynchronous" (a.k.a. "Async") and "Synchronous" (a.k.a. "Sync" or "Realtime") multiplayer. I say "features" because a multiplayer game can incorporate a mix of both Async and Realtime multiplayer features that engage players in different ways.

Async Multiplayer

Async multiplayer means that players don't have to be present and connected at the same time to interact with each other's accounts and resources, to affect shared goals, or to compete.

Most popular browser games of the early 2000s, like "Farmville," "Ikariam," and "Grepolis" had an almost-completely async multiplayer game loop: players had their own "basecamp" to manage (i.e., a farm, or an ancient Greek-like city) and could upgrade it using different resources that were collected over time, stolen, or granted from other players. These resources incentivize players to interact with other player's basecamps: you can help your friends and get rewarded, or ask them to help you speed up what you're doing. These innate social-based mechanics contribute a lot to growing the playerbase organically, as inviting friends provides immediate advantage and faster progression as you get more resources more frequently.

There's also an async multiplayer feature that is extremely common in games, and has been like that since the invention of cabinets and arcades: leaderboards.

These let players compete for the "highest score" without ever fighting each other's directly in a real-time situation, and contribute to keeping players engaged over time. It's important to keep in mind how async multiplayer can be an effective tool to engage players from the socio-competitive side, especially since async multiplayer features are way easier to implement compared to sync ones, as latency becomes almost irrelevant.

Sync Multiplayer

Sync (or "Realtime") multiplayer means that players must be present and connected at the same time to interact with each other's accounts and resources, to affect shared goals, or to compete.

This is the type of multiplayer that lets you play with others simultaneously in shooters, card games, MOBAs, and so on. Realtime multiplayer features engage players "right now" with adrenaline moments and on-the-spot choices, which means that they're very sensitive to latency, and are usually the biggest and most important part of the core game loop of a multiplayer game.

Authority Models

In both Async and Realtime multiplayer games, someone needs to make decisions about how the game or simulation needs to move forward: someone needs to decide who gets hit by a projectile, when to spawn something, or what a player can see. An authority model defines who does this.

There are mainly three authority models: server-authoritative client-authoritative, and distributed authority. Even if the name might suggest otherwise, the network architecture of all these models is "client-server": none of these are peer-to-peer, because there's always a need for a centralized network Host that makes decisions.

Server-Authoritative

In a server-authoritative model, there's one centralized server, and clients connect to it. Every client is usually an individual player: it can be a PC, a console, or a mobile phone. As introduced in Chapter 2, a server is a machine running automatically, usually in the cloud or on-premises. Every client sends the inputs to the server, which validates and processes them, relaying the results to all clients. This means that only the server makes decisions and is the "source of truth" for the current state of the game.

As the server accepts only inputs instead of state changes from the clients (i.e., "I want to pick this item" instead of "I picked this item"), the state of the game can be altered in an intended and secure way, making cheating harder.

See Figure 3-1 for a representation of a server-authoritative model in a dedicated server network topology.

CHAPTER 3   DEVELOPING A MULTIPLAYER GAME

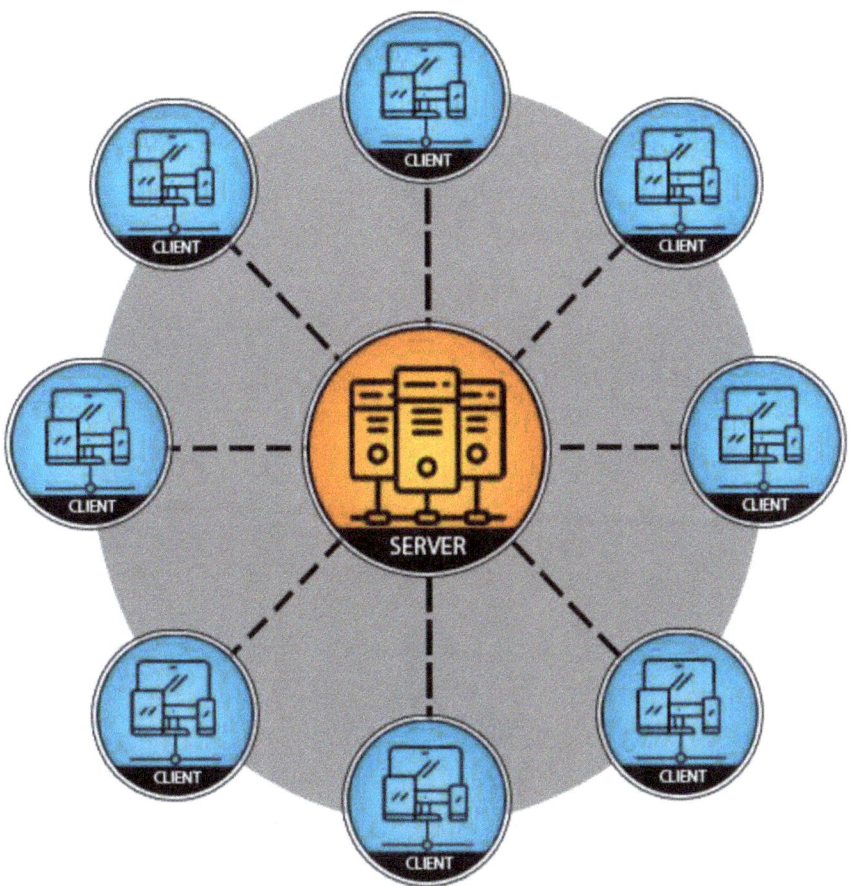

Figure 3-1. *Representation of a server-authoritative architecture. Source:*
`https://docs-multiplayer.unity3d.com/netcode/current/terms-concepts/`
`client-server/`

Since there needs to be a high-performing dedicated server that runs instances of the game and connects multiple players, this model is generally more expensive compared to the others. However, it's also the most secure one as bad actors (i.e., cheaters or hackers) don't have neither physical access to the server, nor remote access to its file system, and therefore can't alter the executable of the game, and its runtime logic, in any way.

Since the server is what connects all players, by design, it is reachable through a public address and port that clients can easily use to connect. Moreover, the entire game session is interrupted if the server crashes or becomes unreachable due to network issues.

Client-Authoritative

In a client-authoritative model, one of the clients is also the server, and is called the "Host"[1]. See Figure 3-2 for a representation of a client-authoritative model in a client-hosted topology. Since the server has absolute decision power, this means that it's easier to cheat in a client-authoritative model, because the Host player is also the server.

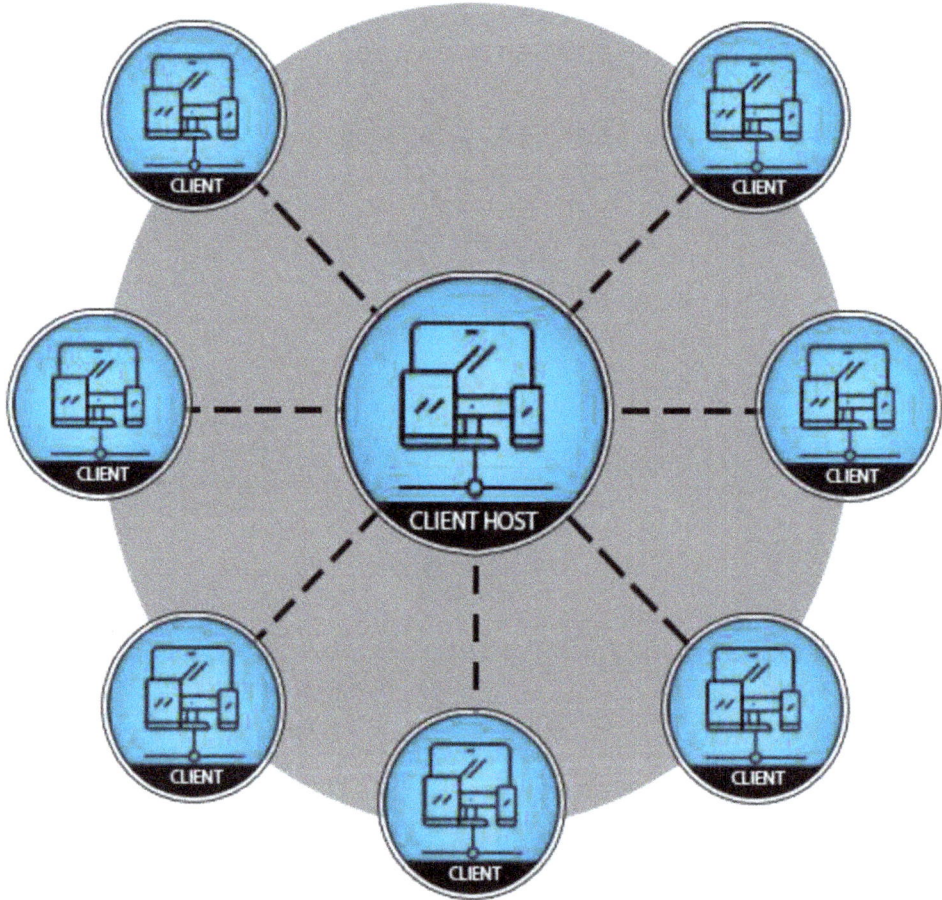

Figure 3-2. *Representation of a client-authoritative architecture. Source:* https://docs-multiplayer.unity3d.com/netcode/current/terms-concepts/client-server/

---

[1] To not be confused by the "Host" of a network, a concept introduced in Chapter 2, which simply represents any device that is part of a network.

The Host also has an unfair advantage as they suffer no latency for the inputs they send and therefore can process their own inputs immediately, while it takes time for other players' inputs to reach the Host.

As all the processing is left to the Host at virtually no cost for the studio behind the game, this architecture introduces a user experience risk: if the Host has a slow or unstable internet connection, or weak hardware, all players will experience lag and similar issues, which ruin the user experience.

Since the Host is what connects all players, it needs to be reachable over the internet. This is usually a problem due to how the Network Address Translation (NAT) mechanism protects the IP addresses of devices in private networks. In Chapter 4, we'll see how to address this.

The entire game session is interrupted if the Host crashes or becomes unreachable due to network issues.

Distributed Authority

Distributed authority is a hybrid between the other 2 models, where every client is responsible for a piece of the simulation. See Figure 3-3 for a representation of a distributed authority model and topology.

In this model, there's no central server simulating the entire game: clients share responsibility for owning and tracking the state of objects in the simulation and have the authority to spawn and manage objects themselves, with additional options to configure ownership permissions ("who can alter what").

All clients run their own partial simulations and communicate their updates directly to other clients through a lightweight central state service (running on a server) that keeps track of state changes of spawned objects and routes network traffic.

CHAPTER 3   DEVELOPING A MULTIPLAYER GAME

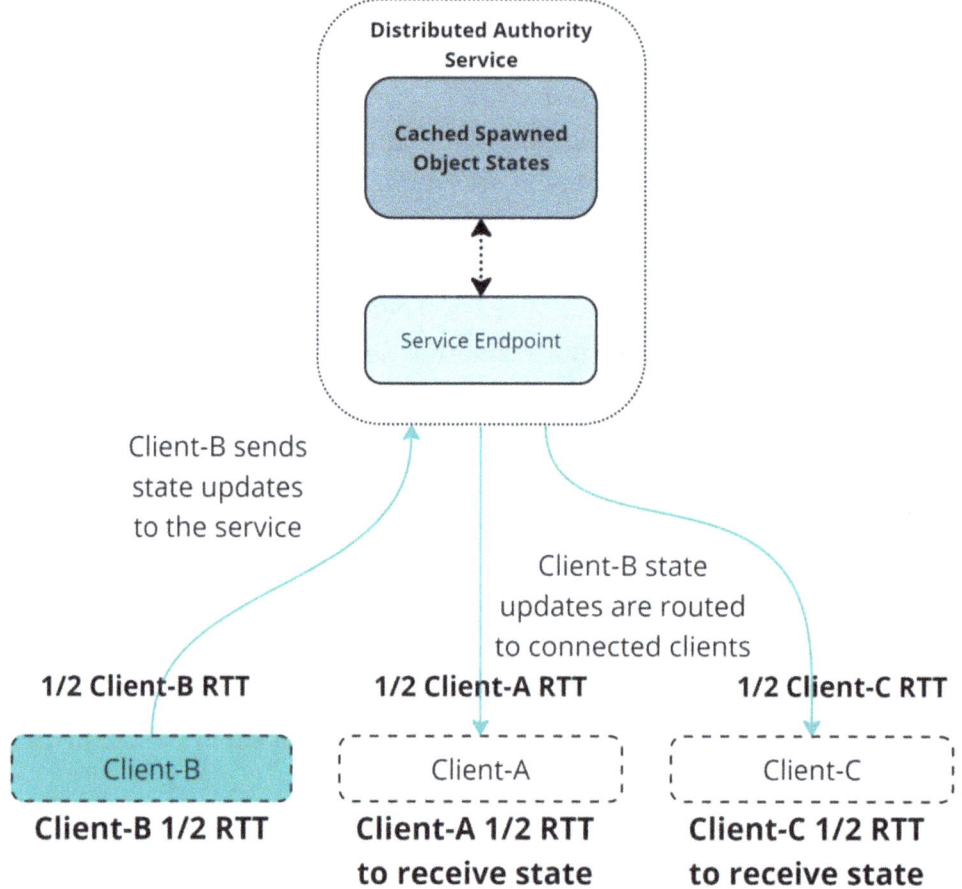

Figure 3-3. *Representation of a distributed authority architecture. Source: https://docs-multiplayer.unity3d.com/netcode/current/terms-concepts/distributed-authority/*

One of the clients is designed as the "session owner" and manages the global game state while they stay connected (like a Host would do in a client-authoritative model), leaving that role to another client when they disconnect. This responsibility transfer is called "Host migration" and allows Distributed authority sessions to survive when a Host leaves.

CHAPTER 3　DEVELOPING A MULTIPLAYER GAME

Choosing the Right Authoritative Model

If you pick the wrong authority model, and depending on what you picked, players will be able to cheat, or will have a terrible user experience due to additional latency, or your code structure will become more complicated than necessary to manage.

These are problems that no team wants to face, so we really need to ask ourselves: "what's the right authority model for my game?". Table 3-1 shows examples and a summary of this.

Table 3-1. Authority model and use cases

	Server-authoritative	Client-authoritative	Distributed authority
Commonly used for…	PvP/competitive, E-sports	PvE/casual co-op, LAN games, two-player fighting games	Social hubs (i.e., Roblox)
Safe to handle money? (i.e., IAP)	✓	✗	✗
Cheap to build and maintain	✗	✓	✓
Impact on user experience (i.e., latency)	Depends on server's specs and network conditions (usually good)	Depends on Host's device and network conditions (usually bad)	Depends on players device

As you can see, server-authoritative is the correct choice for competitive games and money-sensitive operations, as it allows to implement effective anti-cheating measures and provides a better user experience.

It's more complicated to build server-authoritative games as you need to clearly separate the server-side and client-side logic, but it's a must-have for this situation.

Distributed authority is the correct choice for casual experiences, games that don't require a deterministic physics simulation, and casual games where there are tens of players connected at the same time. Client-authoritative models can be used for pretty much everything else, as long as you can afford the aforementioned risks.

Netcode Frameworks

Once you know what authority model you're going to use, the next step is to pick (or build) a netcode framework, which is a software tool or library that provides pre-built functionality to implement multiplayer features in games.

Every framework worth its name provides at least connectivity and synchronization features, but some may even have out-of-the-box lag compensation or backend services (i.e., matchmaking), depending on how popular the ecosystem behind the framework is.[2]

When talking about frameworks, it's crucial to understand that there is no one-size-fits-all solution: each framework works best **only** for a few types of games. As different types of multiplayer games require different types of optimizations, there's a limit to how many of these optimizations can be generalized without making the development experience a nightmare for developers.[3]

This means that choosing the wrong netcode framework is not an option as it will limit what your game can do, or will not allow it to scale well with when the playerbase grows, leading to lag and disconnections that will ruin the player experience and make them hate and bad-mouth your game.

Add to that that if a framework lacks proper documentation, you'll have a hard time when you try to customize features or implement bugfixes, limiting your game's potential for growth. Finally, as you can imagine, changing the netcode framework down the line means rewriting most of your core game loop features as different frameworks use different syntaxes and workflows.

For example, imagine working on a fast-paced First-Person Shooter battle royale for 6 months, only to realize that the framework you picked introduces lag spikes or teleporting[4]/rubberbanding[5] issues whenever it tries to synchronize the position of players that are moving fast (i.e., using vehicles). What can you do at that point?

Option A: you remove vehicles from your game. If this was the core differentiator in a difficult market, your game is now "just another battle royale." Good luck marketing that.

---

[2] Popular netcode frameworks are: Mirror, Photon Fusion, Nakama, Netcode for GameObjects.

[3] If a framework claims to be the solution to all problems, it's probably a jack of all trades, and a master of none.

[4] Characters immediately moving from one point to another in space, without smooth movement.

[5] Movement-related issue in which something teleports very fast back and forth between two points, like a rubber band.

Also, your whole game design now must be redone to take into account the absence of vehicles.

Option B: your engineering team stops working on the game and shifts the focus to making a custom version of the framework that supports fast-paced movement of player objects. Maybe they have the expertise needed to achieve that, or maybe not. They'll find out in the next couple months... Hopefully.

Option C: your engineering team stops working on the game and shifts the focus to changing the netcode framework, throwing most of the past 6 months of work into the trash as all multiplayer-related features need to be redone.

If you had five engineers working on your game at a $10K gross salary for these 6 months, it means you just wasted ~ $300K in option C, potentially more in option B, and your hype marketing budget too in option A. All these options suck.

The real cure here is "prevention": so how do you pick the right netcode framework?

Picking the Right Netcode Framework

As I said, the "best" netcode framework depends on the type and features of the game you're making. The main factors to consider when making the decision are:

1. What Game Engine are you using?

    a. Unity? Unreal? Something custom?

2. What game genre are you developing?

    a. First person shooter? Card game? Something else?

3. Is the game physics-based?

    a. Is gravity important? Can you roll?

4. How many players (max) are going to be together in a single instance?

5. 2? 5? 10? 100?

    a. How important is it to prevent cheating?

6. Is this an e-Sport? Is it a casual co-op game? Is it PvP?

    a. What realtime multiplayer features do you plan to implement?

Chapter 3 Developing a Multiplayer Game

7. Shooting? Driving? Altering the world? Crafting?

    a. How many non-players networked objects are going to be simultaneously in a session?

8. NPCs? Pickable items?

    a. What support is available when things break?

9. Documentation? Communities?

    a. What frameworks are your team already familiar with?

Once you have a precise answer for each of these, choosing the framework becomes a matter of comparing tradeoffs (i.e., licensing costs vs. learning curve) between all frameworks that fit the needs of your project.

As you can see from Table 3-2, PlayerUnknown's Battlegrounds (PUBG) and Ariokan have very different requirements, meaning that the ideal framework for developing one or the other is different.

Table 3-2. Comparison of characteristics of several multiplayer games

	PUBG	League of Legends	Ariokan
Genre	Battle royale	MOBA	Collectible Card Game
Max players/session	100	10	2
Competitive	●	●	●
Fast-paced	●	●	✕
Physics-based	●	✕	✕
Networked entities per session	Players + Vehicles + pickable items + drops	Players + Minions + Wards + Monsters + Drops	Players + cards alterations

Existing vs. Custom Netcode Frameworks

"Should I just make my own netcode framework?"

In general, that is a bad idea. If you think making your own framework is easier than picking one that is an industry standard, you're in for a very expensive (and time consuming) surprise.

There are plenty of solutions out there: all you need to do is pick the right one. Does that justify spending months making your own, unknown netcode framework that you'll have to maintain for years?

Nope. Unless you need to do something non-standard, it's better to stick to the standard tools. The advantage of existing communities, documentation, and tech-familiar talent is priceless, and you need all the help you can get if you want to make your game succeed.

Synchronization of Game State and Events

One of the features every netcode framework provides is the synchronization of state and events. Through the netcode framework, information travels from the server to the clients (and back), informing each device about what is happening in the simulation, what inputs are sent, and the consequences of players' and NPCs' actions. The implementation details of the synchronization flow and system vary by framework, but all implementations are based on the same core concepts: tick rate, networked variables, remote procedure calls, and network messages.

When talking about synchronization, it's important to keep in mind that in a networked environment, there's an instance of each networked object on each device, and each of these instances is treated differently by the local system.

For example, the object that represents a specific player exists both on the player's device, where it is recognized as a local player, and on the server, where it is recognized as a remote player. "Synchronizing" data means copying the state of one instance to the other.

Network Tick Rate

The network tick rate is the metronome of the synchronization system: it determines how many times per second (a "tick") updates and messages are sent on the network, and is measured in Hertz. A network update (a.k.a. "delta") is a message that states how something changed since the last tick.

For example, imagine you have an integer variable named "*number,*" that you want to synchronize over the network. If you change the value of the variable from "100" to "101," this will generate a delta that says: "the value of this variable changed from 100 to 101." With a tick rate of 1, the system will check once per second if a delta for the variable "*number*" was created, and send it to all intended recipients (i.e., the clients, if the delta originated on the server and the system is server-authoritative). With a tick rate of 10, the system will check 10 times per second (so once every 100 milliseconds).

The tick rate has a very noticeable impact on synchronization:

1. A low tick rate introduces additional latency. With a tick rate of 1, inputs and state changes will be processed 10 times slower compared to a system with a tick rate of 10. This means that even in a Local Area Network (LAN), where latency is usually <10ms, the minimum amount of time it takes for synchronized information to reach each device can never be higher than the time difference between ticks.

2. The higher the tick rate, the faster deltas will be sent, and the earlier recipients will get them, resulting in a smoother user experience with reduced latency.

You might be wondering: if a higher tick rate makes information travel faster, why don't we just max out the tick rate to get a better experience?

And the answer is: because processing a tick is a CPU-intensive operation, and sending deltas increases network bandwidth. I made a simple example before, but you must keep in mind that games usually have thousands of variables that need to be synchronized: health, ammo, position, rotation, scale, cooldowns, and so on. Since each networked entity (i.e., a player or an NPC) has information to synchronize, the processing power needed on both the clients and server to check deltas, compress/decompress them, and send/receive them on/from the network can escalate very quickly when multiple entities are spawned. Raising the tick rate too much can have a negative impact on the CPU, slowing down the entire simulation in a vicious cycle I like calling "Spiral of performance death," which leads to stuttering, frame rate drops, and even more stress for the CPU as it tries to compensate for the reduced frames per second.

For this reason, the tick rate of most games sits between 20 and 60, depending on how fast-paced they are.

Networked Variables

Networked Variables are variables whose value can be changed only by the networked entity that has authority over them, and whose changes are automatically synchronized over the network during the next network tick.

Authority Mechanism

Networked Variables are server-authoritative and readable by everybody by default in most frameworks, meaning that only deltas generated on the server are sent during a network tick, while deltas generated on the client are ignored. This helps with cheat prevention, since if a client were to set their own health to the maximum every frame, they would be invulnerable.

Some frameworks let developers specify who has authority over a specific Networked Variable. Listing 3-1 showcases how in the netcode framework "Netcode For GameObjects," you can make a Networked Variable readable only by the server and the owner of the object to which the script is assigned, and writeable only by the server. With this simple change you can reduce bandwidth consumption for the server and all non-owners of the object, and you can implement a more client-side hack-resistant design where only the player knows how much ammo they have left.

Listing 3-1. Example of how to set read/write permissions of a Networked Variable (which Netcode For GameObjects calls "NetworkVariable")

```
public class PlayerState : NetworkBehavior
{
    NetworkVariable<int> ammoLeftInWeapon = new NetworkVariable<int>
    (default, NetworkVariableReadPermission.Owner,
    NetworkVariableWritePermission.Server);
}
```

Callbacks Mechanism

A common feature of Networked Variables in netcode frameworks is the "callback" (or "hook") mechanism, which allows for reacting when the new value of the variable is received. Listing 3-2 showcases how you can implement this mechanism using the netcode framework "Mirror," printing a log on clients when the server changes the value of the health Networked Variable.

Listing 3-2. Example of how to use the hook of a Networked Variable (which Mirror calls "SyncVar") to run code on all clients when the server changes its value

```
using Mirror;
public class Player : NetworkBehavior
{
    [SyncVar(hook = nameof(OnClientHealthChanged))]
    int health = 100;

    //Called on all clients when the value of "health" changes in some
    method on the server
    void OnClientHealthChanged(int oldValue, int newValue)
    {
        UnityEngine.Debug.Log($"[Client] Health changed from {oldValue} to
        {newValue}");
    }
}
```

It's very important to note how the `OnClientHealthChanged` method is called on every client that receives the update, not on the server that made the change to the Networked Variable. The call is managed by the framework in a way transparent to the developer.

Another aspect worth noting is that the class `Player` inherits from `NetworkBehavior`, which is a special class provided by Mirror to identify all networked components. This makes it easier for the system to look for deltas every tick, as the only classes that need to be checked are the ones that inherit from `NetworkBehavior`.

Auto-sync on Join Mechanism

Usually, when a client joins an existing game (a.k.a. "hot joins a game"), the latest value of each Networked Variable is sent to that client, so it can "initialize" the state of all objects in the scene with the current state of the simulation on the server. This is a crucial aspect of Networked Variables, because it allows clients to be up to date with what has happened so far, and is the base mechanism behind the "reconnection" feature.

Supported Data Types

Networked Variables usually only support serializable data types (like C#'s `int`, `float`, `bool`) or data structures entirely made of them (i.e., C# structs that combine `int`, `float`, `bool`).

The reason behind this is that the binary representation of these serializable types never changes, so they can be easily serialized as an array of bytes and added to the payload of network packets. Object references like pointers can't be serialized because they don't represent the same object across different devices. For this reason, both players and networked objects are usually identified by a simple number that acts as an id, and the system automatically uses the id to retrieve the associated object on the local client.

Custom Serializers

Sometimes you might have to write your own custom serializer for advanced use cases, for example, if you want to send the data stored in a Dictionary to another client.

For example, in card games like Ariokan, there are cards that grant "Keywords" to other cards, making them behave differently. Players want to be able to see what cards gave the keyword to the one they're currently inspecting, so we (developers) need to synchronize this information. However, cards and keywords are complex classes with multiple references, variables, and properties, so we need a custom serializer for this. Listing 3-3 showcases how you can implement a custom serializer in Mirror to synchronize the cards that have added a keyword to the card being serialized.

As you can see, a custom serializer is basically made of a "write" method that writes the current state of a complex object to a buffer provided by the framework (`NetworkWriter`), and then uses a "read" method to retrieve and interpret that information from another buffer (`NetworkReader`) when it is received at the other end of the communication, and "reconstruct" the state of an object by looking for local references or data that can't be serialized "as is."

Caution When using custom serializers, it's very important to read everything you write in the buffers. If you forget to do so the buffers will not be cleared properly, and you'll experience serialization issues that might crash the game.

Listing 3-3. Example of how to implement a custom serializer in Mirror to synchronize the cards that added a keyword to the card being serialized

```
using Mirror;
using UnityEngine;
public static class CustomNetworkSerializers
{
    public abstract class CardKeyword : ScriptableObject
    {
        public uint ID;
        //many more fields here which can not be serialized automatically
    }
    public interface ICardKeywordSource
    {
        short GetSourceID(); //gets the ID of the Card that assigned the
        Keyword to the card being serialized
    }
    public static void WriteSerializedDictionary(NetworkWriter writer,
    Dictionary<CardKeyword, ICardKeywordSource> dictionary)
    {
        writer.WriteInt(dictionary.Count);
        foreach (var item in dictionary)
        {
            writer.WriteUInt(item.Key.ID);
            writer.WriteShort(item.Value.GetSourceID());
        }
    }
    public static void ReadSerializedDictionary(NetworkReader reader, out
    Dictionary<CardKeyword, ICardKeywordSource> dictionary, PlayerManager
    cardOwner)
    {
        int dictionaryLenght = reader.ReadInt();
        dictionary = new Dictionary<CardKeyword, ICardKeywordSource>();
        if (dictionaryLenght < 1)
```

```
        {
            return;
        }
        for (int i = 0; i < dictionaryLenght; i++)
        {
            uint keywordID = reader.ReadUInt();
            short sourceID = reader.ReadShort();
            ICardKeywordSource source = null;

            foreach (var card in cardOwner.allMyCards)
            {
                if (card.ID != sourceID){ continue; }
                source = card;
                break;
            }
            dictionary[KeywordsDatabase.GetByID(keywordID)] = source;
            if (source == null)
            {
                Debug.LogError($"Couldn't recognize KeywordSource with ID
                {sourceID} on client");
                continue;
            }
        }
    }
}
```

> **Caution** Some frameworks use a FIFO ("First In, First Out") logic when writing and reading information, meaning that the "write" and "read" instructions that refer to the same piece of information must be in the same order (like in the example). Other frameworks use a LIFO ("Last In, First Out") logic instead, and in that case the "read" instructions must be in the opposite order compared to the "write" ones.

Remote Procedure Calls (RPCs)

In the context of multiplayer, RPCs are networked method calls that we can use to notify "actions" or "events" to other players or the server: an RPC is invoked by a Networked object on one device, but executes on the instance of that networked objects on another device (in addition to, or instead of, the device invoking it), like displayed in Figures 3-4 and 3-5.

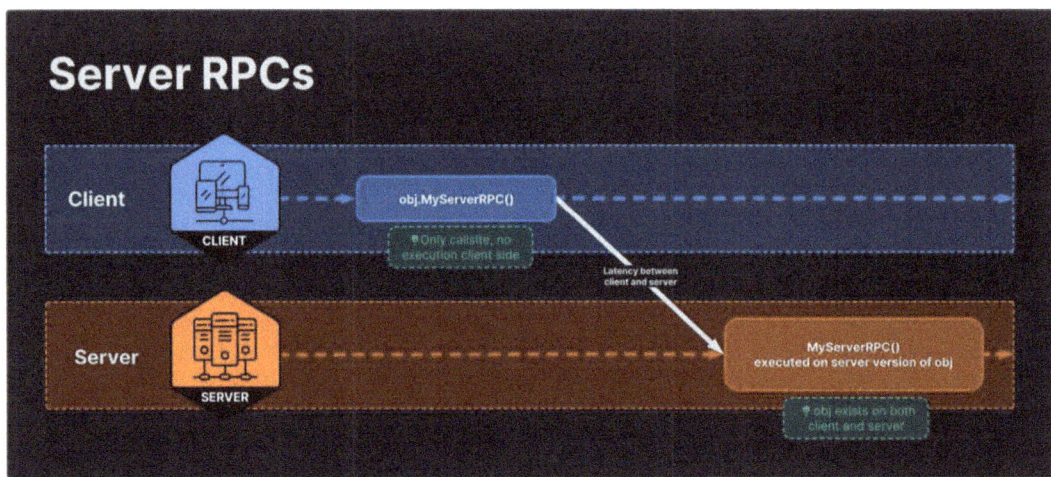

Figure 3-4. Representation of an RPC invoked on client but executed on the server. Source: `https://docs-multiplayer.unity3d.com/img//sequence_diagrams/RPCs/ServerRPCs_Dark.png`

CHAPTER 3   DEVELOPING A MULTIPLAYER GAME

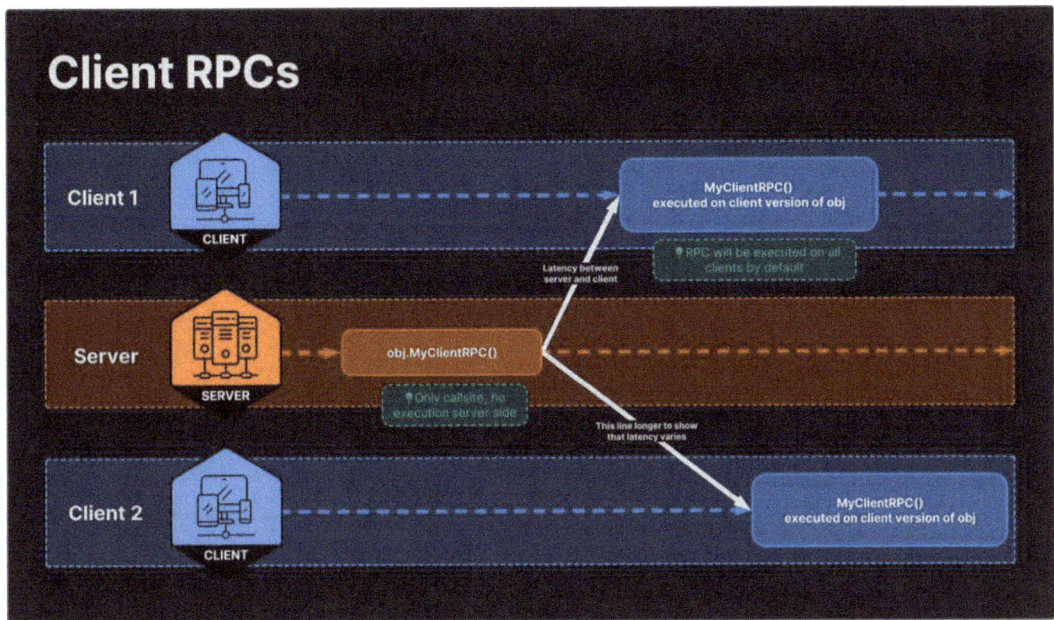

Figure 3-5. *Representation of an RPC invoked on server the but executed on all clients. Source:* `https://docs-multiplayer.unity3d.com/img//sequence_diagrams/RPCs/ClientRPCs_Dark.png`

A classic use of RPCs is to handle player input: for example, when a players want to use a skill, shoot, or pick up an item, they send an RPC to the server stating their intention. The server then processes the input and sends an RPC to all relevant clients to inform them of what happened. Listing 3-4 showcases how to implement a chat system in Netcode For GameObjects using RPCs.

Like Networked Variables, and depending on the framework, RPCs are usually batched and sent when the next network tick ticks. This means that any RPC used for inputs will suffer from a higher "input lag" if the tick rate is low.

The moment you mark a method as an RPC (i.e., using the `Rpc` attribute), you're changing how it is treated by the underlying netcode framework at compilation and runtime: the framework becomes aware of the method's parameters, and serializes/deserializes them over the network when the method is invoked. This means that RPCs need to be carefully designed, as you can only send around parameters that are serializable (or for which you implemented a custom serializer).

Listing 3-4. Example of how to implement a chat system in Netcode For GameObjects using RPCs

```
using UnityEngine;
using Unity.Netcode;
public class ChatManager : NetworkBehavior
{
    //Invoked by a script when player types in the UI of the chat
    (not an RPC)
    public void OnClientSendMessageToServer(string message)
    {
        string localPlayerUsername = "Some username";
        ServerMoodMessageReceivedRpc(localPlayerUsername, message);
    }

    //Invoked on client, executed on the server
[Rpc(SendTo.Server)]
    void ServerMoodMessageReceivedRpc(string senderName, string message)
    {
        /* Here's an example of the type of operation you could do on the
        server to prevent malicious actions from bad actors. */
        string redactedMessage = OnServerFilterBadWords(message);
        ClientMoodMessageReceivedRpc(senderName, redactedMessage);
    }

    //Invoked on server, executed on the server (not an RPC)
    string OnServerFilterBadWords(string message)
    {
        //some logic here to filter out bad words
    }

    //Invoked on server, executed on all clients including the host
    [Rpc(SendTo.ClientsAndHost)]
    void ClientMoodMessageReceivedRpc(string senderName, string message)
```

```
    {
        Debug.Log($"'{senderName}' said: {message}");
    }
}
```

Network Messages

Sometimes you need to send a message that is not tied to a specific instance of a networked object (i.e., for logging, analytics, or profiling information) and therefore can't use Networked Variables or RPCs. In this case, you can use low-level network messages that will act as C# events, and define methods that will be invoked whenever a message of a certain type is received. See listing 3-5 for an example.

Listing 3-5. Example of how to implement a NetworkMessage in Mirror

```
using UnityEngine;
using Mirror;
//note how this is a MonoBehavior, so it's not networked
class Scores : MonoBehavior
{
    public struct ScoreMessage : NetworkMessage
    {
        public int score;
        public Vector3 scorePos;
    }

    void SendScore(int score, Vector3 scorePos)
    {
        var message = new ScoreMessage()
        {
            score = score,
            scorePos = scorePos
        };
        NetworkServer.SendToAll(message);
    }

    void SetupClient()
```

```
    {
        NetworkClient.RegisterHandler<ScoreMessage>(OnClientScoreReceived);
        NetworkClient.Connect("localhost");
    }

    void OnClientScoreReceived(ScoreMessage message)
    {
        Debug.Log($"Received score {message.score} from position {message.
        scorePos}");
    }
}
```

Best Practices for Multiplayer Codebases

Code is a liability, not an asset, and code that is hard to understand is an even bigger liability that slows down development and introduces bugs.

In the codebase of a multiplayer project, where some methods are used only by clients, by the server, or by both, it's easy to get lost in "who does what" when looking at code. That's why it's good practice to use prefixes and assemblies to identify where a specific piece of code is running.

Prefixes

If you look at the code samples in this chapter, you'll notice that many methods of networked classes start with "OnClient" or "OnServer." This is a simple trick you can use to immediately identify where a method is executed. If it starts with "OnServer," you know that such code is meant to be run only if the local game instance is running as a server and that such code should never ever ever run on a client-only instance of the game.

If you see that method referenced in client-only code, it's probably a bug (and vice versa). Any method that does not start with a prefix should be considered as "runnable from anywhere."

This makes debugging way easier, and lets you quickly exclude portions of code when looking for root causes and issues.

As you can imagine, this system only works if you and your team adhere to this naming convention and actively enforce it in code reviews and pull requests, but I guarantee that it's worth the effort.

Role-Specific Code

Prefixes are a way to logically separate code and improve its readability, but they will not stop you from shipping server code in client-only builds (which is a potential security issue). A more advanced way to separate code is to strip it out of builds that do not need it. For example, you could remove all UI-related client code by putting it in a file that is ignored when compiling the server. As displayed in Figure 3-6, in Unity's world, this is done using Assembly Definition Files.

CHAPTER 3   DEVELOPING A MULTIPLAYER GAME

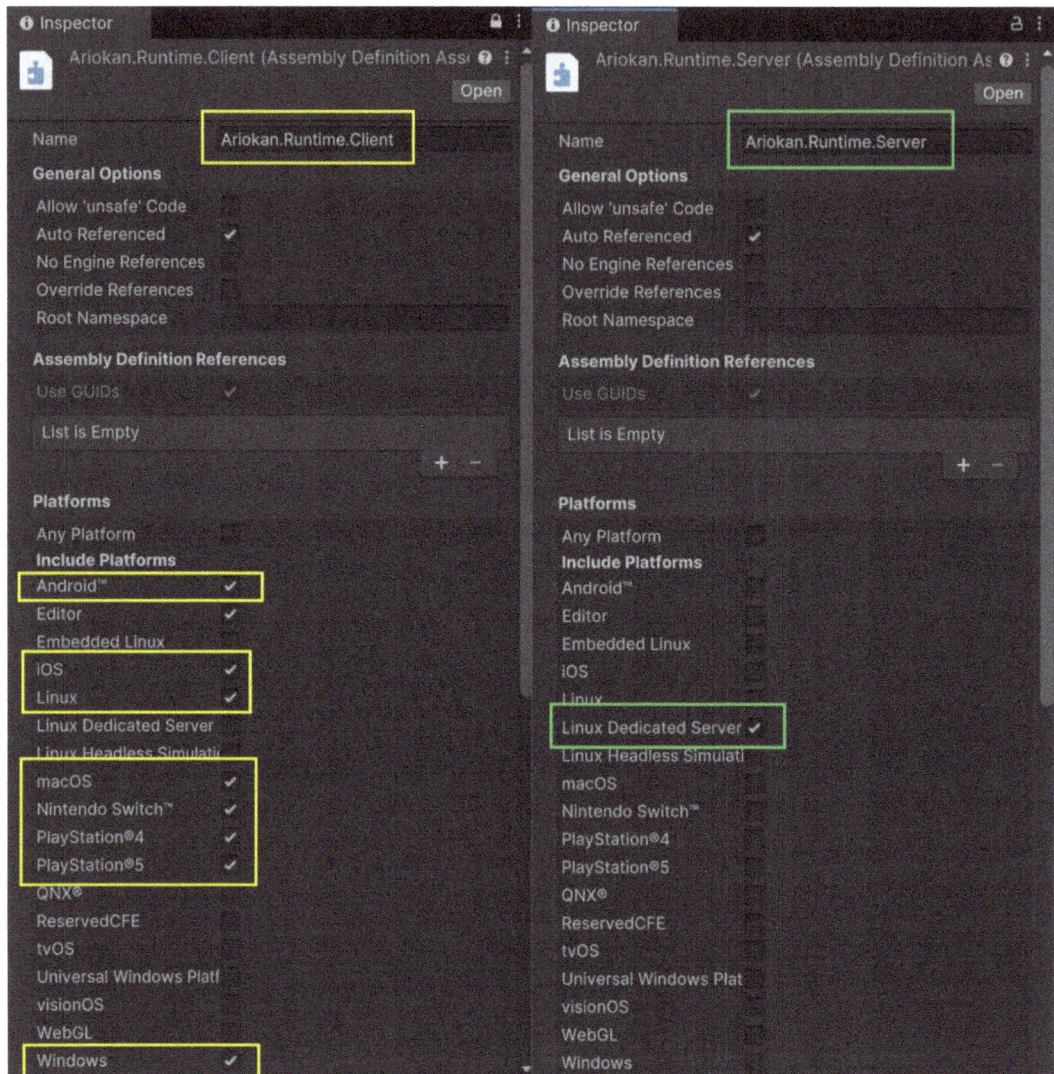

Figure 3-6. *Example of Assembly Definition Files that compile code only for specific platforms, avoiding intra-platforms leaks. The client-specific assembly is ignored when compiling server platforms, and the server-specific assembly does the opposite*

Sometimes you need to remove only portions of code from an assembly or a specific script. In these cases, you can simply use preprocessor directives (i.e., #IF UNITY_SERVER) to define what code should be removed from a build that is/is not a dedicated server build.

Lag Compensation Techniques

Now that you know the fundamentals of synchronization in a multiplayer game, it's time to deal with our worst common enemy and its consequence: latency and lag.

As mentioned in Chapter 2, "latency" is the time information takes to travel from one device to another.

While it is almost negligible in a local network, it becomes a serious problem for our game when players are spread all over the internet, causing a delay commonly named "lag" as the local player waits for information coming from other devices (the input of the local player never has any latency on the local player's machine, and is processed immediately). Since latency can not be removed, the only way to deal with it is to compensate for its effects using several techniques described below.

Note Implementation details of lag compensation techniques described below change from game to game. There's no universal solution that can be copy-pasted across projects, unless they use the exact same systems and inputs.

Client-Side Prediction with Server Reconciliation

"Client-side prediction with server reconciliation" (a.k.a. "CSP" or "client-side anticipation"), is the most basic form of lag compensation technique, and consists in the client using the current state of the game to predict the outcome of the local player's input for non-client-authoritative actions, performing actions immediately without waiting for the server's reply first, and correcting the result later on if the prediction was wrong. This allows the client player to feel as if the game is responding immediately to their input, concealing latency.

For example, imagine you're playing a turn-based card game where every player can play a card only when it's their turn and has enough resources to do so. Assume that the player is connected to the server over a connection that has 100ms of Round-Trip Time ("RTT" or "Ping"), meaning that any information sent from the player to the server will take 50ms to reach the server, and another 50ms to come back, and that the network tick rate is 20Hz.

Without CSP, every time the local player tries to play a card, the game would freeze for 100ms + 1 network tick (50 ms), waiting for the server to reply with a "yes, you can

CHAPTER 3   DEVELOPING A MULTIPLAYER GAME

play it" or "no, you can't." This makes the user experience very clunky for the player, as a delay of that size is very noticeable, as shown in the example described in Figure 3-7.

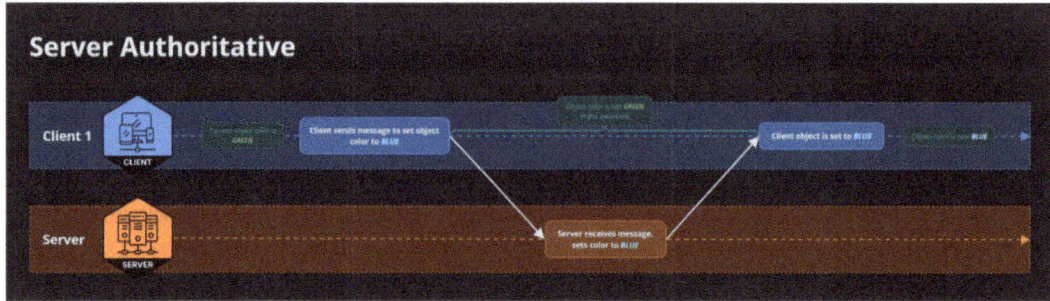

Figure 3-7. *Another example: a player wants to change the color of an object from green to blue, so they click a button in the UI to send an RPC to the server, which changes the object's color. On the client, the object changes to blue 150ms later, when the server responds to the RPC. Image source:* `https://docs-multiplayer. unity3d.com/netcode/current/advanced-topics/client-anticipation/`

To solve this problem, we can implement CSP: on the local player's client, we calculate whether the state of the game allows the player to play a card right now, using the same logic the server would use. If the result is that the card can't be played, we show an error to the player when they try to play the card. If instead the card would be accepted, then we can fairly predict that our "play" action is going to succeed on the server, too. The client sends the request to the server but acts immediately as if the move was already accepted by the server, changing the rendered state of the game (i.e., playing animations). 150ms later, the server replies with the actual result of the action, and the client reconciles the predicted visual state with the server's authoritative state if they diverged (i.e., putting the card back in hand), either by interpolating or snapping to the correct value, following the same logic explained in Figure 3-8.

CHAPTER 3   DEVELOPING A MULTIPLAYER GAME

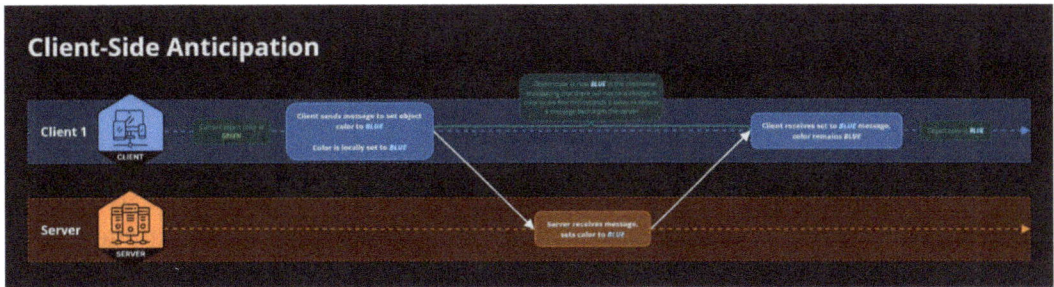

Figure 3-8. *With CSP, when the button is pressed the client immediately anticipates the result of the RPC by visually changing the object to green while it waits for an update from the server. Image source:* `https://docs-multiplayer.unity3d.com/netcode/current/advanced-topics/client-anticipation/`

This model is particularly easy to implement in turn-based games, as every player can usually perform only one action per turn in a slow-paced environment, or in games where all the information needed to calculate whether a move is possible or not is shared with the clients, and it can even be used as part of more complex solutions to improve the responsiveness of the game. For fast-paced competitive games, though, implementing deterministic lockstep can be a more robust approach.

Client Authority

Client authority is a way to reduce latency for the local player by giving complete control over what they're interacting with during a gameplay session. As the player becomes the source of truth for a specific object, we can safely assume that anything they try to do will succeed and that no approval from the server is needed. Many casual and non-competitive co-op games implement client-authoritative movement and controls, but as a result, give up completely on the security aspect as players can do whatever they want with the objects they own.

Deterministic Lockstep

Deterministic lockstep consists of synchronizing a simulation across different devices by sending only the inputs that control that device, rather than the state of the entire system.

This means that instead of synchronizing state (current position, rotation, and so on), we only focus on sending the inputs ("I want to jump," "I want to move to point X") and replay them locally on each client so they achieve the same game state as a result.

The great advantage of this technique is that the bandwidth needed to synchronize the entire game is directly proportional to the number of inputs and players, not the one of networked non-playing character objects, because objects that do not produce any input send no data.

The biggest issue with this type of implementation is keeping everyone in sync, all the time, deterministically: every tick must execute the same way across multiple devices. As we've seen in Chapter 1, it's very easy to break determinism: all it takes to make the simulation diverge is a single input that produces the wrong result and causes a snowball effect for everybody.

There are two common implementations of deterministic lockstep: delay-based and rollback-based.

Delay-Based Lockstep

Since the local player's input is processed immediately, the idea behind delay-based lockstep is that we can delay the local player's input by a few frames to compensate for the time it takes for incoming information to reach our device. Then, in theory, both inputs will "arrive" at the same time and can be executed on the same frame as expected.

For example, imagine that two players in a fighting game are playing over a connection that has 96ms of Round-Trip Time ("RTT" or "Ping"). This means that any information sent from device A to device B will take 48ms to reach the other device, and another 48ms to come back, so the latency is 48ms.

If a game is running at 60 frames per second ("FPS"), every frame will take 16ms, so we can simply delay the processing of the local player's inputs by three frames.

Now, imagine that during frame 1, both players press a button to attack: each player immediately sends a message to inform the other about the input, but waits 3 frames to process it locally. On frame 4, both devices will have all the info, and will process start the attack animation.

As long as every input can travel the network in these three frames, the game simulation can proceed without desynchronization.

You might think that delaying inputs will make the game feel "laggy" for the local player and have a negative impact on their reaction times. However, the reality is that many players won't even be able to notice a few-frame-long delay. For those who can notice it, or are training for offline competitions where there will be no delay, the fact that the delay is constant allows them to get used to it, so they'll still be able to use online play as a method of practice.

The real problem is that the internet is an unpredictable mess: networks are inconsistent, and their quality fluctuates continuously.

So, what happens if the input takes six frames instead of three? Since the game can't proceed without information from both players, it can only stop and wait for the input to arrive, "pausing" during moments of prolonged network trouble. As you can imagine, this is not something players like.

Most delay-based implementations try to monitor the conditions of the network and change the amount of input delay at runtime to match the connection's health, but, since network behavior is very difficult to predict, this often leads to a "too little too late" situation where the delay is kept unnecessarily long after a problem occurred, or is too short when a problem occurs for the first time.

Considering that the quality of the connection between every possible player of our playerbase is completely unpredictable, and that lag-compensation solutions need to be judged based on how they handle bad connections and difficult scenarios (not easy ones), delay-based lockstep is considered a fragile solution whose only advantage compared to its counterpart (rollback-based lockstep) is the ease of implementation.

Rollback-Based Lockstep

Ask for forgiveness, not for permission.

— Grace Hopper, pioneer of computer programming

Rollback-based lockstep (a.k.a. "Netcode Rollback") works like a time traveller that tries to fix the future by going to the past: all inputs from the local player are processed immediately, but when an input from a remote player comes in a few frames later, rollback "corrects the past" recalculating everything affected by that input, based on the frame at which such input was generated.

Let's use the previous example: two players, a local and a remote one, press a button to attack on frame 1 while playing on a connection with 96ms RTT. The input of the local player is processed immediately, but the remote player' takes 48ms (three frames) to arrive.

The input of the local player is processed immediately, and the game continues assuming the remote player has not done anything. On frame 4 the input from the remote player arrives: the system recognizes that it was generated on frame 1 and that the timeline must be rewritten because what was shown to the local player in the last 3 frames is not what really happened.

At this point, the following things happen in order:

1. The game state gets "rolled back" to what it was before frame 1, the frame where the input needs to be applied
2. The inputs from the remote player, and all inputs the local player generated during frames 2 and 3, are applied
3. The game re-simulates all frames forward until it reaches frame 4

All of this happens instantly, in one game frame: all the local player sees is the game state they thought was correct (but wasn't) and gets immediately replaced with the correct game state.

This usually means that the local player sees animations of remote players "skip ahead" a few frames (i.e., a character might suddenly jump mid-air, or be in the middle of an attack).

Contrary to what happens in a delay-based lockstep, where the game pauses to catch up with missing information, there's no way your input can be invalidated or "lost" by network lag. Players can be 200% sure that the inputs they send will be executed regardless of the network quality, enhancing the consistency of online play. Moreover, in a situation when the network is experiencing problems, rollbacks will usually happen in the immediate time around the spike, with no repercussions over the rest of the game. For this reason, rollback-based lockstep is particularly fit for connections where the chances of packet loss are high (i.e., Wi-Fi or mobile connections).

Prediction and Rollback

Rollback-based lockstep solutions can be further improved by including a "predictive" logic: instead of assuming that the player is doing nothing when they don't send any input, we assume that they're "repeating" their last input for the current missing frame. For example, if they were running forward in a first-person shooter, we assume that they're still running forward.

When the correct remote inputs arrive a few frames later, the game checks if they were incorrect. If they are, the game rollbacks to a previous state and uses the new inputs to simulate (and re-predict) the events. But if the prediction was correct, there's no need for a rollback: the game simply updates what it knows to be the last correct input from the remote player.

The advantage of this approach is that the game feels perfect when the prediction is correct, even if there was network trouble.

Surprisingly, this strategy results in correct predictions most of the time because:

1. Players rarely do nothing for long periods of time, and
2. Most players change inputs way less than 60 times per second when playing at 60 FPS.

During a match of a fighting game where players move left and right, you can safely assume that a player changes their walking direction ~6 times per second (a good sample even for very active players).

This means that every second, only 6 out of 60 frames (10%) will include input from the remote player, and what happens during the other 54 frames (90%) can be predicted accurately by assuming that the inputs are the same as the previous frame.

This means that if there is a network issue during any of these 90% "idle" frames in which remote input was unchanged and is being predicted correctly, there won't be any rollback, and players won't notice the network issue.

There's also another aspect to consider, which makes rollback-based solutions compensate even more for lag: the fact that many inputs in games also "lock" the state of the player and prevent them from doing other actions while they're performing the current one. For example, imagine a game where you can't perform other actions while you're jumping: all inputs the player sends while jumping will be ignored and won't change the state of the game. Since rollbacks are visually noticeable only when the state of the game changes, these inputs are completely irrelevant and won't have any visual impact, even if there were network issues or predictions were incorrect.

Lockstep's "Wombo-Combo"

In the world of online multiplayer games, there's no way to get rid of latency, so inputs will always arrive after the frame they were intended for, causing a rollback if the inputs changed the state of the game.

CHAPTER 3   DEVELOPING A MULTIPLAYER GAME

We can fix this by combining the two lockstep approaches in a wombo-combo that solves it all: adding rollback on top of a delay-based solution that uses a fixed, small-enough amount of delayed frames (usually between 1 and 8). This gives enough time to most remote inputs to reach the local player, reducing the need for rollbacks until an actual network issue appears.

Considerations and Limitations

Netcode rollback might sound like the holy grail of lag compensation, and it definitely solves many of the problems related to latency. However, adding netcode rollback to a game is a very complex task.

First of all, even if rollback can be used by any deterministic game regardless of the genre, you have to remember that its bandwidth costs scale with inputs and players, as everybody has to always send its inputs to everybody else in what is basically a star (when server-authoritative) or mesh (when peer-to-peer) topology, which makes it an expensive and non-ideal solution for games with more than 10 players due to how each players increases the probability of a desync that triggers a rollback for everybody.

In addition to that, the rollback algorithm requires additional CPU and RAM to perform "serialization"[6] of the game state for every single frame, in case we need it later. Unless the serialization algorithm is hyper-optimized, which is something that might require changes in how you store/represent data in the various systems of the game[7], this is a resource-intensive operation performed while the game simulates the game logic, meaning that the "frame budget"[8] for the actual game logic is lower than it would normally be.

Moreover, managing things like object lifecycle (creation/destruction), visual effects and sound effects becomes way more complicated as we need to consider that their state might be rolled back at any time: like with animations, we need to be able to "skip" to a certain moment of the sound, or we need to make a destroyed object re-appear.

Finally, the prediction model is good at predicting inputs for short periods, but bad at predicting them for longer periods: it's easier to predict 6 frames into the future is

---

[6] Converting data of the computer's memory to a format that can be saved and loaded.
[7] Michael Stallone, engineer at NetherRealm Studios, estimates that it took two man-years to build serialization systems in Mortal Kombat X when they retrofitted the game with rollback netcode.
[8] The time a game has to process a frame. At 60 fps, the game has 16.6ms to process each frame. If it takes 16.7ms to process a frame, the game will run at 59.8 fps if VSync is disabled, and at 30 fps if VSync is enabled. The frame budget is used for all realtime rendering and calculations.

easier than to predict 30 or 60, meaning that a lag spike of more than 500ms will very likely cause a noticeable rollback for the non-lagging player, changing the course of the game.

To summarize: you need to plan for netcode rollback, and if you do not implement it early in the game's lifecycle it'll take years of work to adapt all the game's systems to it, as widely proven.[9]

Playtesting Techniques

Now that you know how to combine the bricks that make up your multiplayer game, it's time to think about good playtesting practices and techniques so you can validate your implementations quickly.

Running Multiple Instances of the Game

When it comes to playtesting, the main difference between a single-player and a multiplayer game is that you need multiple instances of the game to validate that features work as expected, especially if your game implements a server-authoritative architecture where each device has a different role.

Unfortunately, many inexperienced teams tend to do this in the worst way possible: making builds for every change and running them to test that things work. This is an obsolete and extremely time-consuming practice that kills developer velocity, and it should be used only when testing cross-platform interactions between different instances of your game. (i.e., how the Android version of your game behaves when playing vs. the Windows version of the game on a server running the Linux version of it), or when you need to run tests on the actual devices that will run the game to solve platform-specific bugs.

Nowadays, we have tools to run multiple instances of a game directly from the engine: for example, if you're making your game in Unity you can use both 1st party

---

[9] It took ~eight man-years of time split between many programmers over 10 months for the full rollback implementation of Mortal Kombat X, since it had already shipped. The studio behind Rivals of Aether spent a lot of development time over a few years exploring how to convert their finished game from delay-based to rollback, and eventually gave up, while Mike Zaimont added GGPO, a rollback library, to Skullgirls in about two weeks early in development using his custom engine.

CHAPTER 3   DEVELOPING A MULTIPLAYER GAME

tools like **Multiplayer Play Mode** and third party tools like **ParrelSync,** which allow you to playtest features with multiple local players without making builds, and also let you access debugging tools and in-engine features that would not be accessible in builds. Moreover, as you can see in Figure 3-9, these tools allow you to customize the role and execution parameters of each instance, so you can effectively have a server instance and one or more client instances with different behaviors.

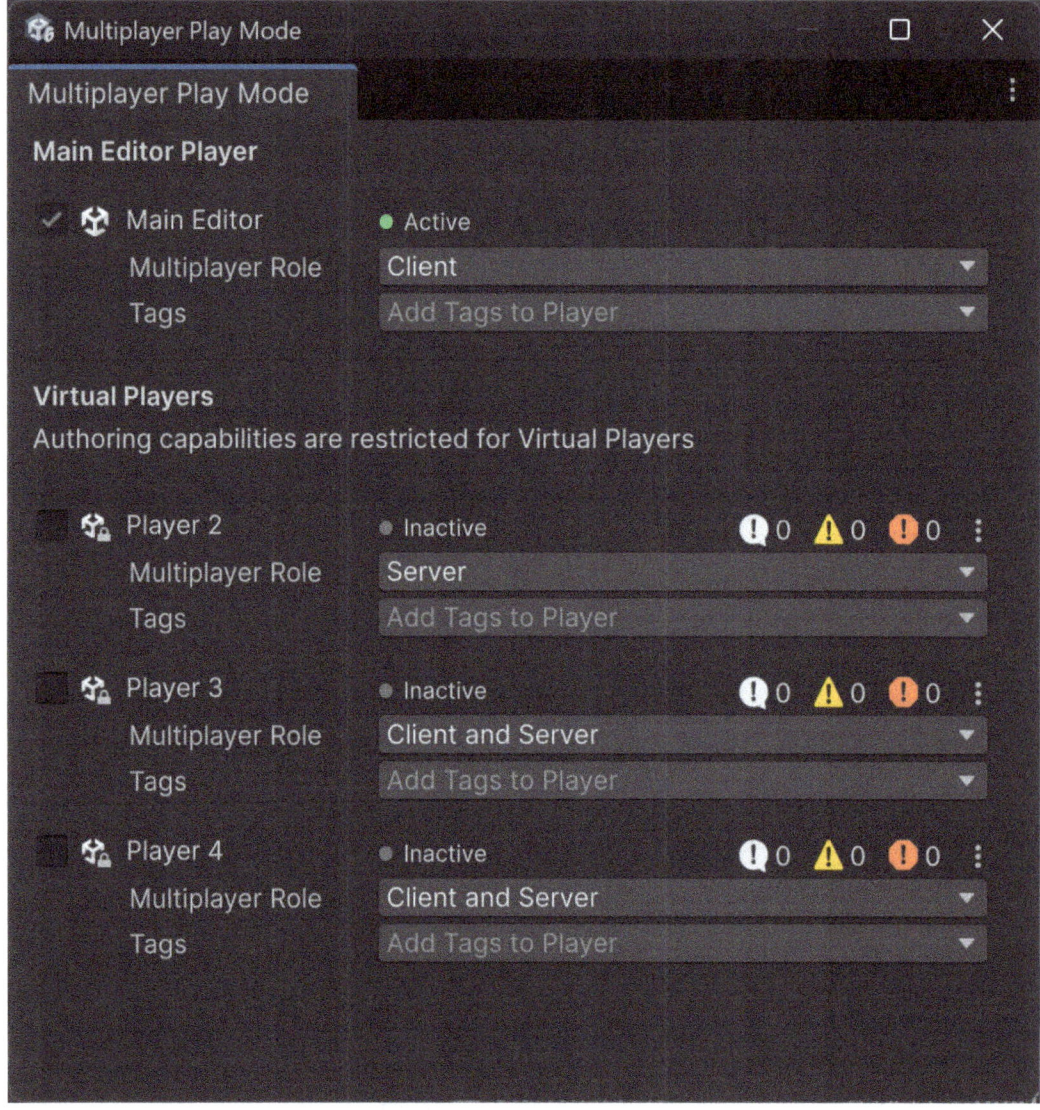

Figure 3-9. *Unity multiplayer play mode, combined with the dedicated server package, allows you to enable multiple "virtual players" with different roles and custom tags so you can customize their behavior*

CHAPTER 3   DEVELOPING A MULTIPLAYER GAME

This is extremely important because every time you test a server-authoritative multiplayer game, you need to run at least one instance as a dedicated server (= with no local players) and one or more as dedicated clients, to ensure that data and code are separated correctly. If you run a single instance as both the server and the client, you'll risk overlooking synchronization issues and problems related to mixed code. Having multiple and customizable client instances allows you to sign in with different accounts in every instance, automate testing steps, and prove that your game works in different scenarios.

Another perk of running multiple instances in the editor is that you can leverage in-editor tools that come with every framework. As you can see in Figure 3-10, the framework "Netcode For GameObjects" has an entire suite of 1st party tools that let you analyze the network traffic of the game in realtime to understand what can be optimized, or that let you inject artificial latency, lag spikes and packet loss into the simulation so you can test whether the implementation of your lag compensation techniques works in real-world scenarios.

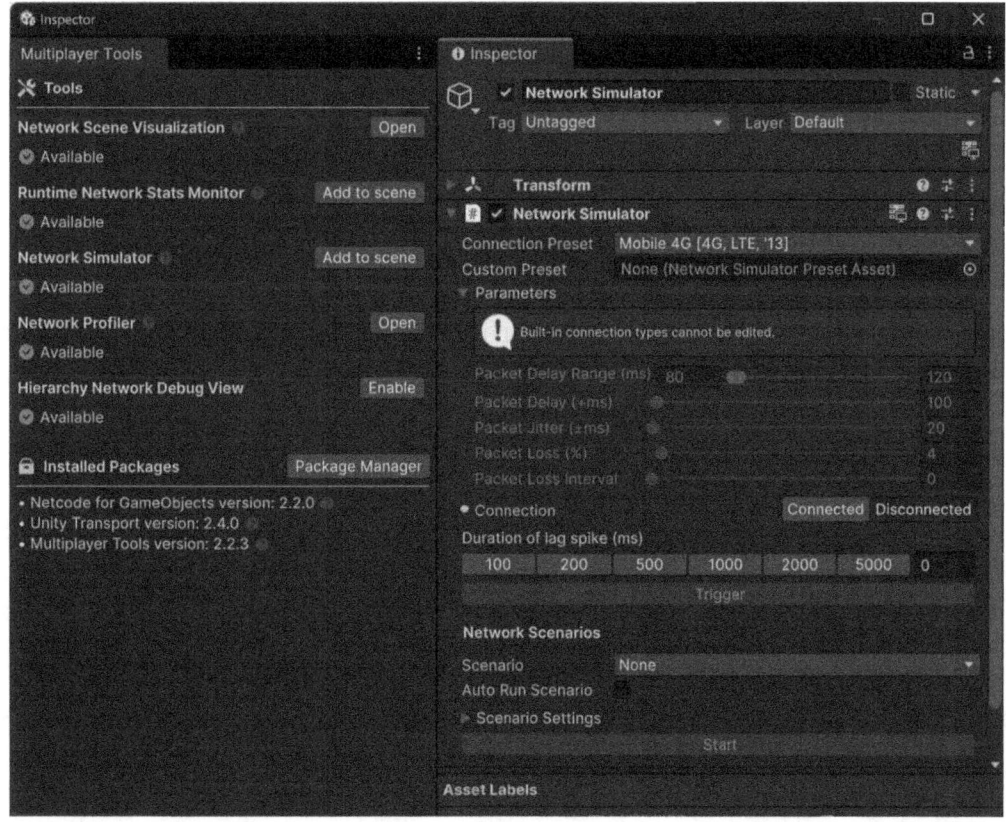

Figure 3-10. *Unity multiplayer tools (on the left). Network simulator (on the right) that allows you to artificially inject lag spikes and test how the game behaves under different types of connection presets*

Host Mode

Running a game in "Host mode" means running a single instance of it both as a server and a client that connects to itself. Even though playtesting in this way does not allow for validating if synchronization and latency-dependent features are properly implemented, given that the instance will have access to both server-side and client-side information, this testing technique can still be helpful in some cases:

1. To run your game in "single player mode," in case you want to provide an "offline" or "practice" game mode to your players, or to test against bots

2. To manually test latency-independent gameplay logic

3. To run automated tests about latency-independent gameplay logic

4. To prototype your core game loop in a way that is scalable to 1+ players

The last point is especially important: at the beginning of a project, you usually want to quickly prototype a core game loop without having to worry too much about architecture.

Host mode lets you set up the networked system, RPCs, Networked Variables, and spawning logic, so you can scale it later on. The alternative would be to develop the full architecture directly (which takes more development time), or to make a single-player version of the game first and "add multiplayer later" which, as discussed in Chapter 1, is not really a viable option.

Meta-Configuration Files

Is it possible to make our game behave differently, even outside of our game engine, or when first and third party tools are incompatible with our tech stack and needs? Absolutely. All we need is a simple yet powerful asset: meta-configuration files.

As displayed in Listing 3-6, Meta-configuration files are simple files that contain "parameters" that your game instance can read at startup time to initialize its own systems and change its behavior.

Listing 3-6. Example of a Meta-configuration file in JSON format that automatically starts a Server instance on port 8887, waiting for three players and with support for bots. This type of file can also be used to store sensitive data like secret API keys, as long as you remember not to push them to your version control system.

```
{
    "OverrideMultiplayerRole" : "True",
    "StartAsHost" : "False",
    "StartAsServer" : "True",
    "StartAsClient" : " False ",
    "MaxPlayers" : "3",
    "Port" : "8887",
    "EnableBots" : "True",
    "AllowReconnection" : "False",
    "ServerIP" : "127.0.0.1",
    "AutoConnect" : "True",
    "Secret API Key" : "<Do not share me>!"
}
```

With meta-configuration files, you can alter what the game does without changing code, for example:

1. Automate steps of your manual testing process (i.e., start a local server, select a skin for a character, load a specific game mode)

2. Make an instance of your project act as server, the other as client

3. Enable developer-only functionality in your editor but not in your builds

The first case is a very common one: maybe you want to start from a specific level of your game, or you want to skip the login, matchmaking, lobby, and initialization process when testing game modes and offline content.

Without a Meta-configuration file, it would take tens of seconds to go through the initialization flow of your game every time you run the simulation. Using a Meta-configuration file you can simply set a flag to "True" and instruct your game to read it to start in an "Auto connect" mode that ignores player login and gives you a random account with some pre-set data. Since you can ship this file with your executable, you can customize the behavior even when outside of your game engine of choice.

CHAPTER 3   DEVELOPING A MULTIPLAYER GAME

The implementation of a Meta-configuration system is trivial: just read the file at startup, store its content in a data structure (i.e., a Dictionary), and make that data structure accessible to the code whose behavior changes based on the Meta-configuration.

If you want to make life easier for your team and prevent mistakes, you can even implement an editor tool for visually editing the configuration, as shown in Figure 3-11.

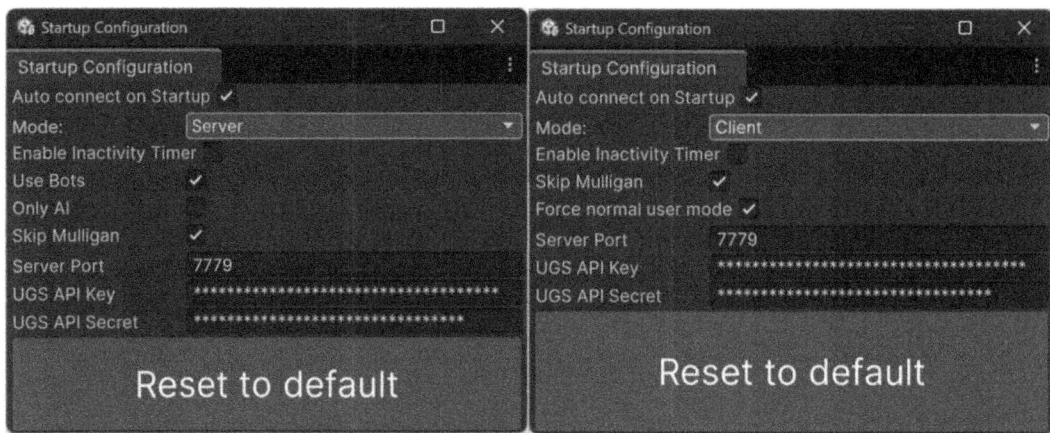

Figure 3-11. UI authoring tool for a Meta-Configuration file. Notice how fields change based on the value of the "Mode" field, which alters the role of the instance and makes some fields relevant/irrelevant

Conclusion

In this chapter, you learnt about all the foundational elements that make up a multiplayer game. You should now have a clear idea of how to architect the networked systems of your game, how to pick the right frameworks based on the game genre you're working on, and how to handle communication, synchronization, and lag compensation for a smooth user experience. You also learnt about testing practices and how to validate real-world scenarios using editor tools.

Now that you know the foundational principles, it's all a matter of getting started: you should already be able to pick up a network framework and, following its specific syntax and rules, implement a multiplayer game in which two players from the same network can send data or messages to each other.

In the next chapter, you'll learn how to connect players from different parts of the world and in different scenarios, protect your game from cheaters, and the foundational aspects of modern multiplayer, live-service games.

CHAPTER 4

Going Global

In Chapter 3, you learnt the fundamental concepts behind the structure and development of a multiplayer game.

In this chapter, you'll learn how to prepare your game for the real world: how to connect players in different scenarios, how to recognize, prevent, and fight back security threats in the context of server-authoritative competitive games, how to change the behavior of your game without making new builds, and how to proper gather analytics that can inform your decision-making.

At the end of the chapter, you'll know the tools and techniques needed to release, operate, and improve a commercial multiplayer game.

Connecting Players in Different Scenarios

Not all multiplayer games are born equal: depending on the distance between players, we need to use different tools and strategies to connect them. This section covers several scenarios that you might have to handle during the development, playtesting, and release phases of your game.

Local Multiplayer

"Local multiplayer" is when multiple players play together using the same device.

An example of this is when you invite friends over to play all together from your couch.

In a local multiplayer scenario, there's no network connection involved and, consequently, no relevant latency to deal with. In most cases, local multiplayer can be implemented without using a netcode framework: all you need to do is separate the input systems of each player, so that the inputs sent by the controller/keyboard of one player do not affect the characters of other players.

CHAPTER 4 GOING GLOBAL

Games like "Overcooked" or "Tekken" use a single camera to render all players at the same time, as displayed in Figure 4-1.

Figure 4-1. *Gameplay screenshot of "Overcooked," where a single camera renders the characters controlled by different players*

Some local multiplayer games also separate the rendering systems of players, "splitting" the screen so that each player can render its own view separately. As displayed in Figure 4-2, "Ratchet: Gladiator" implements a split-screen rendering system for its local co-op mode.

CHAPTER 4   GOING GLOBAL

Figure 4-2. *Gameplay screenshot of the local co-op mode of "Ratchet: Gladiator," a PlayStation 2 game that supports split-screen local multiplayer*

Even though a netcode framework is not necessary to implement local multiplayer, implementing the game's architecture with a netcode framework allows the game to support more types of multiplayer (i.e., LAN and Internet), which lets players play from different devices and/or physical locations, potentially increasing the playerbase.

Tip   When you start developing a local multiplayer game, ask yourself: "Should people play from different devices and locations?" If the answer is "yes," use a netcode framework from the start.

LAN Multiplayer

"LAN multiplayer" is when multiple players play together using different devices connected to the same local area network.

An example of this is when you're at a gaming conference and want attendees to try your PvP multiplayer card game from two different PCs, or when you invite friends over to play and everybody brings their own PC. (also called a "LAN party")

CHAPTER 4   GOING GLOBAL

In a LAN multiplayer scenario, all devices share the same physical location, and the latency is usually pretty low (<5 ms). However, the devices still need to synchronize information with each other, so we must implement a netcode framework that handles connection, synchronization, and communication between them.

But how do players find each other, or the server, in a LAN multiplayer scenario? There are two ways: direct connection and network discovery.

Direct Connection

Direct connection is the most straightforward way to connect to a Host, as long as you know the host's port and IP address: as displayed in Listing 4-1, all you need to do is feed that information into the connection mechanism provided by the netcode framework of your application, and then connect as a client to it.

Listing 4-1. Example of direct connection in Netcode for GameObjects

```
using UnityEngine;
using Unity.Netcode;

public class MyNetworkManager : MonoBehavior
{
    const string defaultServerListenAddress = "0.0.0.0";

    //The device that acts as a server calls this on startup
    public void StartServer(ushort listeningPort)
    {
        SetNetworkPortAndAddress(defaultServerListenAddress, listeningPort,
        defaultServerListenAddress);
        m_NetworkManager.StartServer(); //or StartHost(), if you also want
        the server to be a Client
    }

    //The client calls this to connect to the server
    public void ConnectToServer(string serverIP, ushort serverPort)
    {
        SetNetworkPortAndAddress(serverIP, serverPort, default
        ServerListenAddress);
        m_NetworkManager.StartClient();
```

    }
    void SetNetworkPortAndAddress(string address, ushort port, string
    serverListenAddress)
    {
        var transport = GetComponent<UnityTransport>();
        transport.SetConnectionData(address, port, serverListenAddress);
    }
}
```

All you need to do is:

1. Connect all the relevant devices to the same router (either with a LAN cable or through wi-fi) and ensure they are on the same local area network (you can use the `ipconfig` command in your computer's terminal / shell / command prompt tool to check that, as explained in Chapter 2)

2. Choose which device will start as a server (or host, if it has a player on it)

3. Start the game on it and initialize the server (i.e., calling `StartServer()`)

4. Get the IP of the server/host device using the `ipconfig` command

5. Use the IP and the port number in client devices to connect to the server (i.e., calling `ConnectToServer()`)

At this point, the connection is established between the two devices. If the client fails to connect to the server, it could be because of one of those reasons:

1. *Firewall*: Operating systems and routers usually have a firewall that blocks incoming/outgoing connections by default, especially for non-standard ports. You can try disabling the firewall, or adding an exception to it for the port your game uses.

2. *Internal network traffic is blocked*: As displayed in Figure 4-3, you can try to use the `ping` command in the command line/shell of a client to send a message to the server and see if it replies. If the server is unable to reply, your router might be blocking
```

CHAPTER 4 GOING GLOBAL

the internal traffic of the network. If that's the case, you can try using another local network or disabling the router's internal protections from its settings.

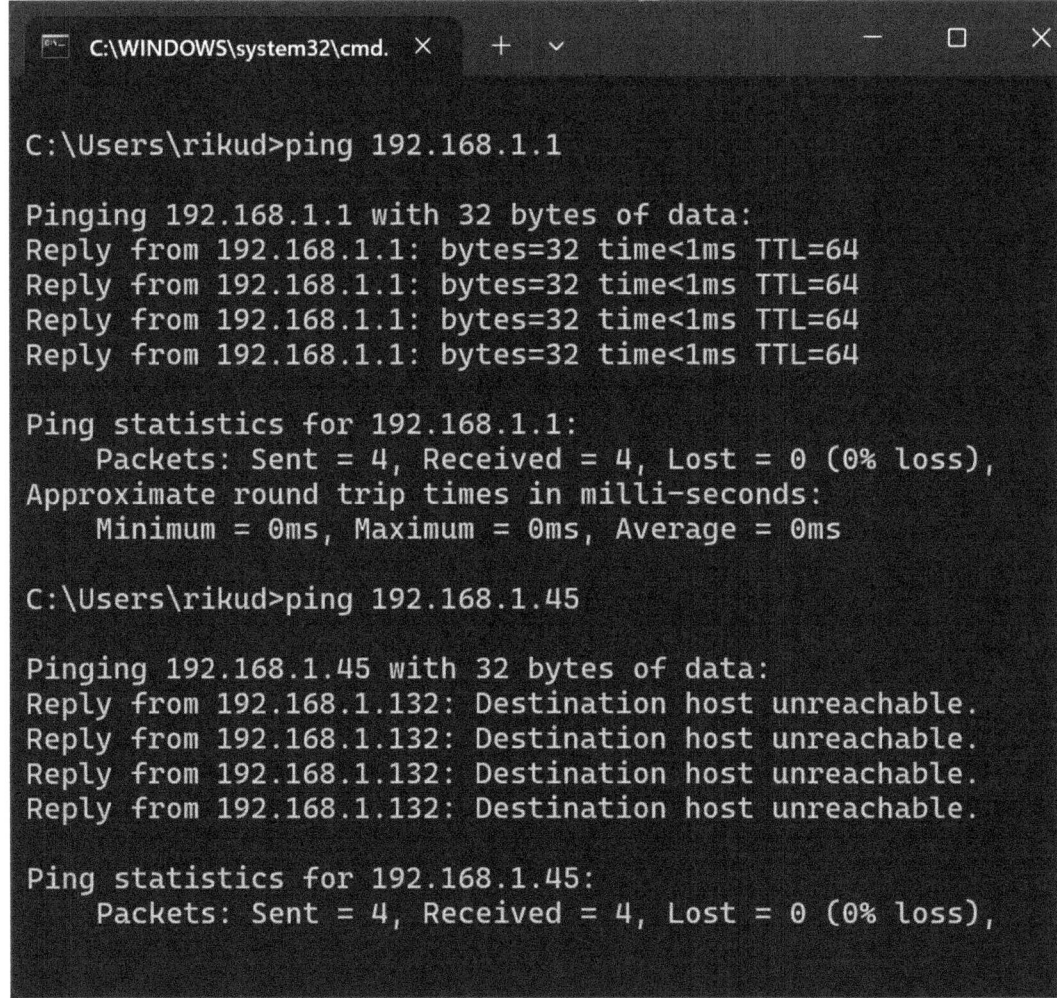

Figure 4-3. *Example of using the* `ping` *command to check whether a host in the same network is reachable or not. In the example, the host with IP 192.168.1.1 is reachable, the one with IP 192.168.1.45 is not*

Network Discovery

Network discovery is a mechanism that lets devices discover and gather information about other devices on the same network, automatically, using protocols like Simple Network Management Protocol (SNMP) and broadcast messages.

Some netcode frameworks implement network discovery, which makes it easier to play in LAN as you don't have to manually retrieve the IPs and ports of the device that is acting as a server: once the network discovery implementation retrieves this information, the client uses a direct connection to connect to the server.

Online Multiplayer

"Online multiplayer" is when multiple players play together using different devices connected to different local area networks interconnected by the internet (which is considered a "Wide Area network," or "WAN," itself).

An example of this is when you're sitting on your gaming chair and want to play with a friend that lives in another building, city, or country.

As discussed in previous chapters, in an online multiplayer scenario, latency is usually high, variable, and troublesome. All problems related to LAN multiplayer are present and exacerbated, especially the ones related to firewalls: as multiple routers are involved in routing traffic from one LAN to another over a WAN, and public IP addresses must be used, it's extremely difficult to connect two devices directly. That's where tools like dedicated servers, port forwarding, NAT punchthrough, and relay servers come to the rescue!

Rented Dedicated Servers

When it comes to connect players from different networks, dedicated servers rented from hosting providers are one of the most straightforward, and expensive, options: the provider will ensure that their server is reachable by devices outside of the server's network, and will offer secure ways to gather the IP address and port of the server, which every client will use to establish a direct connection with it.

Managing the servers' infrastructure is what you pay the provider for. If you have a dedicated server in your network and want to expose it to the internet, you'll have to do all the firewall, security, and port forwarding setup yourself.

Port Forwarding

Port forwarding is a technique that picks a public port on the router that protects the LAN the server is part of, and makes that port forward all traffic to the server in the LAN. For example, it's possible to map the public port 12345 of the router so that all the incoming traffic is redirected to the server.

While port forwarding sounds like a solution in theory, in practice, it exposes your LAN to potential attackers: the moment you start advertising your router's public IP and forwarded port, hackers will happily try to see if they can exploit it to gain access to your LAN and its related systems.

In addition to that, setting up port forwarding requires access to the router itself and its settings, which is something many players only have at home. Public WiFis, mobile and school/corporate networks do not let their users access the settings of the router that easily. Even when a user has access to the router, they still need some technical knowledge to set up port forwarding. The combination of these factors makes port forwarding impractical in most cases and real-world scenarios.

Relay Servers

Relay servers are a middle ground between dedicated servers and manual port forwarding: a relay server is a lightweight dedicated server running in the cloud, with port forwarding already set up, that only relays data between all clients connected to it, without any further processing.

Contrary to a standard dedicated server, a relay server does not run an instance of the game and is incapable of running any game-related logic: as you can see in Figure 4-4, it simply works as a middleman that relays information back and forth between its clients.

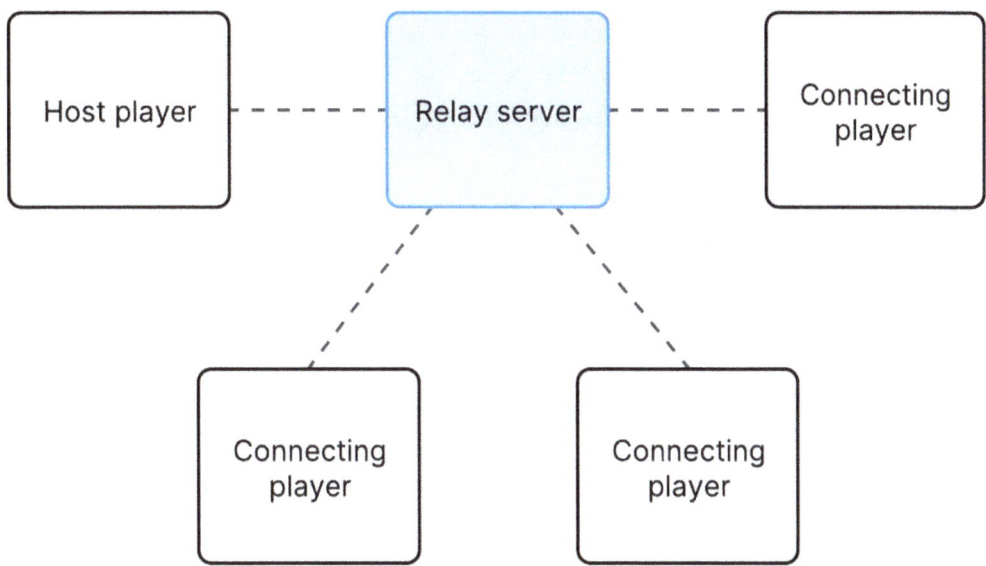

Figure 4-4. *Example of a relay server that connects multiple clients to the server (Host player). Source:* `https://docs.unity.com/ugs/manual/relay/manual/relay-servers`

Everyone, including the host, connects only to the relay server. Whenever a package is sent, the relay server redirects it to the intended recipient: the clients and the actual server running the game never communicate directly with each other. Contrary to port forwarding, this method guarantees communication but heavily increases the round-trip time of packets, worsening all latency-related problems of the game, making it ideal only for casual, non-competitive games where one player is also the host. Since relay servers also cost money, they're usually combined with NAT punchthrough and used as a fallback when it fails.

NAT Punchthrough

Network Address Translation (NAT) punch-through (a.k.a. "hole punching"), is a technique that tries to open a direct connection between client devices, without port forwarding. When successful, it connects clients directly to each other and allows them to exchange packets without intermediaries.

Unfortunately, its success rate depends both on the NAT punchthrough implementation and the NAT type used by the clients' networks, and as a consequence, it fails 15-30% of the time.

For this reason, NAT punch-through is typically only used with a relay fallback: a client tries to connect to the host by NAT punching. If that fails, it instead connects to a relay server. This lowers the workload of the relay server (= lower costs) and ensures that all clients can connect to the host.

Finding Remote Players

So far, we've talked about methods that let players connect to the Host. But what about the ways to find the right number of players needed to start the match, and tell them what to connect to?

Matchmaker

A matchmaker is a queue-based system that groups players based on some criteria, with the goal of gathering enough of them to start a match.

When a player wants to play a match, they create a "matchmaking ticket" and enter a matchmaker "queue" with it. When enough players are in the queue, the matchmaker removes the tickets (and related players) from the queue and creates a group. Then, it instantiates a session on a dedicated server (or in one of the client's devices and a relay server, if the game is client-hosted) and tells every player in the group to connect to the server's IP address and port. The clients receive this information and connect to the server. At this point, the matchmaker's job is done. Figure 4-5 shows an example of a matchmaker screen.

CHAPTER 4 GOING GLOBAL

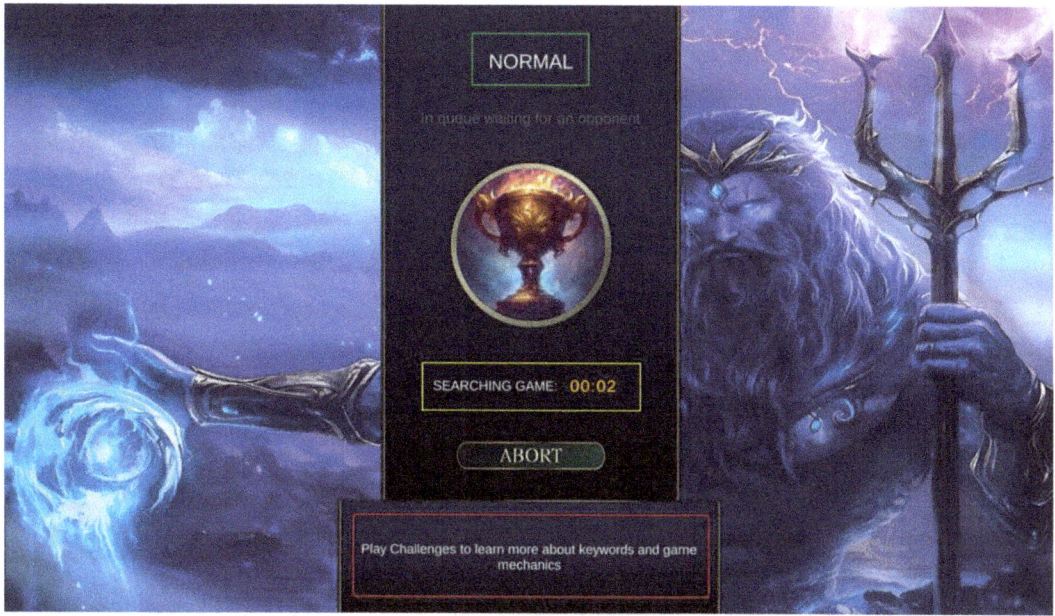

Figure 4-5. *Matchmaker screen of Ariokan's unranked queue. The green rectangle displays the type of queue, the yellow one shows the time spent in the queue, and the red one displays tips to entertain players while they wait*

The one described above is the most basic implementation of a matchmaker, but modern systems have more features and allow developers to

1. Have separate queues (i.e., one for ranked games that impact the player's skill level, called "Elo,[1]" and one for unranked games)

2. Group players based on metadata (i.e., their Elo)

3. Dynamically adjust these rules/restrictions if not enough players can be found within a certain time limit (this is called "rules relaxation")

The most important part to keep in mind is that a matchmaker needs enough concurrent players queuing up at the same time in order to start a match. This can be hard to achieve, especially for new games with a low number of concurrent players (a.k.a. "CCUs"), and often becomes a death sentence the moment reviews start mentioning that queue times are "very long" (which, for the average user, means "more than 1 minute").

---

[1] The Elo rating system is a method for calculating the relative skill levels of players in zero-sum games such as chess or esports.

For this reason, I highly discourage you from releasing your game with only a pure matchmaker implementation, unless you want your game to be labelled as a "dead game" by your community after a couple of days.

Instead, you should "fake it until you make it": after a certain time in the queue (i.e., 30 seconds), if not enough players have been found yet, your player should be matched with bots of their same skill level.

This technique has several advantages:

1. It lets players actually play the game instead of staring at a counter for minutes.

2. It helps with onboarding and early-game retention as the bots can be designed to lose the player's first match of the day in order to boost the player's confidence, motivation and will to play. (reduces churn)

3. It reduces the risk of your server's infrastructure imploding in case of a successful launch on day one.

As your community grows and CCUs increase, you can steadily remove the bots and make players play against each other without waiting ages: the end goal is to make your players have a great experience, even if the community is small, not to make them play against bots indefinitely. In Chapter 7, we'll talk about ways to make credible and challenging bots that can help with this.

Lobby

A lobby is a system that allows players to form groups by inviting each other or by advertising the lobby itself so that players can join, and allows its members to share information.

Lobbies are used for a wide variety of use cases both in casual and competitive games, especially for those features related to social groups. If you are part of a private lobby, you can send an invite code to your friends so they can join the lobby, forming a group with you, or you can set the lobby as public so that any player can join it without the code.

As you can see in Figure 4-6, players within a lobby can share information about themselves (i.e., what character they're selecting for the game) or the game flow (i.e., the IP address and port of the server they'll connect to). The lobby can also hold information not tied to any player, such as the game mode that will be played, or other restrictions that limit access to players that match the criteria (i.e., those whose Elo is too low). In Chapter 7, you'll find a detailed example of how to use a lobby in conjunction with a matchmaker to do a "party matchmaking" system.

Figure 4-6. BossRoom's lobby screen. The "room name" is the lobby code, and information about other players (characters and "ready" status) is visible

Matchmaker and lobbies streamline the multiplayer experience as players can find each other without having to know technical information such as their IP addresses.

Security and Anti-cheating Strategies

Whenever there's a game worth cheating, there's going to be a cheater. This is true for all types of games, be it online or offline.

In the context of digital games, we can safely ignore cheaters that "do no harm," which is the common case for many single-player premium offline games (who cares if you make yourself invulnerable in "Clair Obscur: Expedition 33," or if you can save infinitely in "Fear and Hunger 2"?).

Cheaters become a relevant problem only if they ruin the fun for other players, raise the churn rate of paying users, or damage the in-game economy of our game. For this reason, the amount of effort we put into anti-cheating measures needs to be proportional to the amount of players' pain and revenue loss we prevent.

Why Do Players Cheat?

If you know the enemy and know yourself, you need not fear the result of a hundred battles.

— Sun Tzu, The Art of War

The first step for us to win in the everlasting war between game developers and cheaters is to understand the psychological motivations behind cheaters' behavior. It turns out that since cheaters are human beings too, what motivates them boils down to three simple things: money, social status, and self-realization.

When a black-hat hacker comes across a popular and vulnerable game, they'll exploit its vulnerabilities to create cheats that they'll either resell to cheaters or use themselves to extract money from the game (i.e., by earning huge amounts of premium currencies and then reselling the accounts at a discount, or by giving themselves an unfair advantage in pay-to-earn games). This usually impacts the economy negatively, as it creates inflation for premium currencies and reduces the amount of revenue of developers, which see a decline in in-app purchases related to premium content players would normally have to pay for.

Some people want to feel better than they are, especially in competitive games. They cheat to get to higher ranks and be recognized by peers for skills they do not really have. These cheaters are dangerous because they undermine the core concept of competitive gaming, devaluing the entire ranked experience and pissing off competitive players, which impacts engagement and retention. All they want is recognition without effort.

Finally, there's the category of cheaters that simply want to feel powerful at the expense of everyone else: these people enjoy crushing their enemies, bending the game rules, and one-shot everything that steps on their path to self-realization, ruining the fun for every human being unfortunate enough to come across them.

CHAPTER 4 GOING GLOBAL

A critical point to understand is that the first two categories of cheaters are attracted only by popular games: their desires can't be fulfilled by almost-unknown games that don't have enough players yet, so they usually do not show up in the early phases of a project, giving you more time to prepare for them, as you can see in Figure 4-7.

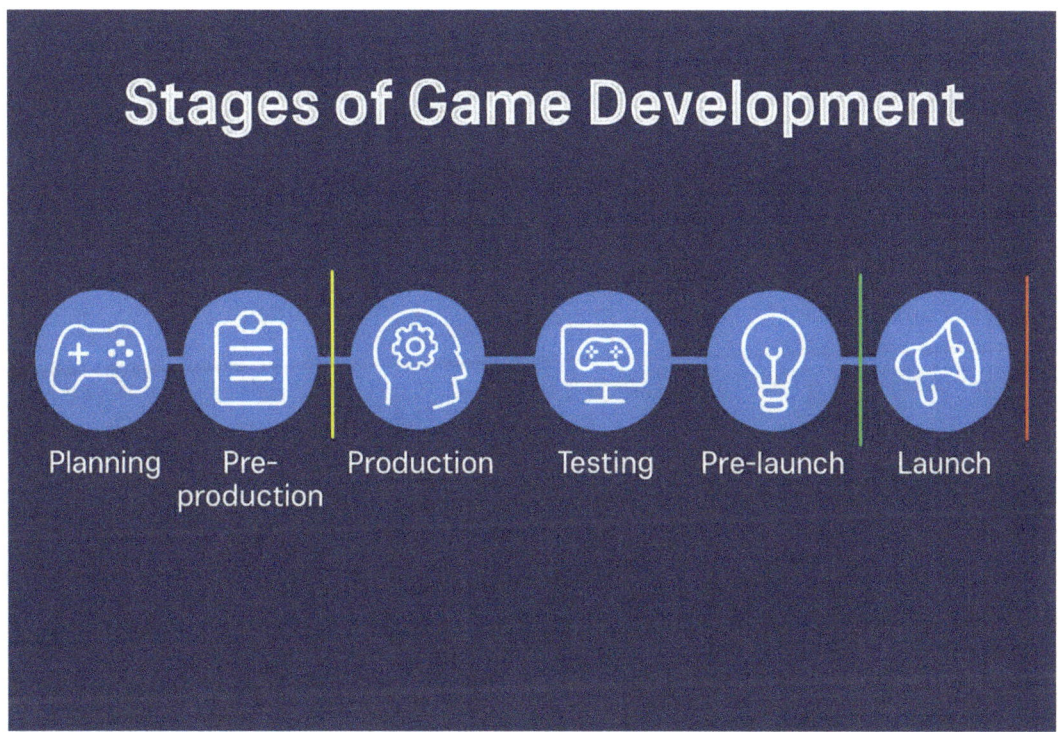

Figure 4-7. Most cheaters won't show up until you release to a broader public, but most teams worry about cheating when it doesn't matter (yellow bar), or when it's too late (red bar). Plan your anti-cheating efforts accordingly or you'll waste time and budget for nothing

How Do Players Cheat?

To know your Enemy, you must become your Enemy.

— Sun Tzu, The Art of War

Cheaters can only succeed in vulnerable games. The less vulnerable your game is, the harder it will be for cheaters to achieve their goals, and the healthier your overall community and in-game economy will be.

CHAPTER 4 GOING GLOBAL

To understand how to protect ourselves, we first need to know our enemy's attack plan, or the cheat they might try to implement. In the world of multiplayer games, there are mainly two types of cheats: "local" and "state-changing" ones.

Local Cheats

Local cheats leverage information already available to the local client to give them an unfair advantage without changing the state of the game for other players.

For example, "wallhacks" cheats let a player see through walls or in "fog of war," revealing the position of enemies that might be hiding nearby (see Figure 4-8). That's similar to "peeking" cheats, which let you know what cards the opponent is holding or what you'll draw. Another example is "aimbots," a cheat that automatically aims your gun at the most vulnerable parts of your enemies.

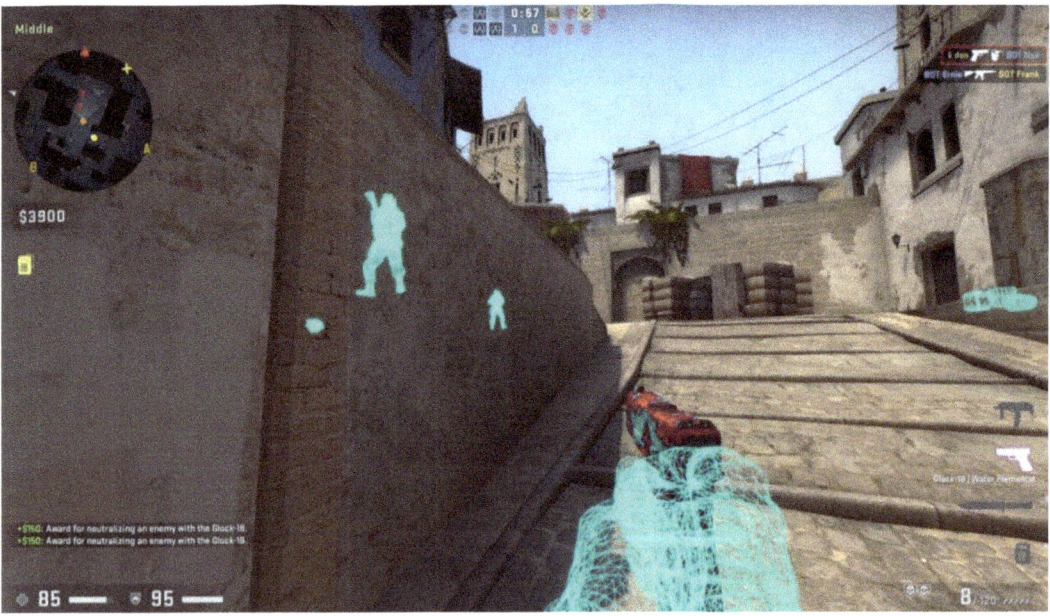

Figure 4-8. Wallhack cheat showing enemies and objects that would normally be invisible from the local player's perspective

The problem with local cheats is that they're hard to detect, as they're based on information that is already available to the client, and do not "alter" the actual state of the game. You could start looking at shooting/movement patterns (i.e., to detect aimbots), but it'd be mostly guesswork with the risk of false positives. That's what most anti-cheating software does nowadays: they look for patterns and try to detect suspicious behaviors. However, many players hate to have anti-cheats running on their machines, because they're particularly invasive and CPU-consuming processes that slow down the device.

That's why the best way to fight this type of cheat is prevention: clients must know only the information strictly needed to run their part of the simulation.

For example, in a card game like Ariokan, the local player does not need to know "what" cards the opponent has in their deck, or in their hand, to render the state of the game. The only piece of information needed is "how many" cards are in each location. By removing the "what" information, peeking cheats become useless. As you can imagine, though, this requires additional logic in the code, as every player needs to be informed only about the details of their cards, and not the ones of the opponent.

State-Changing Cheats

State-changing cheats alter the global state of the game to give an unfair advantage to a player. For example, cheats that let you set an enemy's health to 0, or to grant yourself invulnerability, are state-changing cheats.

As these cheats alter the inputs and in-memory data of the game's process to work, they are effective only in games that use a client-authoritative setup (i.e., peer-to-peer, distributed authority, client-hosted), and they're the reason why truly competitive and play-to-earn games, where obtaining rewards legitimately is crucial, always use a server-authoritative architecture.

How to Prevent Cheats and Deal with Hackers

The supreme art of war is to subdue the enemy without fighting.

— Sun Tzu, The Art of War

Dealing with cheaters and hackers is a cat-and-mouse game, and the key to victory is in discouraging the enemy: the more difficult (and low-rewarding) it is to cheat in your game, the lower the chances that someone will put some serious effort into breaking your defenses.

Making your game server-authoritative and minimizing the information clients have access to is a great starting point, but it's not enough to protect it from cheating. This section also highlights several anti-cheating techniques that you should apply as soon as possible to secure your game.

CHAPTER 4   GOING GLOBAL

Implementing Server-Authoritative Gameplay

Never trust the client.

—Any experienced engineer who made client-server applications

As mentioned in the "Authority Models" section of Chapter 3, the only[2] a way to protect your game from state-changing cheats is to implement a server-authoritative gameplay flow and run it from a secure dedicated server.

This is the golden rule: it doesn't matter how secure you think your game is, if a client is making decisions because they are given server powers (like in "Host mode"), they can (and will) cheat.

To reiterate: in a server-authoritative environment, the server assumes that the player is always trying to cheat, and that every input needs to be validated. Clients send only inputs to the server, which validates and processes them, relaying the results to all clients. The server is the only one that makes decisions and is also the "source of truth" for the current state of the game. As the server accepts only inputs instead of state changes from the clients (i.e., "I want to pick this item" instead of "I picked this item"), the state of the game can be altered in an intended and secure way, making cheating harder.

So, how does this work in practice? How does a server-authoritative system look like, compared to a client-authoritative one? Listing 4-2 shows an example of a server-authoritative implementation for a damage system:

Listing 4-2. Example of a health manager in a Server-authoritative damage system with the framework Mirror in Unity

```
using UnityEngine;

/// <summary>
/// The potential cause of a direct damage to a player
/// </summary>
public enum DirectDamageCause : byte
```

---

[2] Technically, you could also use a blockchain to keep the state of the game in the form of transactions. However, given that blockchains are extremely slow and still suffer from the "majority attack," this method is impractical in fast-paced scenarios.

```csharp
{
    Attack,
    Effect
}

public struct DirectDamageData
{
    public GameObject source;
    public DirectDamageCause cause;
    public short amount;

    public DirectDamageData(GameObject source, DirectDamageCause
    damageCause, short damageAmount)
    {
        this.source = source;
        cause = damageCause;
        amount = damageAmount;
    }
}

///<summary>
///The health manager of a player.
///</summary>
public class HealthManager : NetworkBehavior
{
    const short MaxHealth = 1000;

    [SyncVar(Channel = Channel.Reliable, OnChange = nameof(OnClientHealth
    Changed))]
    short health;

    [Client]
    void OnClientHealthChanged(short oldValue, short newValue)
    {
        if (isLocalPlayer)
        {
            //update only the local player UI
        }
```

CHAPTER 4 GOING GLOBAL

```csharp
        else
        {
            //update an healthbar on top of the character of a
            remote player
        }
    }
    public override void OnStartServer()
    {
        base.OnStartServer();
        OnServerGameStarted();
    }
    [Server]
    void OnServerGameStarted()
    {
        health = startingHealth > 0 ? startingHealth : MaxHealth;
    }
    [Server]
    public void OnServerHeal(short amount)
    {
        //If damage is actually relevant
        if (amount == 0) { return; }
        //If you're not already dead
        if (health < 1) { return; }
        health = (short)Mathf.Clamp(health + amount, 1, MaxHealth);
    }
    [Server]
    public bool OnServerDamageWithEffect(GameObject sourceOfDamage,
    short amount)
    {
        var damageData = new DirectDamageData(sourceOfDamage, Direct
        DamageCause.Effect, amount);
        return OnServerDamage(damageData);
    }
```

```
/// <summary>
/// Damages the player
/// </summary>
/// <param name="damageData"></param>
/// <returns>True if the player dies because of the damage</returns>
[Server]
public bool OnServerDamage(DirectDamageData damageData)
{
    //If you're not already dead
    if (health < 1) { return false; }
    health -= damageData.amount;
    if (health > 0)
    {
        return false;
    }
    OnServerDied();
    return true;
}

[Server]
void OnServerDied()
{
    //Respawn the player at a random location
}
}
```

In the example above, the HealthManager is the component that server-authoritatively manages the health of an entity (i.e., a player). There are two elements that make it server-authoritative:

1. The health variable, which is a SyncVar (see "Networked Variables" in Chapter 3 for reference). In Mirror, SyncVar's value is synchronized with clients only when the server changes its value, so if a client tries to change its health variable, the other player's (and the server's) simulations won't be affected

2. The structure of the script, which handles the initialization and alteration logic of the health variable in server-only methods defined with the [Server] attribute (which in Mirror prevents the execution from client-only instances)

The combination of these makes it impossible for clients to alter their health in an impactful way: even if they hacked the health variable and set it to the maximum amount, the change would never be synchronized. In this script, the only client-related responsibility is updating the UI (with OnClientHealthChanged) whenever the value of health changes on the server.

Extra data like DirectDamageData and DirectDamageCause is optional, but it lets us determine where the damage is coming from in case we need to check for invulnerabilities against certain types of damage or damage dealers. Listing 4-3 showcases how another component can interact with the HealthManager in an actual gameplay scenario.

Listing 4-3. Example of a component that can deal damage in a Server-authoritative damage system with the framework Mirror in Unity

```
public class DeathZone : NetworkBehavior
{
    int damage = 10;

    void OnTriggerEnter(Collider col)
    {
        if (isServer)
        {
            OnServerTriggerEnter(col);
        }
        if (isClient)
        {
            OnClientTriggerEnter(col);
        }
    }

    void OnServerTriggerEnter(Collider col)
    {
        var healthManager = col.GetComponent<HealthManager>();
        if (healthManager != null)
```

```
    {
        if (healthManager.OnServerDamageWithEffect (gameObject,
        damage))
        {
            Debug.Log("I killed something");
        }
    }
    }

    void OnClientTriggerEnter(Collider col)
    {
        //play some VFX, sound, etc...
    }
}
```

The goal of the component in the example above is to damage objects when a collision happens. The `OnTriggerEnter` method is called by the physics engine whenever an object collides with the object this component is assigned to. When that happens, this script checks whether the simulation is running on the server, with the `if (isServer)`, and in that case, damage is dealt to the colliding entity's HealthManager. Note how the client doesn't do any actual damage, and focuses on playing a visual representation of the collision (i.e., an explosion). This is because only the server is responsible for altering the state of the game: any damage coming from a client instance would be valid only on the local client and ignored by everyone else.

So, how would the client-authoritative version of the `HealthManager` look like? To get there, we just need to shift the responsibility of calculating the value of `health` and of respawning from the server to the client, as displayed in Listing 4-4.

Listing 4-4. Example of a health manager in a client-authoritative damage system with the framework Mirror in Unity

```
///<summary>
///The health manager of a player.
///</summary>
public class HealthManager : NetworkBehavior
```

```
{
    const short MaxHealth = 1000;

    [SyncVar(Channel = Channel.Reliable, OnChange = nameof(OnClientHealth
    Changed))]
    short health;

    [Command]
    void CmdUpdateHealth(short newHealth)
    {
        //Commands are RPCs run on the server, but invoked by the client.
        health = newHealth;
    }

    [Client]
    void OnClientHealthChanged(short oldValue, short newValue)
    {
        if (isLocalPlayer)
        {
            //update only the local player UI
        }
        else
        {
            //update an healthbar on top of the character of a
            remote player
        }
    }

    public override void OnStartClient()
    {
        base.OnStartClient();
        OnClientGameStarted();
    }

    [Client]
    void OnClientGameStarted()
```

```
{
    health = startingHealth > 0 ? startingHealth : MaxHealth;
    CmdUpdateHealth(health);
}

[Client]
public void OnClientHeal(short amount)
{
    //If damage is actually relevant
    if (amount == 0) { return; }
    //If you're not already dead
    if (health < 1) { return; }
    health = (short)Mathf.Clamp(health + amount, 1, MaxHealth);
    CmdUpdateHealth(health);
}

[Client]
public bool OnClientDamageWithEffect(GameObject sourceOfDamage,
short amount)
{
    var damageData = new DirectDamageData(sourceOfDamage,
    DirectDamageCause.Effect, amount);
    return OnClientDamage(damageData);
}

/// <summary>
/// Damages the player
/// </summary>
/// <param name="damageData"></param>
/// <returns>True if the player dies because of the damage</returns>
[Client]
public bool OnClientDamage(DirectDamageData damageData)
{
    //If you're not already dead
    if (health < 1) { return false; }
    health -= damageData.amount;
    CmdUpdateHealth(health);
```

```
        if (health > 0)
        {
            return false;
        }
        OnClientDied();
        return true;
    }

    [Client]
    void OnClientDied()
    {
        //ask the server to respawn
        CmdRespawn(Vector.Zero);
    }

    [Command]
    void CmdRespawn(Vector3 respawnPosition)
    {
        //Respawn the player at the desired location
    }
}
```

Can you see the core flaw? As the client is the one telling the server when to update the health and to respawn (through the RPCs CmdUpdateHealth and CmdRespawn, respectively), the client could send whatever value they want as a parameter of the RPCs, or not send them at all, effectively dodging all damage as the server trusts it to notify when damage is dealt. They could also cheat the respawn position, teleporting in an unreachable spot, or close to the game's objective (i.e., close to the flag in a "capture the flag" game mode).

That's why we need to be extremely careful with what we allow the client to do. In a competitive setting, we should never trust what's coming from the client, we should never give them authority over game-impacting data and actions, and we should always double-check the inputs they send.

Securing Network Communications

Usually, games do not send sensitive information around, but when they do, they expose themselves to a type of attack called "Man-In-The-Middle" ("MITM"). When a hacker finds an unsecured connection between a server and a client, they can temporarily interrupt it to put themselves in the middle of the transfer and pretend to be both the original receiver (from the point of view of the original sender) and original sender (from the point of view of the original receiver) of the packets, gaining access to info traveling over the connection.

Once the hacker has access to the packets, they can inspect them to capture sensitive data (i.e., passwords, e-mail addresses, IP addresses) or even alter them to display misleading or malicious information (i.e., links that can steal your browser's data). The hacker basically becomes a relay server, making the connection slower.

However, if the connection is secure, meaning that the information traveling on it is encrypted in a unique way between each client and the server, the packets intercepted will be unreadable by the hacker, rendering this type of attack useless.

Luckily, some frameworks provide the option to encrypt the network traffic at the transport-level. For example, the Unity Transport library can be set up to encrypt the connection between the server and the client while ensuring the authenticity of participants through pre-generated certificates and encryption keys, effectively preventing MITM attacks.

Tip Always use encryption when sending passwords, session tokens and other sensitive information. MITM attacks are very frequent and dangerous, especially on public networks (i.e., free Wi-Fi at conferences and restaurants).

Protecting the Memory

The portion of RAM ("Random Access Memory," the working memory of a device) allocated to a game process is a gold mine for cheaters, as it stores information like players' positions, objective locations, stats, cooldowns, and so on. As stated previously in this chapter, "local cheats" read this information to give the local player an unfair advantage. If the game is client-authoritative, the same technique can be used to make state-changing cheats. But how can a cheat find relevant information in the wide vastity of the computer's RAM?

Identifying Memory Locations

You can imagine the RAM's structure like a group of contiguous blocks identified by a hexadecimal address and with a minimum size of 1 byte (as most processors can't address less than that). When an application starts, the operating system assigns a portion of the available RAM to that application, which then starts using it to store its own info and can ask the operating system for more when needed.

Every variable, together with all objects we instantiate during a gameplay session, is stored in the RAM, usually in fixed positions from the beginning of the RAM portion assigned to an application (the "Game's memory"), and all an hacker needs to do to edit this data is their precise position within the game's memory.

Some tools like ArtMoney and CheatEngine allow players to scan the game's memory for specific values, and determine their address: imagine you're playing an FPS and have 31 ammo in your gun, and want to turn it into 200.

All you need to do with these tools is:

1. Search the RAM for all addresses containing the value "31" and represented as 4 bytes (since `int` variables are usually 4-bytes long across languages): this will very likely return thousands of addresses.

2. Go back to the game and fire a bullet (so now you have 30).

3. Go back to the tool and re-scan the same addresses, filtering by the new value (30): this will give you way fewer results than before.

4. Repeat steps 2 and 3 until you only get one result: that's where your "ammo" variable is stored in the memory (i.e., 0x112233AA).

5. Edit the value the address points to, making it to 200.

6. Congratulations! Now you have 200 bullets in your weapon, and you know the exact address at which this information is stored (see Figure 4-9 for an example).

CHAPTER 4 GOING GLOBAL

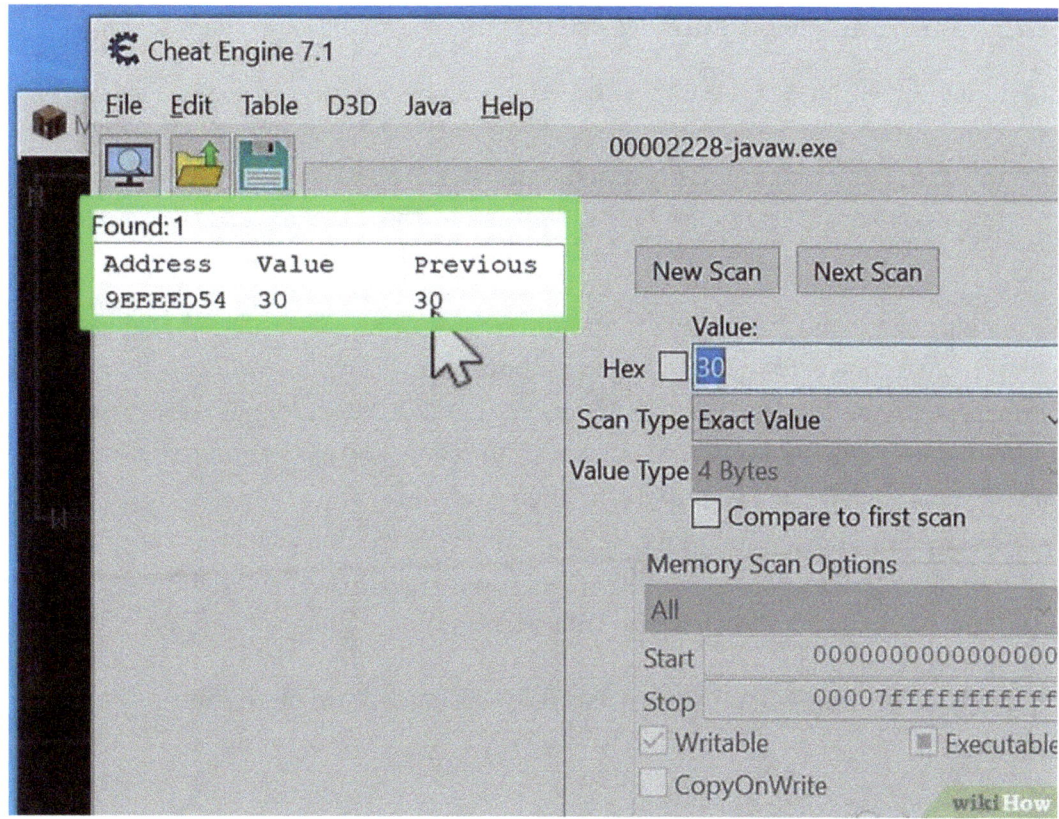

Figure 4-9. *Example of a successful memory scan. The value can now be changed to alter whatever data it represents. Source:* https://www.wikihow.com/Use-Cheat-Engine#/Image:363032-25.jpg, *License: Creative Commons 3.0, no changes made*

Even though the exact address changes every time the game runs, it can be calculated as an offset from the address of the object it belongs to, plus all previous variables. As you can see in Listing 4-5, if a "gun" object starts at address 0x11223300, and the int ammo variable is the first one declared in the object, the address of ammo will always be equal to the starting address of "gun." Following the same logic, the address of subsequent variables will vary depending on the size of the previous ones. Even the address of the gun object will change every run, but CheatEngine and similar tools allow us to use the same process to detect the starting address ("entry point") of the application. Once we know that, we can deterministically calculate every other offset at every run, automatically, and save it in a "cheat table" for fast reference.

CHAPTER 4 GOING GLOBAL

Listing 4-5. Example of addresses calculation

```
class Gun //the object itself stats at 0x11223300
{
    int ammo; //starts at Gun's address (+0)
    int maxAmmo; //starts at Gun's address + the size of ammo (4 bytes)
}
```

At this point, if the game is client-authoritative, you can make state-changing cheats with this technique. If the game is server-authoritative, the change will only be visible to the local player, and the moment we fire our next bullet, the server will use the unhacked value of ammo, re-synchronizing it with the client and overwriting whatever hacked value we have in the memory, nullifying the hack.

A pretty easy and zero-effort way to deal with these types of cheats is to apply a technique called "memory scrambling": all you have to do is add variables at the beginning (or in the middle) of a group of variables:

Listing 4-6. Example of changing variable's addresses through memory scrambling

```
//Before scrambling:
class Gun
{
    int ammo; //At +0 from Gun's start -> 0x11223300
    int maxAmmo; //At +4 from Gun's start -> 0x11223304
}

//After scrambling:
class Gun
{
    bool canFire; //At +0 from Gun's start -> 0x11223300
    int ammo; //At +1 from Gun's start -> 0x11223301
    int maxAmmo; //At +5 from Gun's start 0x11223305
}
```

This messes up the memory layout, making existing cheat tables useless unless the hacker spends some time recalculating them. The more often you do this, the more annoying it'll be for hackers to re-do the calculations, and they might eventually give up.

Another way to make it harder to do memory hacks is to store values through projected properties, as you can see in Listing 4-7. By storing an altered version of the value in a property, hackers can do memory scans for the wrong value only. Properties, being code that is executed on the fly when invoked, cannot be "memory scanned" like normal variables.

Listing 4-7. Example of projected memory value property. Instead of storing the actual value, we store an altered version of it. Using the previous example, if a hacker searches "31" as the value of ammo, they'll never find it

```
struct ProjectedInt
{
    int projectedValue; //if RealValue is 31, this is 33
    public int RealValue
    {
        get => projectedValue + 2;
        set => projectedValue = value - 2;
    }
}
//and then we use 'ProjectedInt ammo;' instead of 'int ammo;'
```

If you want to make it even harder to access memory and reverse engineer your game, there are more advanced techniques that you can apply. However, most of them have the disadvantage of flagging your game as a virus, and/or have a high chance of breaking the execution flow of your code. You should consider applying these techniques only if you really really really need it:

1. Add fake entry points that change dynamically, to defeat cheat tables.

2. Detect debuggers (like Cheat Engine) using APIs like `IsDebuggerPresent` and `System.Diagnostics.Debugger.IsAttached`, or by measuring time between instructions at runtime with a `StopWatch` to see if the execution is taking a bit too much (which is often a symptom of somebody pausing the code to inspect it through a debugger).

3. Running your game in a custom virtual machine, which makes it way harder to find memory addresses.

Caution if your game is made with Unity these techniques are going to be particularly risky, as going from C#->IL(->IL2CPP->Assembly) already introduces several layers of complexity that can mess up entry points. Use IL2CPP compilation as a first layer of protection, as it changes the game's compiled code from IL to Assembly which is harder to reverse engineer. If cheating becomes a serious problem, consider Virtualization.

Protecting Code

An executable file (i.e., .exe in windows) is a non-human-readable binary file generated from human-readable non-binary-code (literally, text), through a software called "compiler." The executable is what players install and run on their machines, and once the executable is in the hands of players, they can do whatever they want with it. Like a child breaking an object to understand how it works, cheaters can try to analyze your game's executable to understand patterns and "reconstruct" the original code that was used to generate it, then edit it to make cheats. Tools like ILSpy allow any user to do that: all they need is a copy of your game on their PC, and some coding knowledge.

Before we talk about how to protect our games' code, let's have a look at attack techniques.

Code Patching

Code patching is the most basic form of hacking code, and consists of making minimal changes to existing logic so that we can always produce the result we want. It can be used to automatically validate checks (i.e., to always answer "yes" to your "Does this player own my game?" check), or to always assign specific values.

Let's do a practical example: imagine you have a C# method, and that you use a disassembler to get to the Assembly code showcased in Listing 4-8.

Listing 4-8. Example of C# method and its simplified representation in Assembly

```
//C#
void SetPower(int power)
{
    this.power = power;
}
//Equivalent (simplified) Assembly code generated that represents that
method in the binary executable, displayed by the disassembler.
...
// 'edi' is 'this.power', 'eax' is the new value
mov edi, eax
ret //end of 'SetPower()'
...
```

Now, a hacker could simply change the assembly code so that it always assigns 100 to power, as displayed in Listing 4-9

Listing 4-9. Example of modified Assembly code

```
...
// Always set 'power' to 100
mov edi, 100
ret
...
```

Once the code is modified in the disassembler, the hacker can make a new executable with the modified code, creating a "patch," replacing the original one. This removes the burden of having to do memory scans with tools like Cheat Engine, making cheating easier.

Code Caves

Code caves consist of injecting code that changes the behavior of the game. Using the previous example, we could add a JMP ("Jump") instruction to jump to a specific marker (a.k.a. "Label," in Assembly), as shown in Listing 4-10:

Listing 4-10. Example of modified Assembly code with code cave, and C# equivalent

```
...
JMP MyCave // jump to custom code
...
mov edi, eax // do the original behavior
ret
MyCave: <custom code> // do what I want
JMP <address of ret of original function> // jump back to the original
function
...
//C#
void SetPower(int power)
{
    MyCave(power);
}
void MyCave(int power)
{
    this.power = power;
    // party hard here, i.e., auto-cast your most powerful skill.
}
```

This example is simplified, but the technique is real. To protect against the custom assemblies generated by both code caves and patches, you should generate a checksum of your exe file and compare it with the one of the exe that the player is trying to run: if they differ, the player's executable has been modified.

Code Obfuscation

Code obfuscation is one of the most effective ways to protect your code: it consists of replacing the names and variables of every function with nonsense gibberish, which completely hides the original semantic meaning of the code, before compiling the executable. Listing 4-11 shows an example of this.

Listing 4-11. Example of code obfuscation

```
//Original C# code
void SetPower(int power)
{
    this.power = power;
}
//Obfuscated version
void Ag749sjdfoPsodjdfj(int ksdsdfsdk8342r23g)
{
    this.b98dhsfspawbs = ksdsdfsdk8342r23g;
}
```

As you can imagine, figuring out what obfuscated code does is a true nightmare for hackers. Unfortunately, most obfuscation tools have the side effect of breaking Reflection-based code, which is any code that identifies other variables and methods by their literal string names in the code (i.e., RPC markers of most netcode frameworks), so implementing them in a mature project/large codebases is often extremely risking.

Separating Assemblies

Another way to protect your code is not to ship it with your executable if it's not necessary. For example, the client-only executable of your game should never include server-only code. If you ship the server-only code too, you're giving hackers a way to study the behavior and logic of your game, making it easier to identify attack vectors and ways to break your defenses.

If you're using Unity, you can use assembly definition files and platform-specific compilation rules to only include what is needed.

Avoid Storing "Secrets" in Code

Most web and services APIs require that you invoke them by sending a "secret," a string that lets you authenticate with your API provider and access the systems tied to your account. Unfortunately, many developers forget that anything bundled in the executable can be read by hackers, so they store secrets in constants within the code, and even push it to version control systems like GitHub (where leaks happen every day).

The golden rule of thumb is this: never ever store your secrets, passwords, and API keys in user-facing code and executables, and never push them to your version control system. The right way to handle secrets is through secrets manager software, or through local files read by secure cloud functions running on your servers: instead of letting your players' client application send a request directly to the API that needs the secret, let it send a request to a cloud function you own instead. The cloud function can then read from a local file (or a secure database) the secrets needed to perform the request, send it to the service, and relay the response back to the client.

Caution Whoever gets access to your secrets can send requests as if they were you, and make you pay for them. This constitutes an extremely dangerous financial risk that can literally bankrupt your studio in a few hours. If a secret is leaked, which includes "pushed to your version control," immediately replace it.

I Detected a Cheater, What Should I Do?

When your systems detect a cheater, your first instinct might be to tell them that they're cheaters, and to hit them with a glorious strike of the ban hammer. However, this is usually counterproductive: if you ban a cheater right when they started cheating, they'll know how you found out, and will adjust their tools to cheat more stealthily next time.

Instead, what you should do is to punish them after a few hours/day, and never tell them *how* you found out they were cheating. If you know that they're actually cheaters, you don't owe them any proof.

Live Service Games

Many of the most successful and remunerative multiplayer games nowadays (i.e., League of Legends, World of Warcraft, Genshin Impact, Fortnite, and Final Fantasy XIV) all have one thing in common: they continuously release new content and implement a set of UX, UI and economy design strategies that keep players coming back for more content on a daily basis.

Any game that does the same is a "Live service game" (a.k.a. "Game as a Service" or "GaaS"): a game designed to keep people playing for as long as possible in the hopes that, at some point and possibly repeatedly, those players will pay for in-game content. This strategy lets studios get, in theory, more revenue per player than they would by just selling the game.

The idea is that if a player comes back daily because we reward them with bonuses and currencies through limited-time events, their "fear of missing out" (a.k.a. "FOMO") will push them to login at least once every day to redeem rewards, complete limited-time events, and maybe to interact with other parts of the game, leading to spending at some point. The most unethical and hated live service games also slow down story progress intentionally, increase the cost of resources exponentially, or create difficulty spikes to push players into buying in-game bonuses and premium items that accelerate progress and/or provide an actual advantage. Especially on mobile, where this type of title and psychological dark patterns are frequently exploited, the UI is often designed to point out at microtransactions as often as possible to remind players that if they spend those $10, they could progress faster, and increase purchases.

While this sounds like the holy grail of monetization (often at the expense of your soul), and worked fine for the 2010s decade, the reality of years 2020 – 2025 is that Live Service games that are also Free-To-Play (which is often the case) are extremely hard to monetize even if you have a strong brand and are building a sequel: we'll talk more about this in Chapter 5.

Regardless of that, there's a couple of interesting (and totally ethical) techniques used mainly by GaaS that every developer should know about, especially since they can be reused even in the context of multiplayer games that don't publish new content regularly, and in the context of single player games.

Remote Configuration

Very often, developers of multiplayer games need to rapidly disable buggy features content, make balancing changes, or restrict access to players who are playing an old version of the game. Most studios do this by making a new build every time, pushing it to the marketplace (Steam, Google Play, etc.), and asking players to download it to continue to play.

However, this approach is slow: it can take hours to make new builds, and even days for a marketplace provider to approve the new build. Moreover, it doesn't guarantee that your players will actually update their local build (some won't do it on purpose so they can exploit old vulnerabilities).

Luckily, nowadays there's a way to dynamically change the behavior of your game without making new builds: you can use a "remote configuration" system, which is an online service that lets your application download new game's data at runtime, so that you can change the application's behavior without making new builds. Remote configuration is especially useful in mobile games, where you don't want players to update their apps multiple times after their first install.

The implementation of a remote configuration tool is pretty simple: you upload a file (i.e., a JSON) on a server, and make your game download that file on startup and in critical paths (i.e., before joining a match). The game then uses the content of the file to enable, disable, or overwrite a specific part of itself. As you can see from Figure 4-10, the great advantage is that the file can be remotely edited at any time through an online dashboard, so builds are no longer needed except when you want to add more functionality and data that the file doesn't cover yet.

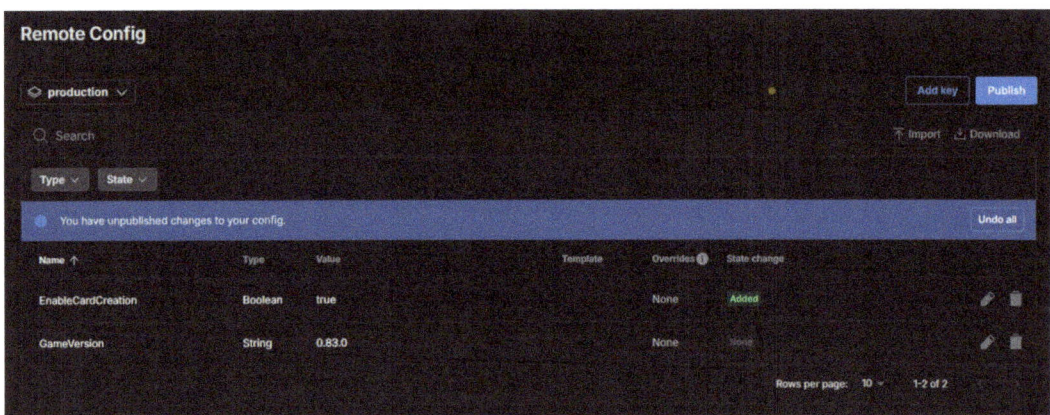

Figure 4-10. Dashboard to edit variables of a remote configuration in realtime, using Unity Remote Configuration service. By clicking "publish," the updated values are saved in cloud so clients can download them when they request the Remote Configuration

Feature Flags

A "Feature flag" is a Boolean variable of a remote configuration file used to enable or disable a feature or behavior of the game. These are extremely useful for two reasons:

1. They prevent long-living branches in repositories with multiple collaborators, as features can be merged while they're still work-in-progress without showing up in the game until the flag is enabled.

2. To enable/disable specific parts, behaviors, or content of the game in case a bug is fixed/detected, without making a new patch, which is very handy in competitive games and e-Sports, as you can see in Figure 4-10.

The only "downside" of feature flags is that they need to be planned in advance, as your code needs to have a bunch of 'if (<flag in remote config is true>)' to be able to react to the changes in the configuration.

Over The Air Updates

In gaming, an "Over The Air" update (a.k.a. "OTA") is simply a game update that happens through a remote configuration, without making a build. For example, a System designer could set the maximum health of a player to 50 instead of 100 by simply editing a remote configuration. When a match starts, the server reads the remote configuration and uses the latest value to initialize the player's health.

The more your game can leverage OTA, the less builds you'll need to make to iterate, which can save you a lot of time and increase your iteration speed. As OTA updates are usually very small in size, players will also be happy that they don't have to re-download gigabytes of executables every time you want to change something.

Game Analytics

Before you release a game to a wider audience, you need to be sure that you're able to collect information that you can later use to understand what about your game is working well and what needs to change. This can be done through analytics frameworks, little libraries that track and anonymize players' data, in a way compliant with privacy laws like GDPR, so you can inspect it in a dashboard or with queries to get insights about the behavior of your players, the economy, and the balancing.

These libraries usually let you record analytics in the form of "event + parameters." Table 4-1 shows the structure of a hypothetical matchEnded event that tracks when a match between two players ended, and some information useful for balancing.

Table 4-1. Structure of a matchEnded event that tracks when a match between two players ended, and some information useful for balancing

Parameter	Description	Type	We track this to...
GameVersion	Current version number of the client side game.	string	Filter/aggregate other parameters based on game version
Duration	How long the match lasted (in seconds)	int	Calculate average match duration, which impacts many design decisions
GameMode	Game mode played in this match	int	Filter/aggregate other parameters based on game mode
WinCondition	How did the match end?	int	Understand what strategies players prefer
WinnerTeamID	Who won?	int	Helps identify advantage given by elements like "starting position on the map"
WinnerCharacter	What character did the winner use?	int	To calculate win rates of specific content
LosingCharacter	What character did the loser use?	int	To calculate lose rates of specific content, especially vs. specific characters
Timestamp	When did this match happen?	date	To filter/organize data in charts
Turn	On which turn did the game end?	int	Helps understand if matches have time to develop or if they end too early/late

As tracking everything is often costly, we need to focus our development and monetary efforts on tracking those metrics that give us actionable insights, which means that analytics should help us answer specific questions that we need to ask ourselves first.

Here's a list of what I consider evergreen questions that any studio should have answers for through analytics, no matter the game genre:

1. How many active users do we have?

    a. Where "active" = "that performs relevant actions within the game" (i.e., playing matches). Many studios consider "active" those users who simply did a login, which is a mistake as it doesn't tell you anything meaningful about your players' behavior and how engaged they are.

2. What is the % of users that go from signup to the end of the onboarding flow?

    a. Extremely important to understand if your user acquisition initiatives are going to move the needle or not and increase the "network effect" of your game. If most of users quit during the onboarding, they'll never interact with other players.

3. What are the drop-off points of the onboarding flow?

    a. Helps you understand *what* is wrong with the onboarding flow, so you can fix/simplify/rework it.

4. How many users are still playing after their 1/7/14/30/90 days since they started?

    a. This is called "retention," and tells you what features you need to add to keep engagement high and let users "come back for more." First-time-user-experience (FTUE), daily login bonuses, weekly events, monthly passes, tournaments, social features, and ranked leaderboards are all features that affect retention at different drop-off points. If your retention is low, you'll need to spend more budget on user acquisition to keep the numbers of monthly active users high.

5. What are the drop-off points of the story/progress mode?

    a. If all players drop at the start of "Chapter 3" of your 5-chapters adventure, there's no point in adding more chapters: you need to fix Chapter 3 first.

6. How long is the average match?

    a. From match start to match end, considering only time spent in the Game. If long, then your game is not suited for mobile due to battery life and network instability.

7. How long is the average play session?

    a. From login to logout, including time spent in the Metagame. Gives you a good hint about how many matches a user goes through during a session, and if they do something in between.

8. How many users play game mode X instead of game mode Y?

    a. Gives you an idea of how your user traffic is split between game modes (i.e., story vs. multiplayer mode, or PvP vs. PvE)

And here's also some examples of game-specific metrics

1. (Ariokan): How many players create cards in addition to just "unlocking" the ones made by somebody else?

2. (League of Legends): What is the win rate of <character>?

3. (Overknights): What are the most used components on player-modded cards?

4. (PUBG): How many players die in the blue zone?

5. (Roblox): How many mini-games are published by players during their first week?

You might have noticed that most of these questions require that you collect individual events at different points of the user journey of an individual player to understand their behavior. Once you collect several, apparently unrelated, events, you can build a "funnel," which is a graph capable of telling you how many users "trigger" a specific event that is part of a series, like you can see in Figure 4-11.

CHAPTER 4　GOING GLOBAL

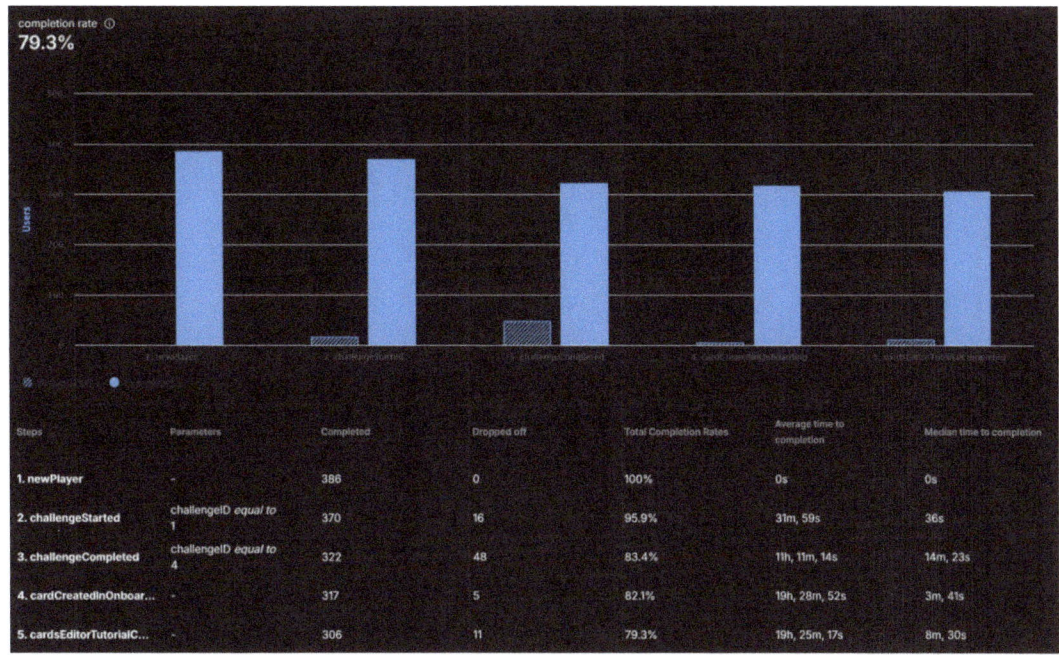

Figure 4-11. *Example of Onboarding flow analytics funnel from Ariokan. Note how the system also tracks the time between one event and the other, giving actionable insights about the time it takes to complete each step*

For free-to-play games, another important metric to track is "Customer Acquisition Cost recovery time," which answers the following question: "How much time does it take to get back from a player the money I spent to make them a player?"

This is an important driver of profitability, because if you spend $10 to make someone play your game, and it takes 6 months for them to do their first $10 microtransaction, you'll likely run out of money before you can become profitable. On the other hand, if they can "repay" their cost in a few days, then you'll likely to be able to reinvest those into acquiring new players, growing your playerbase fast. At that point, it's all a matter of retention!

Tip　Add analytics as soon as possible once you have a working core game loop. If you release without analytics, you'll miss very precious data that can be critical to further refine your game.

CHAPTER 4 GOING GLOBAL

It's easy to get lost in data, so always remember to track what you need to make choices. And if you want to do balancing, and need to track content competitiveness-related metrics (i.e., Win rates of characters), remember to always send the events from a server: many players tend to ragequit games when they lose, and if this happens, they might not send all the events you need to do a proper assessment.

Conclusion

In this chapter, you learnt how to prepare your game for the real world: how to connect players in different scenarios, how to recognize, prevent, and fight back security threats in the context of server-authoritative competitive games, how to change the behavior of your game without making new builds, and how to proper gather analytics that can inform your decision-making.

You know how live service games handle updates in a way that does not disrupt players or require them to download new executables, and what metrics you need to keep an eye on to improve your game over time.

In the next chapter, you'll learn about the different ways to monetize your game.

CHAPTER 5

Monetization

In this chapter, you'll learn about the different ways to monetize your commercial game so you can make a sustainable business out of it.

At the end of the chapter, you'll know the pros and cons of every revenue model, and you'll be able to choose the one that best fits your game, community, and needs.

Why Is Monetization Important?

Unless you're making games as a hobby, monetizing your game is what allows you to make a business (and a living) out of it. Without monetization, the only way to sustain the development of your game is to burn through your personal, publishers', or investors' savings, which is unsustainable in the long term and will eventually lead to the closure of your studio. On the other hand, if you monetize your game successfully, you enable your studio to sustain itself, make more games, and run experiments to find your next genre-defining hit.

Revenue Models

A "revenue model" describes how you make money with your product. A game can use one verticalized revenue model, or mix elements from several ones to catch revenue from different types of players and target audiences.

To better understand revenue models, it's important that you know some commonly used monetization-related terms first, which I explained in Table 5-1.

CHAPTER 5 MONETIZATION

Table 5-1. *Monetization-related terms*

Term	What is it	Calculated as...
User acquisition ("UA")	One or more initiatives that bring you new players	N/A
Customer acquisition cost ("CAC")	Money you need to spend to get one player to play your game	Money spent in UA / new players coming from UA
CAC recovery time ("CACRT")	How much it takes for a player to repay its CAC	Time elapsed between the 1st login of the new player, and the transaction that repays its CAC
Cost to serve ("C2S")	Operative costs tied to the player (i.e., servers, storage)	Amount spent in services, utilities, and customer support for the average player
Lifetime Value ("LTV")	How much you can earn from a player over time, on average.	(Average revenue coming from a player / average lifespan of player) - C2S
Average revenue per daily active user ("ARPDU")	Average revenue earned from a user over a single day	Total revenue / Daily Active Users (DAU)

Premium

Pros:

- Immediate revenue that the studio can reinvest
- CACRT = 0 (investors will love that)
- Players don't have to deal with microtransactions, and you don't have to implement them.
- Can apply discounts to sell more in certain periods of the year, or during certain events

Cons:

- No way to monetize players after the initial purchase, so LTV is at most equal to the base game's price, and can go lower (or even negative) if players have a perpetual C2S, which is often the case for online games.

- It's very hard to raise the price above the launch price without causing players backlash, except when transitioning from "Early Access" to the full release.

- High barrier to entry for friends who play together, as it's hard to convince an entire group of players to buy the game.

"Premium" is a revenue model that consists of blocking access to your base game behind a paywall: if a player wants to play your game, they must buy it first.

Almost all offline-only and single-player games are premium, because there are no expectations that the player will invest more money into a game that has an actual "end." However, this revenue model is compatible with online games too, and in fact, it has been successfully used in 2024 by games like *Helldivers 2* and *Palworld*, which, by June 2025, made $370M+ and $400M+, respectively, in gross revenue.

Downloadable Content ("DLC")

The price of Premium games is established at release and can only go lower over time, so if a studio wants to increase their revenue without making an entirely new game, they can make DLCs that provide additional content such as levels, characters, cosmetics, and weapons.

DLCs are also one way of keeping Premium games "fresh" after their initial release, as they can lure back players who have abandoned the game, get more LTV from them, and reignite the community interest towards the game with free content and marketing buzz, as you can see from Figure 5-1.

CHAPTER 5   MONETIZATION

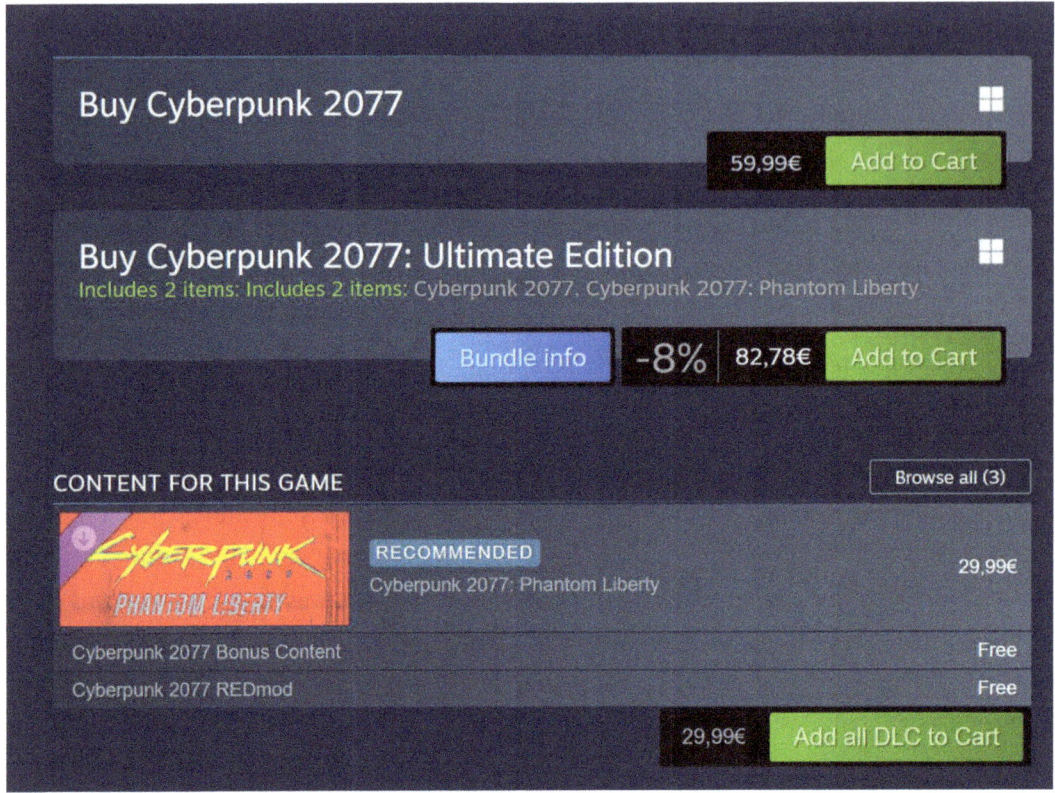

Figure 5-1. *Cyberpunk 2077, a Premium game that also offers paid and free DLCs*

Free-to-Play

Pros:

- Lowered barrier of entry as no payment is required upfront, especially for friends who play together
- Plenty of ways to monetize players after the initial purchase

Cons:

- No immediate revenue the studio can reinvest
- 95-97% of players will only incur costs, no revenue
- Devaluation of perceived value as the game is free
- Players have to deal with microtransactions, and you have to implement them

CHAPTER 5   MONETIZATION

On the opposite end of the spectrum compared to where Premium is, we have Free-To-Play (a.k.a. "F2P") games.

As you can see in Figure 5-2, F2P is a revenue model that consists of giving away access to your game for free, and monetizing players during the rest of their user journey through aggressive in-app microtransactions or advertising. This makes it easier for players to play the games and invite their friends, as they don't have to pay anything upfront.

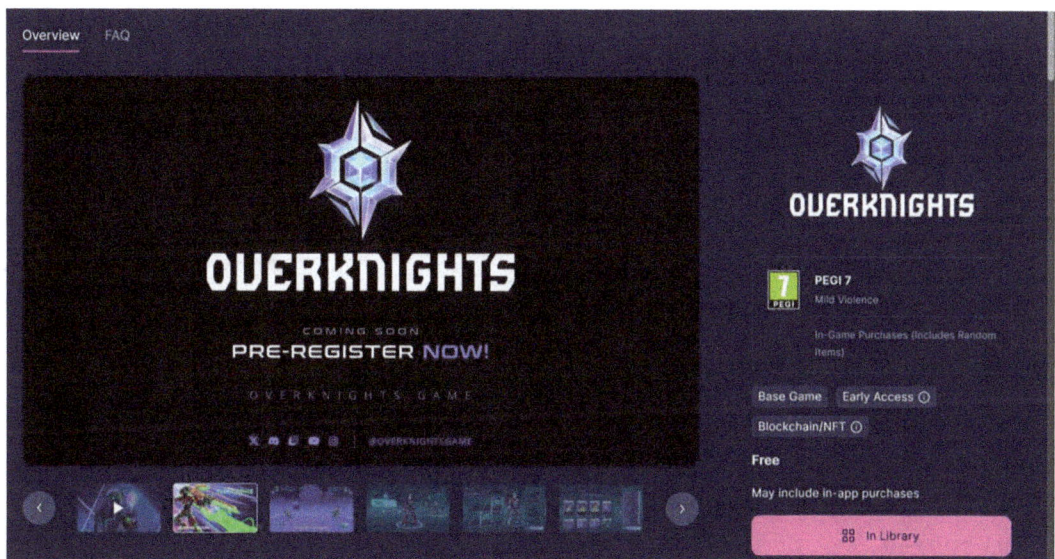

Figure 5-2. *Overknights, a F2P game*

The hope of getting more players and lower UA costs is what leads many studios making multiplayer games to fall into the trap of going F2P.

Why do I say "trap"? Before we dive into the details, let me share a bit of history: this model used to work extremely well across desktop and mobile platforms in the 2010–2020 decade because UA was extremely cheap as developers could track users' preferences and behaviors extremely well without their consent, which made advertising networks very effective and cheap. With the advent of Apple's changes to IDFA ("Identifier for Advertisers") and the introduction of App Tracking Transparency, UA costs exploded, and strategies had to change.

In the golden age of F2P, many now-popular videogames like *Fortnite* and *League of Legends* built their success on this model in the PC market. However, nowadays PC F2P games are extremely hard to monetize even if you have a strong brand and are building a sequel, as the outstanding monetization failure of "*Legends Of Runeterra*." and the 2025's scandal about *Hextech Chests* in *League Of Legends*, proved. On the other hand, the Mobile market heavily revolves around F2P games, also because in-app advertising is an option for apps belonging to that market.

And now, a personal note: if you're developing for PC/Console, I strongly recommend avoiding the F2P path if your only reason to take it is the hope of getting more players. You give up revenue and hurt your game's perception because players give zero value to what they get for free. I see the difference every day: most people who got *Ariokan* for free during the open alpha phase of the project are way less engaged than those who spent $30 to get it when it became a Premium game. Those who put in the money care about the game's success much more, are helpful to other members of the community, are not scared by the bugs they come across, and try to get the most from everything the game puts on their plate.

That said, let's dive into how F2P games try to squeeze value out of players.

In-App Purchases

In-app purchases (a.k.a. "IAP" and "Microtransactions") are transactions that players can perform within the application to get something in return. For the studios, they are a way to increase the LTV of players, and for players they're a way to progress faster or unlock content.

When I say that F2P games are "extremely hard to monetize," I mean that data shows that, on average, only 3-5% of players convert to paying players in F2P games: so 97-95% of them never repay their UA cost (infinite CACRT!) but they still have a C2S because they play with their friends on your servers.

The players that spend huge amounts of money in microtransactions are called "whales," and they're the only reason why F2P games do not shut down. But guess what? Due to the sunk cost fallacy, whales tend to get attached to games where they already spent money on... So newer F2P games have to be very very very convincing if they want to lure those whales away from the games they're playing.

And what do these whales usually buy through microtransactions?

Premium Currency

"Premium currency" is a currency that can usually be obtained only through IAP, and is used to unlock everything else.

CHAPTER 5 MONETIZATION

The reason why this currency exists when players could simply pay with real money is the same reason why casinos give you chips in exchange of cash: they create a mental separation between the player and their money, and are not perceived as "real" cash by players, even if they are it, as you can see from Figure 5-3.

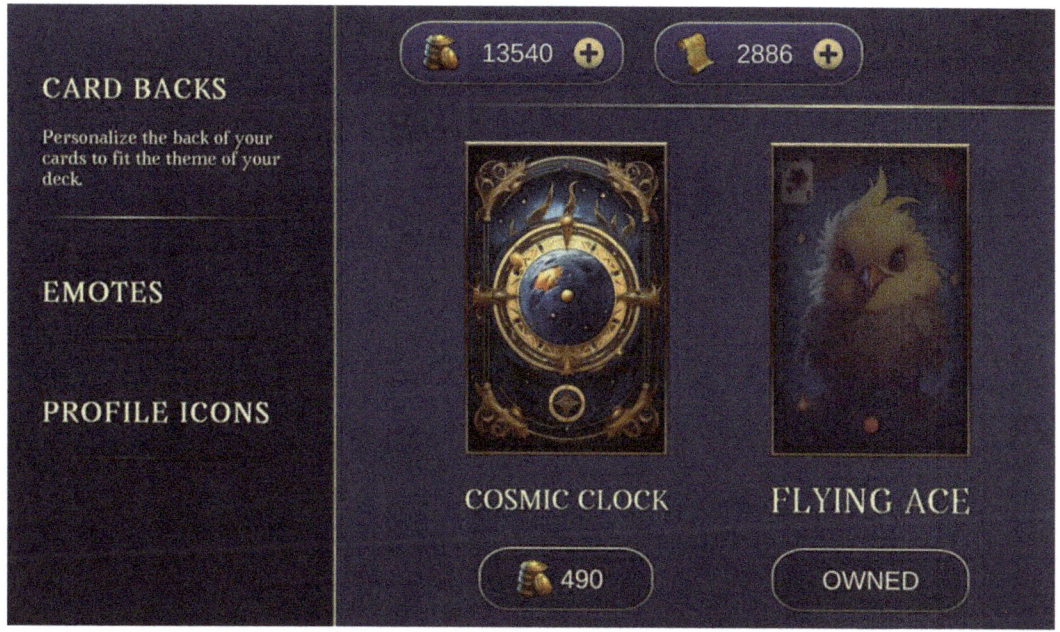

Figure 5-3. Example of premium currency in action from Ariokan. How much real money does the "Cosmic Clock" cost?

From a psychological perspective, for a player it's way more painful to say: "I spent $50 on a hat for my character" than: "I spent 500 gems on a hat for my character." Moreover, it opens up more design space if your game economy is balanced, as you could go one step further and give your players a "clothing wildcard" to buy the hat, turning "I spent $50 on a hat for my character" into "I spent 1 clothing ticket on a hat for my character." This will also allow you to give more limited Premium Currency as in-game rewards that can also be purchased with real money in the store of your game.

Cosmetics

Cosmetics are among the most common forms of monetization in F2P games, and consist in visual content that let a player "customize" their own visual identity. Some examples are profile icons, special clothes for characters (a.k.a. "Skins") and visual effects or emotes that let you mock the opponent, as you can see in Figure 5-4.

CHAPTER 5   MONETIZATION

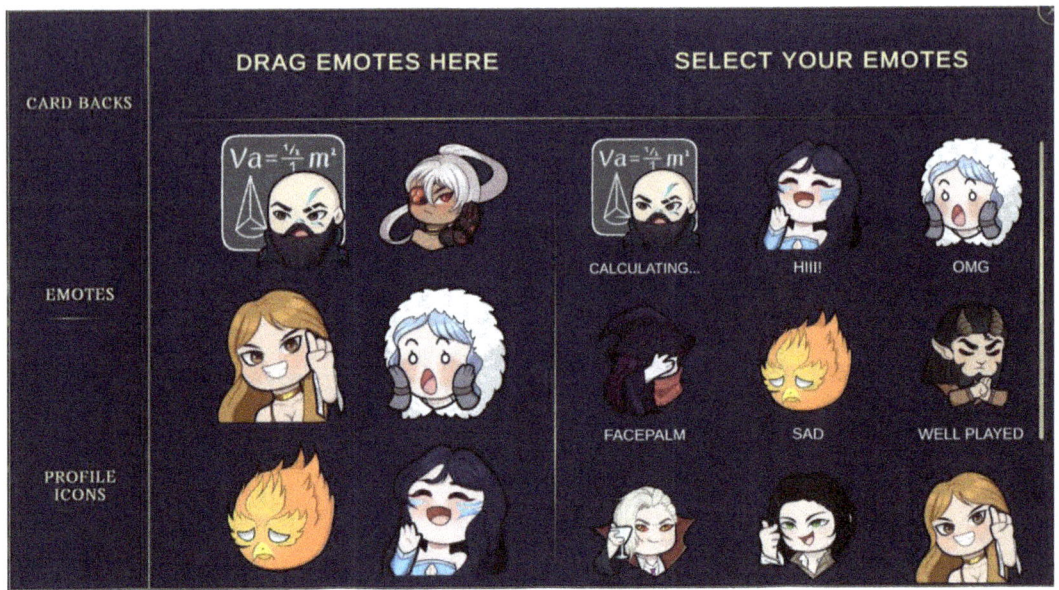

Figure 5-4. Unlockable animated emotes in Ariokan

An important note about cosmetics is that they can be very expensive to make in some games, which sometimes makes it even harder to gain sustainable profit margins in F2P games.

Boosters

Boosters grant you currencies or bonuses that make you progress faster than you normally would. For example, some games like "*Morimens*" require you to spend Metagame-only resources to access parts of the core game loop (i.e., play a level), and let you replenish such resources by spending premium currency, as you can see in Figure 5-5.

CHAPTER 5   MONETIZATION

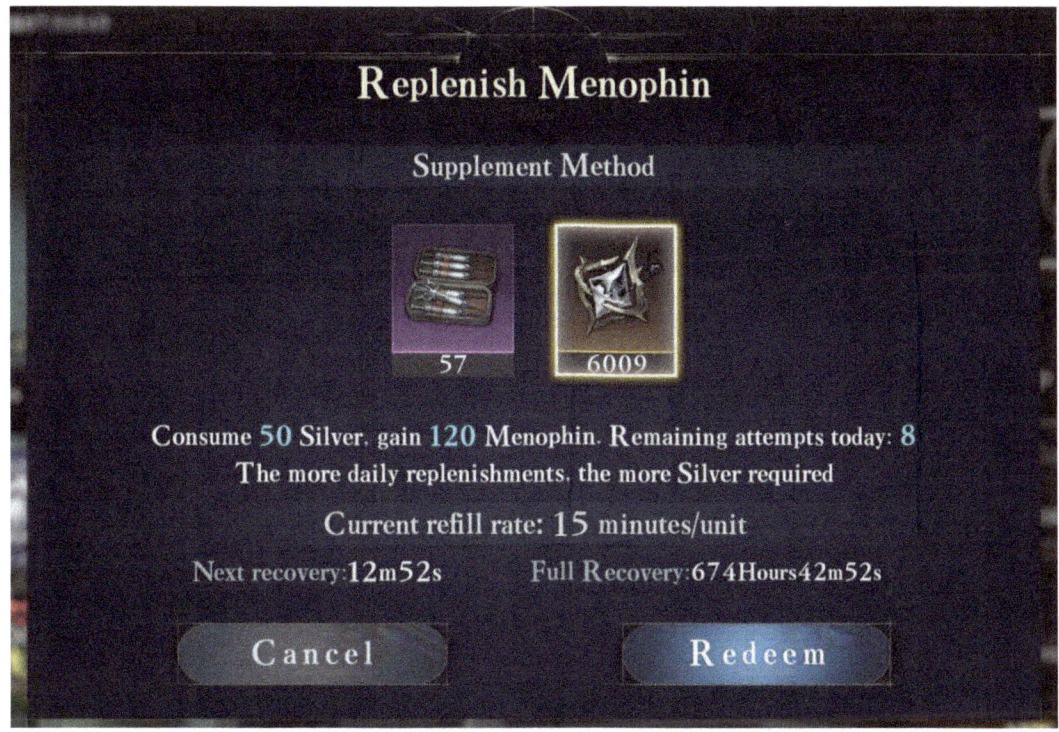

Figure 5-5. *Screenshot of Morimens' energy replenishment screen, which lets you spend a premium currency ("Silver") to replenish energy ("Menorphin")*

But what if you run out of the Premium Currency? Don't worry, as you can see in Figure 5-6, the game has got you covered with a booster pack that you can buy for 300 "*Silver Prime*" (another premium currency).

CHAPTER 5   MONETIZATION

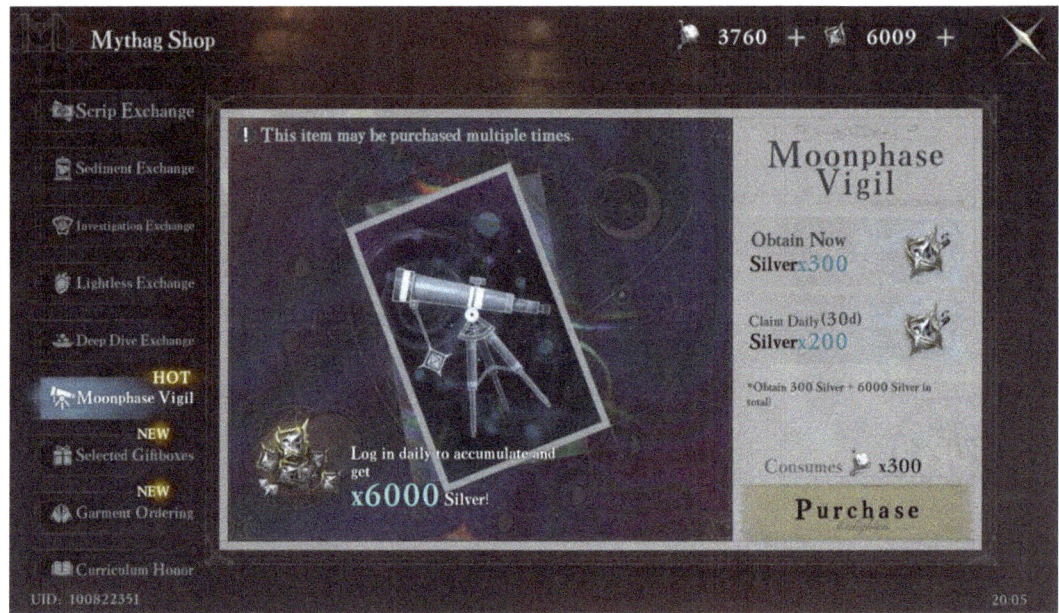

Figure 5-6. *Silver booster pack in Morimens. Notice how this requires another premium currency to be unlocked, distancing your mind even more from the real money you're paying ($4.99 in this case)*

Boosters can also make players level up or unlock content faster, and are a good product to sell to people who don't have a lot of time to play and need to squeeze as much play value as possible from a single play session. A good tactic that you can implement to increase sales is to also use premium currency as boosters, making it possible to unlock non-premium content with it.

Caution   Always respect players and their time. Don't make your game impossible to beat to sell more boosters. Players, especially on Desktop and Console platforms, will notice if you're forcing them into buying boosters. This predatory tactic might increase margins in the short term but erodes players' trust in the long term.

CHAPTER 5 MONETIZATION

Seasonal Passes

Seasonal passes are a very well received form of monetization, which consists of providing rewards to players based on how many points they obtain through the tasks (i.e., daily quests) they complete, and provide even better rewards if players pay for the premium upgrade of the pass, until the pass expires.

As you can see in Figure 5-7, seasonal passes tend to:

1. Be time-limited, in the sense that progress resets after some time (i.e., the duration of a ranked season).

2. Be split into two tracks (one free, and one premium), each one with multiple "levels." The rewards on the free track tend to be minimal, while the ones on the premium track can be very generous and impactful.

3. Let players redeem all premium rewards of previous levels once the premium track is unlocked. This makes it worth upgrading the pass even on the last day before the reset.

4. Be affordable compared to individual premium items.

Figure 5-7. Seasonal pass in Morimens. Notice how the "Advanced Topics" rewards are locked unless you pay for the Extra Curriculum, which costs premium currency, and both passes are time-limited to increase urgency

133

I strongly recommend implementing seasonal passes as they have a very positive impact on D14 to D30 retention. The only "blocker" stopping you from implementing them is that your economy needs to be varied enough: you need multiple currencies, especially consumable ones, that you can provide in passes; otherwise, you'll end up giving away a lot of premium content like cosmetics.

Loot Boxes and Gacha

Loot boxes are a consumable virtual item that contains a randomized selection of the items previously described (i.e., cosmetics, boosters), or actual in-game content (i.e., characters, weapons, or cards). The idea is that players can buy (or obtain) a box, open it, and find something useful and/or rare.

It's important to note that in the late 2010s, loot boxes started to be regulated worldwide as studios were often using predatory tactics and dark patterns to create a "gambling-like addiction" to loot boxes, especially in younger audiences.

As a consequence, if you want to implement them today, you need to be careful and comply with the several (and different) regulations of all the regions in which your game is released.

Some common regulations force you to:

- Show the draw probability of all rewards that can be found in the boxes
- Not sell loot boxes directly
- Even though it's mostly ok to give them as "gifts" when players purchase something else, or in exchange for premium currency.

Gacha games are games where characters and equipment are almost exclusively gained through loot boxes (called "banners") that provide increased chances to find a specific character or piece of equipment during a limited period.

Games like "*Genshin Impact*" and "*Morimens*" fall under this category, and most characters in those games can only be unlocked by spending premium currency to turn the fortune wheel, as you can see in Figures 5-8 and 5-9.

CHAPTER 5 MONETIZATION

Figure 5-8. *Gacha character unlock screen in Morimens. Notice how you can use multiple premium currencies (blue rectangle) to try to unlock ("awaken") this character, and the event is time limited (green rectangle)*

SSR Item Base Drop Rate: 3.03% (Including Guaranteed Rate: 5.00%)			
Type	Name	Type	Name
Awakener	Castor UP!	Awakener	Liz
Awakener	Tinct	Awakener	Winkle
Awakener	Jenkin	Awakener	Casiah

(When neither Rate-Up nor Guarantee is triggered, all Awakeners or Wheels of Destiny share the same base probability.)

SR Item Base Drop Rate: 15.85% (Including Guaranteed Rate: 25.00%)			
Type	Name	Type	Name
Wheel of Destiny	Duty's Gravitas	Wheel of Destiny	Elevated Focus

Figure 5-9. *Partial drop rate table in Morimens for the banner in Figure 5-8. The game must disclose those to comply with regulations and avoid fines, limiting predatory tactics*

Ads-Based

Microtransactions are just one of the ways a F2P game can be monetized. Another popular one is in-app advertising, which consists of partnering with an advertising network to display player-relevant ads in your mobile or browser game[1] that players can watch or click in exchange for rewards. The more ads players interact with, the more you earn.

Mobile games like Candy Crush Saga generate plenty of revenue through advertising, as players watch ads to get boosters (i.e., extra lives), paying with their time instead of money.

Advertising, when done well and not as an ad-spam machine, adds another layer of monetization and is particularly effective in F2P and Freemium models. Some apps even use very frequent ads to nudge users towards buying a premium version of the game that doesn't include ads.

Freemium

Pros:

- Same as F2P, but with higher chances of monetization

Cons:

- Same as F2P, but with the additional burden of having to enable/disable features based on what the player has paid (and ensure compatibility in matches between players that have paid for different things)

Now that we've learned about the two ends of the monetization spectrum, it's time to have a look at the intermediate models. A Freemium revenue model consists of giving away your full game for free (like F2P), but in locking some features behind a paywall. Contrary to F2P, where a non-paying player can do everything a paying player can do, the Freemium model limits what you can do until you pay for the premium features or content (i.e., additional levels or game modes).

---

[1] Desktop and console players are outraged by the use of ads, and will react very negatively if you try to show ads in their games on these platforms.

Subscription

Pros:

- Immediate revenue the studio can reinvest
- CACRT = 0
- Players don't have to deal with microtransactions, and you don't have to implement them.
- Can apply discounts to sell more in certain periods of the year, or during certain events
- Predictable recurring revenue

Cons:

- Extremely high barrier to entry as players know they have to commit to paying every month, which is even higher for friends who play together, as it's hard to convince an entire group of players to buy the game recurringly.

A subscription model consists of letting players pay a specific amount of money every month to keep accessing the game. It's usually combined with other approaches (i.e., premium, freemium, and time-limited demos), and it's a perfect way to monetize Massively Multiplayer Online ("MMO"): games that let players share experiences and live adventures all together, forming guilds and even communities where digital versions of real-life activities happen (i.e., weddings and hangouts). It's not a coincidence that *"World of Warcraft" and "Final Fantasy XIV,"* which both fall under this category, successfully use a mix of premium, free demos, and subscription to make players come back every month to their digital community.

Tip Subscriptions work best in games that can make players feel the Fear Of Missing Out (FOMO) and sunk-cost fallacy. A game is a good candidate for this model if it relies heavily on spending time with friends in the digital world, or can make you lose all your progress if you don't renew the subscription.

CHAPTER 5   MONETIZATION

Licensing

Pros:

- Immediate revenue the studio can reinvest.

- CACRT = 0.

- Revenue is not affected by the number of sales, so if it doesn't sell well you still earn good money.

Cons:

- Revenue is not affected by the number of sales, so if it sells a lot you lose the upside.

Licensing consists of selling the rights to commercialize your game on a specific store/platform to somebody else for a flat amount. Instead of earning money from players, in a licensing model, you earn from whoever buys the rights to sell and/or distribute your game.

An example is Microsoft's *"PC Game Pass,"* which lets you access hundreds of Premium games as long as you pay a monthly subscription, as you can see from Figure 5-10. The platform (i.e., Microsoft, in the case of the *PC Game Pass*) pays the studio a flat amount of money to have the game included on their platform, either as an exclusive that can't be sold in other stores, or as part of the existing offering.

Figure 5-10. Example of game licensed to the Game Pass

CHAPTER 5 MONETIZATION

Secondary Markets

Pros:

- Potentially endless revenue

- Can be easily combined with F2P to lower entry barriers

Cons:

- Unpredictable revenue that depends entirely on volume of transactions

Some games allow players to sell digital items earned by playing (i.e., the ones coming from loot boxes) to other players, taking a cut of the transaction. This is called "operating a secondary market," and some stores like Steam even offer built-in functionalities that allow games to do that, as you can see in Figure 5-11.

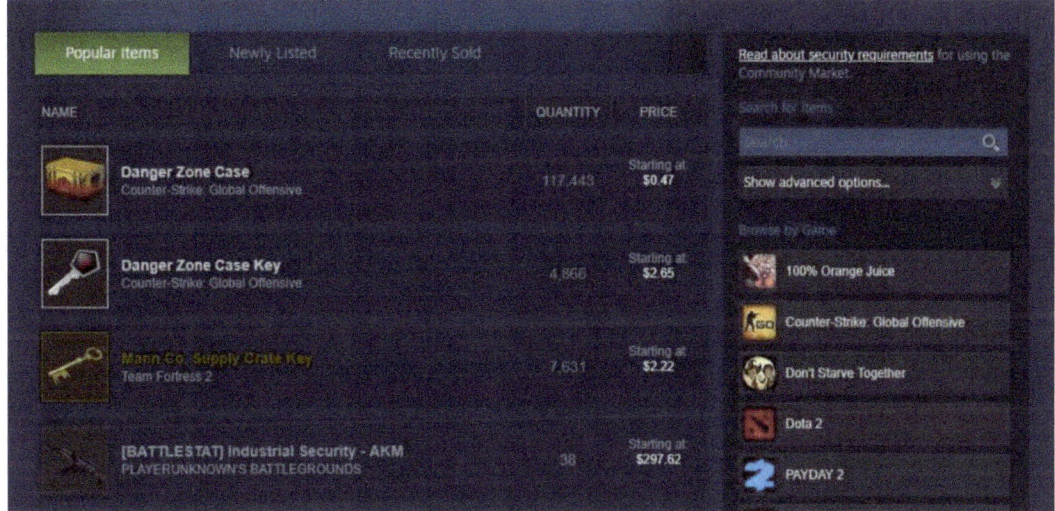

Figure 5-11. *Steam's secondary market*

The interesting thing about secondary markets is that a studio might continuously earn without doing anything apart from giving the item to a player once. If the item is in high demand, a lot of transactions will occur, and the studio will earn money from each of them. Since this revenue model is unpredictable, it is often used in tandem with other ones.

Summary

Table 5-2 summarizes the differences between the aforementioned revenue models.

Table 5-2. *Summary of the differences between revenue models*

Revenue model	Revenue depends on...	Monetized players	Barrier to entry	Effort to implement monetization
Premium	Copies sold	100%	High	None
Free-to-play	In-app purchases	3-5%	None	High
Freemium	In-app purchases/game upgrades	0-100%	None	Very high
Subscription	Subscribers	100%	Very High	Low
Licensing	B2B deal	N/A	Low	None
Secondary markets	Volume and price of content-related transactions	N/A	Platform-dictated	Platform-dictated

Should I Make a Demo?

A demo is a feature and/or time-limited and incomplete version of your game, whose only purpose is to let someone try the game before they can make a purchase. My recommendation is to always include a demo if your game is not F2P or freemium, because it can help you lower the entry barrier for those potential customers who are unsure about your game, as you can see in Figure 5-12.

Keep in mind that you can still run demos for premium and subscription-based multiplayer games, in the form of "free weekends": you let players access the game for a couple of days (usually a weekend, as people don't work) and then lock access again so that only paying users can play.

CHAPTER 5 MONETIZATION

Figure 5-12. Galactic Fighters, a Premium game that also offers a paid DLC. Note how the studio also offers a discounted bundle for getting both, and even provides a demo for those who are unsure about liking the game

Distribution

Once you have figured out your revenue model, the next step is to figure out where to expose your game so players can buy it. In one word, you need to figure out "distribution."

There are mainly three ways to distribute a game: through a third-party physical store, through a third-party digital marketplace, or through a first-party channel (a.k.a. "Direct to consumer").

CHAPTER 5   MONETIZATION

Physical Distribution

As you can imagine, physical distribution is impractical and not worth it in most cases unless your target audience is mainly made up of collectors who want to have physical copies of the games they buy. It comes with logistics challenges and increased prices that many Indie and AA studios simply can't afford. Since the advent of digital marketplaces, most players have accepted the convenience of digital marketplaces and ditched physical media entirely. It's not a coincidence that gaming PCs nowadays are sold without a DVD reader.

Digital Distribution

With the advent of *Steam* as a publishing platform in 2005, studios started selling games through digital platforms, as players started looking for a more convenient way to discover, buy, and play games.

Nowadays, platforms like *Steam, Google Play Store,* and the *Epic Games Store* let studios publish games for a little-to-none fee and immediately tap into a pool of millions of players eager to buy games. The great advantage of these platforms is that they cover every simple step of the customer's journey, from discovery to post-purchase assistance, theoretically removing the burden from the studio. For example, *Steam* takes care of exposing games through its discovery queue, handles the purchase process in a secure way, and handles refunds. It also provides features that let studios build communities, talk with players through announcements and discussions, and gather feedback through reviews.

From a technical standpoint, digital marketplaces also offer important features such as patching tools, online storage, and a myriad of services that nowadays all players expect to be implemented in a game, such as the possibility to store save files in the cloud so you can resume playing from the same level regardless of the device you're using, or the possibility to play with your friend.

Finally, they also provide features related to the promotion and commercialization of the game, letting studios create dedicated pages for the games, manage pricing, discounts, and marketing initiatives.

It would take years for a studio to implement this set of features, and digital stores know this. That's why most of them take a relevant cut of the revenue (~10–30%) as a fee to cover their own operating costs and the services they provide.

Apart from the price cut, another problem that afflicts most digital marketplaces is the lack of curation: since anybody can pay the store fee to publish their game, the number of new games published on these platforms every day keeps growing at an alarming rate, making it harder for good games to be found among tons of shovelware[2]. This also makes it harder to justify the high revenue cut.

To get an idea of how serious this problem is, have a look at Figure 5-13: you can see that in 2014 the average number of games released in a day in a year was 4.69, while in 2024 it was 51.39. That's 11 times more.

The worst part is that most of those games are categorized as "limited games," which means that they haven't sold enough copies / reached certain player metrics that give Steam confidence that a reasonable number of players are actually engaged with the game. Tl;dr: it's a nice way to say that they're either garbage nobody wants to play, or games that were not marketed properly.

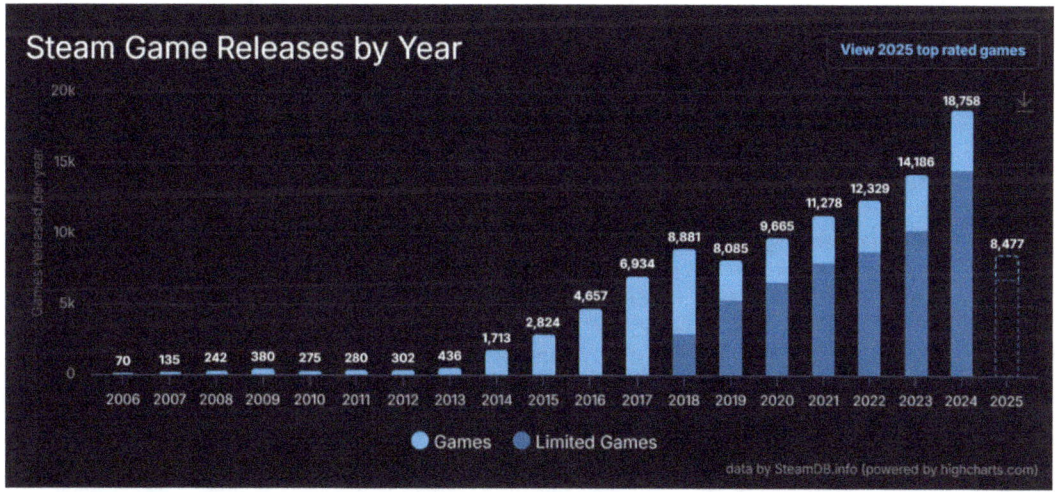

Figure 5-13. Steam game releases by year according to SteamDB

---

[2] Games that are just copy-pasted and reskinned versions of existing games/not worth playing/published as quick cash grabs that provide no real value. Basically "garbage software."

Direct to Consumer ("D2C")

An alternative to digital marketplaces is doing D2C campaigns to sell your game through your own channels. In the digital world, this usually boils down to selling through your game's website or a custom launcher.

While this option provides the highest margins compared to other ones as it removes many middlemen from the equation, driving potential buyers to your own website, and convincing them that it's safe to put their credit card info in your forms, can be a tough challenge. That's why few studios go this way, and try to negotiate better deals with digital marketplaces instead of investing in their own distribution platforms and channels.

Pricing

"How much should my game/subscription/in-app purchase cost?"

This is an important question, with a non-straightforward answer: "it depends."

A few factors that can help you identify the right price for your game and its content are:

- Replayability
- Planned discounts
- Your studio's track record
- Length of the game (in hours)
- The platform you're selling the game onto
- Your target audience and their purchasing power
- What is socially acceptable (price tag of similar products)

Unfortunately, how much time and money you spent developing the game is not something that should have an impact on its price: players don't care if it took you $100K or $10M to develop the game. They care about getting good value for money, and they won't be happy if you try to sell the game at an exorbitant price to compensate for bad planning/execution that made the costs of the project go up.

Your studio's track record plays an especially important role, because if you built trust with an audience previously and proved that you can make good and finished games, it's going to be easier to sell new games at a higher price. That's why some studios intentionally release games for free and with no monetization.

> **Tip** If in doubt, set a higher price. Doing discounts later on is easier than rising prices.

Regional Pricing

When it comes to pricing, one size doesn't fit all, especially if you're planning a worldwide release. If you target very varied audiences (i.e., LATAM and USA), you need to consider that the purchasing of each audience is different.

That's why digital marketplaces often offer the possibility to set a price that automatically adjusts depending on the buyer's country, as you can see in Figure 5-14.

This neat little feature allows players that live in countries with a lower purchasing power to access your game at a reduced price compared to the "standard" one, which, in many cases, would be prohibitively expensive.

Following the same logic, it's a good practice to apply regional pricing also to in-app purchases.

CHAPTER 5   MONETIZATION

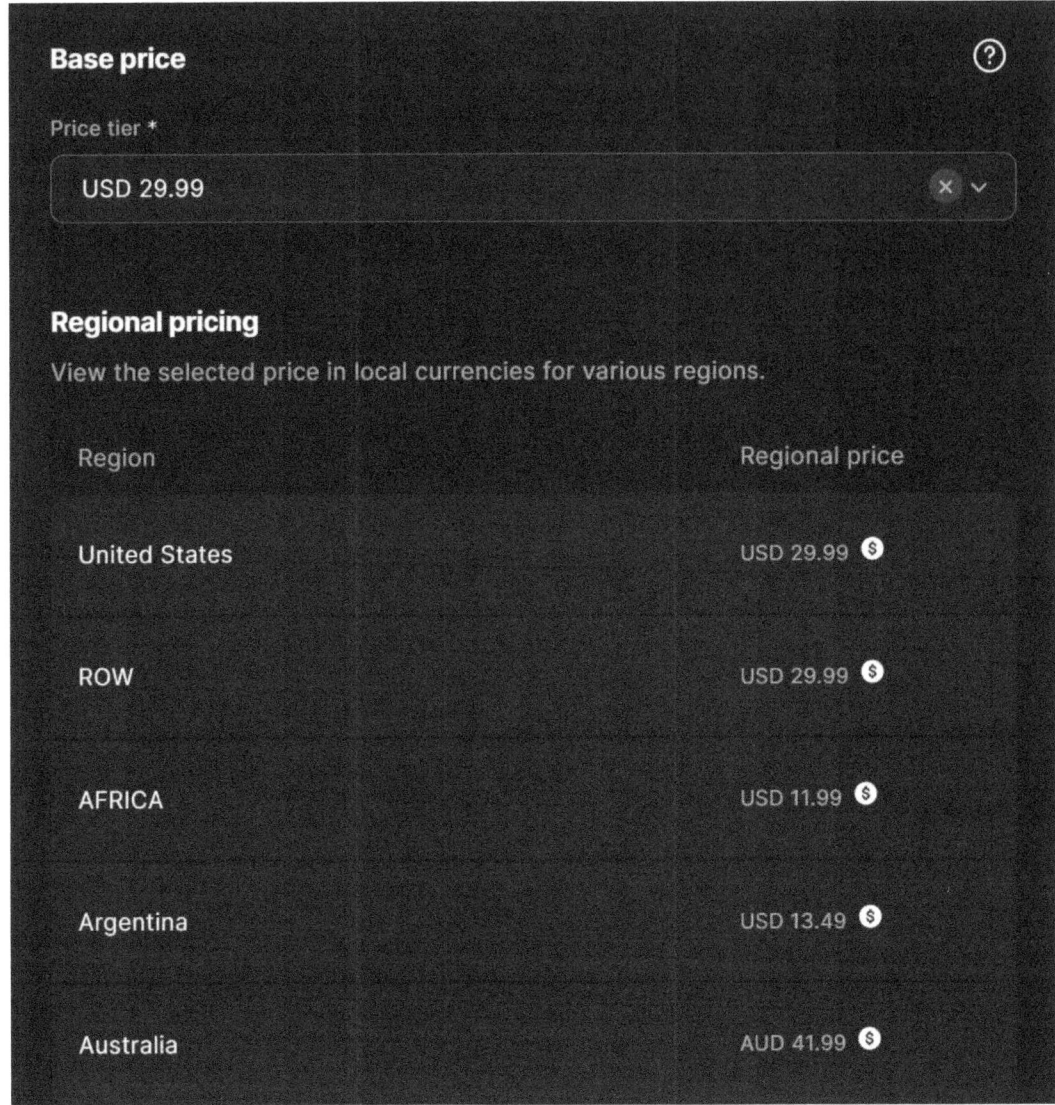

Figure 5-14. Regional pricing configuration in the Epic Games Store. Note how Africa, Argentina, and Australia have different pricing compared to the standard tier targeting the United States

Discounts

Practically speaking, discounts are a way to temporarily lower the price of your game so you can tap into the FOMO of potential buyers and convince them to make a purchase before the price for something they might want goes up again.

Digital marketplaces let you set up discount campaigns, and even bundle products together (i.e., main base and DLCs) in a discounted bundle.

Discounts can also provide a good reason to reignite interest in your game and attract new players in the later stages of your game's lifecycle.

Getting your game into 10+ game bundles is another way to discount your game, but that should be considered your last resort, suited for games that no longer manage to attract an audience: games in such bundles are heavily discounted, and your margins will be very slim.

Tip 1   A 10% launch discount can help you build an initial audience faster. If you manage to get traction in the early days, there's a good chance you can build on top of that momentum.

Tip 2   If your game's theme revolves around holidays (i.e., Halloween), running discounts during these holidays can help you increase sales more effectively than running discounts at other times of the year.

Conclusion

In this chapter you learned that monetizing games is necessary for your studio's survival, and you explored how to monetize your game through different revenue models. You also got familiar with distribution platforms and the different ways to get your game in the hands of players.

You should now know how to identify the right price for your game, and how to adapt it for countries with different purchasing power.

In the next chapter, you'll learn how to optimize your game's build to reduce the cost to serve and increase your revenue margins, especially when running dedicated servers.

CHAPTER 6

Optimizing Your Multiplayer Game

In this chapter, you'll learn how to optimize the bandwidth, CPU, and RAM consumption of a multiplayer game, especially when running a dedicated server, to make your runway last longer and increase the potential playerbase of your game.

At the end of the chapter, you'll know about different optimization techniques and tradeoffs that you can apply in your project.

Why Is Optimization Important?

Optimizing your game means that it takes less resources to store it and run it at a stable framerate. In the context of multiplayer, it also means that you don't need a hyper-fast network connection to play online.

It is common knowledge that optimizing your game is beneficial to the studio, but why is it?

The main reason is that the lower the technical requirements of your game, the higher the chance that a potential player can run it on their machine, which leads to more potential sales and network effects. This is universally true for games, where the optimization revolves around optimizing for low processing power (CPU) and memory consumption (RAM and VRAM). In the context of multiplayer games, there's also another variable for which we need to optimize: the amount of data sent over the network (bandwidth).

If a multiplayer game is not optimized for bandwidth, the amount of traffic a relay or dedicated server will need to handle is going to be higher, increasing costs. A huge amount of traffic will also be harder to handle for weak network connections (i.e., those of mobile phones), increasing lag spikes and all issues related to latency.

In both cases, your studio will lose money or players. So, what can we do about it? And are there optimization techniques specific to multiplayer games?

Server Density

"Server density" is the number of matches that can simultaneously run on a dedicated server, and it's obtained by the formula displayed in Figure 6-1:

$$Density = Min\left(\frac{ServerCPU}{MatchCPU} \times 100, \frac{ServerRAM}{MatchRAM} \times 100, \frac{ServerBandwidth}{MatchBandwidth} \times 100\right)$$

Figure 6-1. *Server Density formula. Variables starting with "Server" indicate the amount available on the physical dedicated server machine. Variables starting with "Match" indicate the amount required by one game instance running on the server*

For example, if running a match among 10 players takes exactly 20% of a $100/month server's CPU, RAM, and bandwidth, then you can only run up to five simultaneous games on the same server, for a total of 50 concurrent users ("CCUs"). However, if after a new release of the game the RAM required to run the match goes to 50% of the server's total RAM, then you'll only be able to run two concurrent games, even if the CPU and bandwidth requirements stay the same. That's 20 CCUs per machine, meaning that you now need 2.5 servers to serve the same number of players you could serve before.

Since every server costs your studio money, optimizing for server density lets you save a lot of money.

Optimizing Servers

The sections below give you practical optimization tips that have an impact on one or more resources.

Pick a Lightweight Operating System

Impacts: CPU, RAM

The operating system is the core of your dedicated server, and one of the most impactful choices too: different operating systems have different resource requirements.

Nowadays, most providers offer you just two operating systems: Windows and Linux.

Simply put, the rule of thumb is to go with Linux unless you can't build a dedicated game server that targets that operating system. The reason is simple: Linux is faster, needs less CPU and RAM to run, and you don't have to pay somebody a license when you're running Linux on a machine.

On the contrary, Windows for servers is slow and RAM-heavy and requires you to pay a license to Microsoft. At the time of writing, a Windows server on Unity's Game Server Hosting (formerly "Multiplay"), a provider of dedicated servers, costs $0.046 per hour, which translates to $402.96 per year for just the license of a single server instance running all 24/7, without including CPU, RAM, and Bandwidth.

Remove Media Files

Impacts: CPU, RAM

It's easy to make a build and upload it to servers as it is, but it's also very expensive in the long term.

Since the purpose of a dedicated server is to make data flow between players, and run the gameplay logic in a secure way, they don't even need many of the assets that are at the core of their client counterpart: VFXs, and media files like sounds, soundtracks and images are completely useless on a server as there's nobody watching or hearing them play when a server is running.

The good news is that you can get rid of them, but before telling you "how", here's a list of problematic consequences that will happen if you keep these assets in your build:

- Increased build times: The useless assets need to be processed during the build. This takes time, will slow your build pipeline and increase the run time of your build automation (if you have one). If you use a service or CI/CD for build automation, your costs will increase as it will run for more time.

- Bigger builds: Your server builds will include the assets, meaning they'll add up to the size of the build. This increases your storage costs and makes the patching process slower as the binary difference between files increases.

- Longer load times: Depending on how your assets are referenced by objects in the game levels, the server will load them. This can cause your servers to load up slower, or to freeze in the middle of a game session.

– RAM and CPU waste: Loading resources takes space and CPU power. Media files like soundtracks and high-quality textures will eat up your server's RAM. In the best case, this makes you pay more for server's resources. In the worst, your server instance will crash and disconnect all players, who will then get angry and go play something else.

As you can see, there are plenty of good reasons to get rid of media assets in dedicated server builds. So how can you do that?

If your game is made with Unity, all you need to do is use the "dedicated server" build target as displayed in Figure 6-2, which will strip out a lot of unneeded media assets and systems from the build, helping you get optimized builds out of the box.

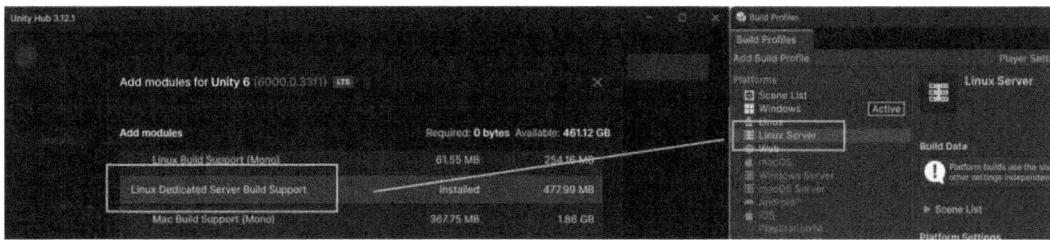

Figure 6-2. On the left, the Unity Hub shows the installation panel for the Dedicated Server Build support module. On the right, the dedicated server Linux build target enabled by the module

And yes, this means you need to keep a separate build of your game that targets a different operating system than the client. At the end of the day, a dedicated game server is just another platform you publish onto, so you should start this multi-platform conversion early on to avoid surprises later and make sure your game runs on Linux without issues.

If you're not using Unity, then you might need to manually implement the optimization that the dedicated server build target does. For example, you could implement a "strip media algorithm" that, in its simplest implementation, goes through all the media files referenced by objects of your levels, at build time, and replaces the references to a 1x1 white pixel image (for textures) or a 0.1 seconds empty SFX (for SFXs and soundtracks), then restores the references back when the build process ends. This way, you won't cause NullReferenceExceptions when running the game on the server, as references are practically kept, but you'll avoid building the real assets that make the build heavy to store, load, and run.

CHAPTER 6   OPTIMIZING YOUR MULTIPLAYER GAME

Caution   If your server-side game logic needs meshes for the colliders of the map, hitboxes or realtime deformations, you can't get rid of them in the build. You can still get rid of other media assets.

Remove Client-Only Scene Objects

Impacts: CPU, RAM

Client-only scene objects (i.e., UI elements) have no reason to exist on the server either, and keeping them would be just a waste of resources. Some engines let you mark objects as "client-only" or "server-only" so they can be excluded from their counterpart builds. As you can see in Figure 6-3, in Unity this is achievable through the "Multiplayer Roles" feature of the "Dedicated Server" Package, which lets you specify what builds should include an object.

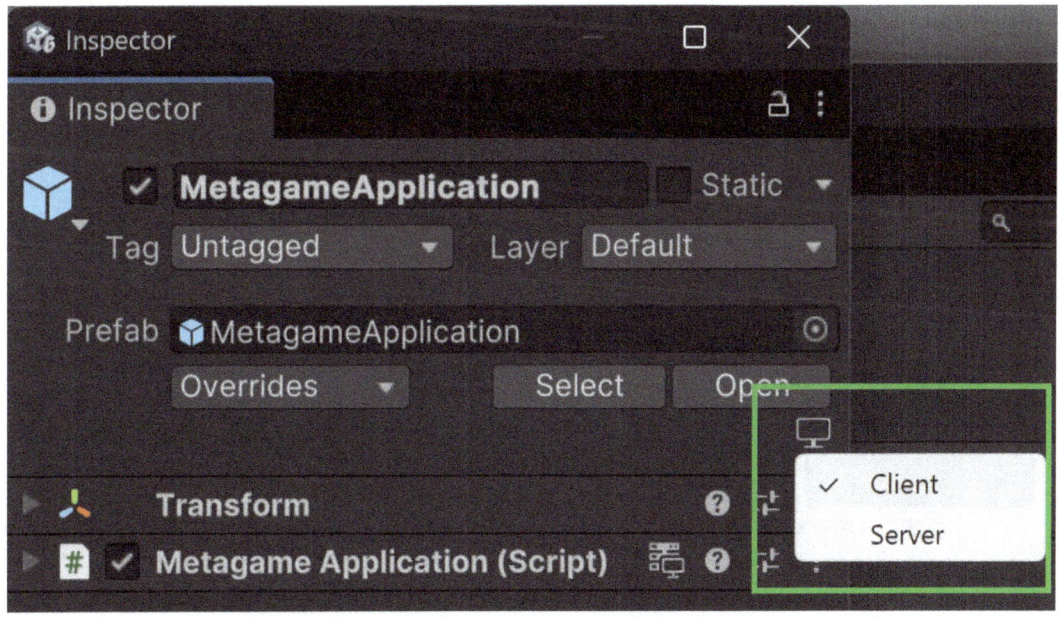

Figure 6-3. *A GameObject excluded from server builds through multiplayer roles*

Limit the Framerate

Impacts: CPU

If you see that your server's CPU usage is consistently above 90%, it's very likely because the framerate of your server build does not have a cap, meaning that the server will try to process as many frame updates as possible every second.

This impacts both the cost of hosting it, and the tick rate (how frequently networked data is read, processed, and sent over the network during a second).

It's crucial to limit the game's frame rate because a server starving for CPU needs more time to process network ticks, as mentioned in the "Network tick rate" section of Chapter 3.

The right cap depends on the type of game you're developing. You should test different numbers and see how the system reacts. A good cap is usually in the 20-120 FPS range, while the tick rate can be much lower.

If you're using Unity, all you need to cap the framerate is add the script in Listing 6-1 to a GameObject in the first scene loaded on your server build.

Listing 6-1. Example of how to set a target framerate, removing the V-sync and setting a target frame rate for the application. vSyncCount is only needed on builds not running in headless mode

```
using UnityEngine;
public class FPSLimiter : MonoBehavior
{
    [SerializeField]
    int target = 60;

    Void Awake()
    {
        QualitySettings.vSyncCount = 0; //remove the V-sync
        Application.targetFrameRate = target;
    }
}
```

Caution If you're using Unity, consider that the frame rate impacts all Unity systems. You could also set the framerate to -1 to remove the cap again.

Run in Headless Mode

Impacts: CPU

As mentioned in Chapter 2, to save costs and exploit the full potential of the physical resources of a server, applications on these machines usually run in "headless mode," which means that they never perform any rendering or look for local user input, saving processing power that can be used to perform faster calculations.

Once you have the build of the game, you can run it in headless mode from the command line, as displayed in listing 6-2.

Listing 6-2. Example of how to run a Linux build of a Unity game in headless mode

```
./MyGame.x86_64 -batchmode -nographics -logfile GameLog.txt
```

Here's a detailed explanation for each parameter:

- `./MyGame.x86_64`
    - is the Linux build of the game ("`./`" indicates to search it in the current folder)
- `-batchmode`
    - runs the application in "headless" mode, preventing rendering and user inputs
- `-nographics`
    - Instructs the game to not initialize a graphics device and makes it possible to run the build on a machine that does not have a GPU. It will also disable logging.
- `-logfile <target file>`
    - re-enables the log, which will be written in the <target file>

By initializing the game in this way, you can avoid wasting CPU resources, initializing devices that are not going to be there or checking for user inputs.

Caution If your server-side game logic requires texture processing, you can't use the `-nographics` argument.

CHAPTER 6   OPTIMIZING YOUR MULTIPLAYER GAME

Use the Smallest Data Type Possible

Impacts: CPU, RAM, Bandwidth

> *Size doesn't mean everything.*
>
> —Teemo (League Of Legends character)

In multiplayer games, the size of your data matters a lot. Every additional byte used to represent information requires additional CPU time, memory, and bandwidth to be processed and sent around.

As a consequence, a quick and effective way to lower the waste of resources is to optimize how you represent data transmitted frequently and stored repetitively across objects.

As you can see in Listing 6-3, in C# you can make an `enum` inherit from `byte` instead of `int` (which is the default), if they have up to 256 entries. Why 256? Because that's how many different elements you can represent using one byte (which is made up of 8 bits, and therefore allows for 2^8 combinations).

Listing 6-3. Example of enum inheriting from different data types

```
enum MyEnum { a, b, c } //it's an int, takes 4 bytes
enum MyOptimizedEnum : byte { a, b, c } //takes 1 byte
```

An `int` variable is represented with four bytes, which becomes useful only if your enum can have around four billion values (2^32), which is usually not the case, so using an `int` instead of a `byte` in this case always causes a 3-bytes waste.

That might not sound a lot, but imagine that in your game an entity uses five enums to represent different data (i.e., what kind of damage it deals, what type of weapon it uses, etc.). That's now a 15-bytes waste per instance of that entity.

If you have 1.000 instances of that entity, that's ~14KB of memory (RAM) wasted for no good reason. If this data is networked, and sent around every second, then it's also 14KB/s additional bandwidth wasted, together with the processing power (CPU) needed to read, compress, and transmit it. The problem gets worse if the unoptimized data is part of a very frequently represented entity (i.e., the record of a player in a database), where the memory waste can quickly escalate to the order of Gigabytes.

Tip Always think about the constraints of your data to determine the right data type. For example, are you storing your health as a byte (1 byte/variable) or int (4 bytes/variable)? If it can't go lower than 0 and higher than 255, you're wasting 3 bytes.

Note Some netcode frameworks automatically optimize data at serialization time. That is, Netcode for Entities heavily delta-compresses primitive types (for GhostFields and Input fields, but not for RPCs), so this optimization may only reduce CPU & RAM requirements.

Synchronizing Only What Is Needed

Impacts: CPU, RAM, Bandwidth

A common mistake that studios make is to synchronize everything over the network. That means UI, VFXs, textures, media, and other potentially "static" data that could be retrieved locally at runtime.

As a reminder, you only need to synchronize "State" (i.e., My power is 9001", "I have 10 health points") and "Events" (i.e., "The game started", "Player X died"), because all other data is usually data that any client can deterministically recreate/retrieve locally given some basic information without the need to synchronize the entire state of objects along the network.

For example, your particle systems must not be part of a networked object, because you can spawn them locally: you can have a local database of VFXs on the client, and when a certain event happens on the server, you can propagate it to clients. Then the client recognizes the event and instantiates whatever VFX it needs where the event happened.

With this system, in addition to removing all VFX and media from the networked objects, effectively preventing their unneeded synchronization at runtime, you also prevent issues related to UI positioning and latency.

To get practical, imagine you're working on a clone of "Chess", the famous 1v1 PvP game, and imagine that you're trying to synchronize everything like a beginner would do.

CHAPTER 6   OPTIMIZING YOUR MULTIPLAYER GAME

You'd synchronize the two players + one network object per piece (there are going to be 32, 16 for each player). And since you want every player to see the board, you'll synchronize the board object as well, which is basically the UI.

Since you want everything to be server authoritative to avoid cheating, you'll also tell clients from the server when to play a sound, whenever something is getting moved or destroyed.

As you can see in Figure 6-4, this approach doesn't work at all: it has visible latency and UI scaling positioning issues. Because if you try to synchronize the UI, what you end up with is a UI that is instantiated on a server, which usually doesn't have any screen, so your UI is going to break if it scales with screen resolution. And even if it worked, both players would see the UI from the same perspective (i.e., both would look at the board from the perspective of the white player).

The user experience is also going to be bad because players will hear sounds later compared to animations or when they perform an action, due to latency.

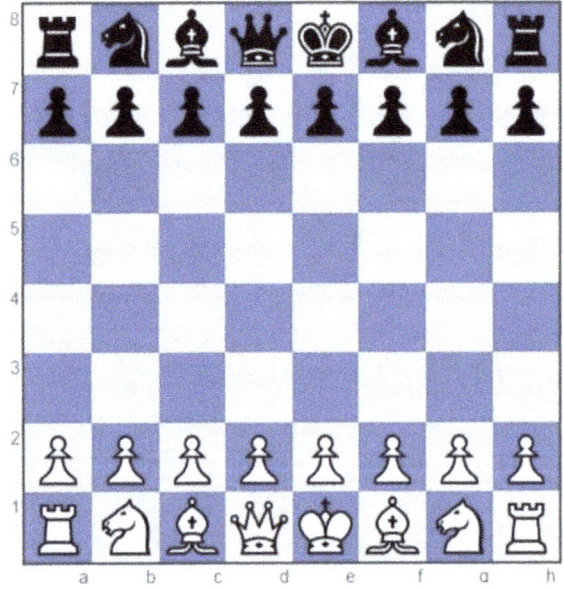

Figure 6-4. *Chessboard and summary of why it is a bad idea to synchronize everything*

The solution is to synchronize only what is needed, as you can see in Figure 6-5, using a standard approach: synchronize just the two players and one networked object per piece, with some additional data, rendering the UI and the board locally.

CHAPTER 6   OPTIMIZING YOUR MULTIPLAYER GAME

Every player has its own UI[1], and plays sounds and animation based on events, or whenever the "alive" flag of a piece changes.

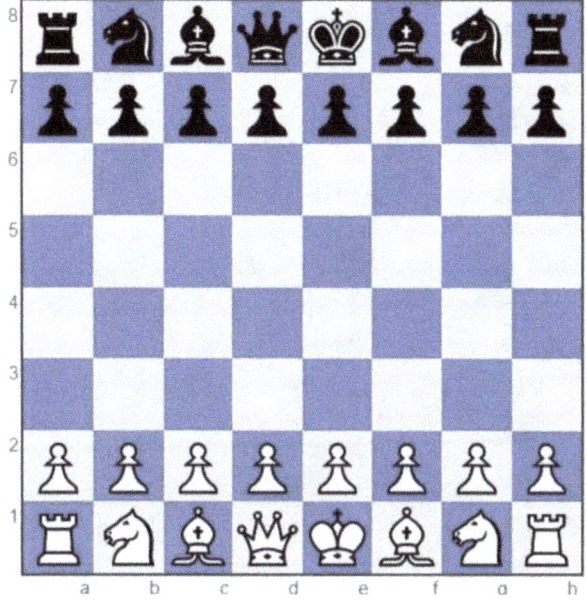

Example: Chess
Standard approach

- Synchronize:
  - 2 players
  - 1 networked object per piece (32)
    - Vector2 position; [8 bytes]
    - bool ownedByPlayer1; [1 byte]
    - bool alive; [1 byte]
  - UX: Prediction + reconciliation

Uses 3,1KB/second with a tick rate of 10
Supports 16 unique pieces per player

Figure 6-5. Chessboard implemented with a standard approach

Assuming you're synchronizing this data with a tick rate of 10 (so 10 times per second), with this approach, you send 3.1 KB/second and can support 16 unique pieces per player, which is what you have in standard chess.

But what if there was an even better way to implement this multiplayer game?

Store Data in Non-conventional Ways

Impacts: CPU, RAM, Bandwidth

If you think out of the box, you can come up with creative (and sometimes very optimized ways) to store and represent information.

For example, you might realize that you do not need to synchronize players' pieces individually: instead, you can synchronize the entire board state (not UI) as an array of 64 byte (1 per square), each telling you what piece is in it.

---

[1] This introduces some challenges, because you need to have different initialization logic for each player to change their "perspective" based on the color they're playing, but it's a necessary evil.

159

CHAPTER 6   OPTIMIZING YOUR MULTIPLAYER GAME

Every byte can represent up to 256 unique values, ranging from 0 to 255 (when unsigned), so if its value is 0, that means that the square is empty. If a byte is between 1 and 127, it means that the cell contains a piece of the white player, and if it's above 127, then it contains a piece of the black player, as you can see in Figure 6-6.

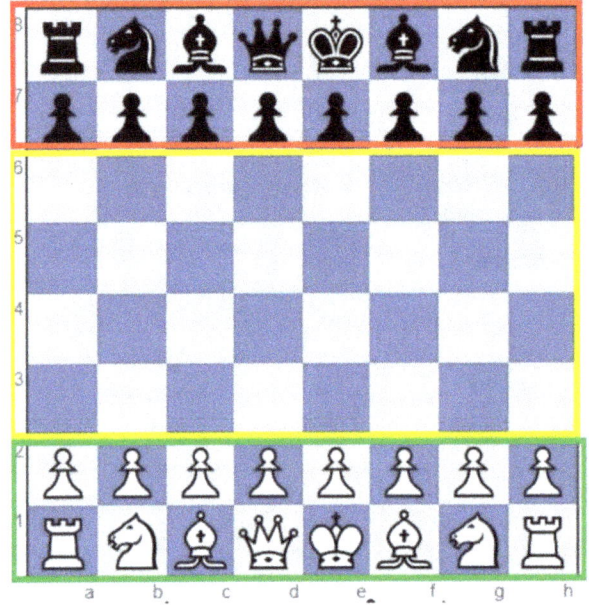

Figure 6-6. Chessboard implemented with an even better approach

The great advantages of this approach are that

- It uses 80% less bandwidth per second (0.6KB/s vs. 3.1KB/s).

- It gives you more design space as you can use the extra values in the bytes to invent new types of pieces that do not exist in standard chess (up to 127 pieces compared to 16).

These are huge advantages, not only in terms of money saved but also in terms of content that you can add to your game.

As you can see, it's really important to think about how we model our data and how to optimize the content of our game and logic of our game.

> **Tip** Bitmasks are also a powerful tool when it comes to group data. For example, a 32-bitmask lets you store up to 32 status effects (i.e., slowed, stunned, poisoned), one in each bit, with just 4 bytes.

Delta Updates

Impacts: CPU, Bandwidth

Most of the time, we don't need to synchronize data every tick. That's why pretty much all netcode frameworks implement "delta updates", sending around only the data that changed, saving bandwidth and CPU. However, there are certain data structures like lists that, by nature, need to be re-synchronized entirely when an element is added, moved, or removed. If you want to save bandwidth, be sure to use data structures that support delta updates as much as possible.

Conclusion

In this chapter, you learned how to optimize your game's build and startup settings to reduce the cost to serve and increase your revenue margins, especially when running dedicated servers. You're now aware of different optimization techniques, and can probably apply a couple ones in your game already. Give it a try!

In the next chapter, you'll learn about how to implement some common, but advanced, multiplayer features.

CHAPTER 7

Common Multiplayer Features

There are some advanced multiplayer-related features that many popular games implement nowadays, and whose implementation might not be trivial. In this chapter, you'll learn how to implement them.

Bots

Be it for shortening matchmaking time, or for testing and onboarding purposes, every multiplayer game has bots: fake players that try to act as real players during a match. In order to do that and do it while providing a positive experience to the player, bots need to match the criteria detailed below.

Bots' Logic Always Runs on the Server to Reduce Latency

After all these chapters, it should be clear to you that the less latency-dependent elements a game has, the easier it is to provide a better user experience. That's why bots' logic always runs on the same device acting as the server.

As a consequence, bot players should always connect to localhost to not be unnecessarily influenced by latency, and their logic should always run server-authoritatively: since they're already there, there's no point in dealing with client-to-server RPCs. All they have to do is call server-side methods and can skip all validation steps normal players have to go through when declaring an action.

Bots Should Be Able to Do What Players Can Do

In order to be useful companions or opponents, bots need to be able to mirror all players' actions that have an impact on the state of the game or other players. For this to happen, we need to architect our codebase in a way that makes it compatible with bots that are playing directly on the server.

This can be achieved by moving the logic of server-side RPCs called by players to intermediate server-only methods that can be called by both the server-side players and bots, as you can see in Listing 7-1.

Listing 7-1. Example of server-side code that handles the "play a card" action and can be called both by human players and bots. The actual logic is in OnServerPlayCard, while cheating-related checks are only in the RPC called exclusively by players

```
using Unity.Netcode;
public class Player : NetworkBehavior
{
   List<int> myCardIDs; //all cards' IDs of the player/bot
    void OnClientTryToPlayCard(int cardID) //client-side method called by
    the player
   {
       ServerPlayCardRpc(cardID);
   }
   void OnServerActAsBot() //bot's logic
   {
       //some code here that lets bots figure out what to do
       int cardID = 10;
       OnServerPlayCard(cardID);
   }
   [Rpc(SendTo.Server)] //the player calls this method
   void ServerPlayCardRpc(int cardID)
   {
       //sanity checks here for player-performed actions
       if (myCardIDs.Contains(cardID))
       {
```

```
            OnServerPlayCard(cardID);
            return;
        }
        //this is a cheating attempt, or an error
    }
    //the bot calls this method directly, as it doesn't cheat
    void OnServerPlayCard(int cardID) {/* play the card! */}
}
```

Once you have this structure in place, you can drive the behavior of a bot by simply calling the server-side method related to the specific action you want the bot to perform.

Tip Bots should be among the first features you implement in your game. This will make it easier to architect the setup code and player actions in a compatible way, and to set up automated tests.

Bots Need Different Skill Levels

In order to accommodate the different needs of both players and developers, it's important that your bots have different "skill levels" that impact *what* they do and *how* they do it.

For example, new players should play against "easy" bots that are going to make mistakes and play in a suboptimal way so players can win easier and learn the ropes of the game without being crushed. More experienced players will likely get bored easily if they face the same type of bots, so you can make them play against more fine-tuned, "hard" bots that try their best to win.

A good criterion that can help you identify the right type of bot that a player should match is the player's ELO score: the higher, the more "expert" the player is.

It's also important to have a "test" difficulty level to use in automated tests: bots with this level are simply idle until the system (the tests, in this case) explicitly tells them to do something. This lets you drive the behavior of the bot based on what you'd like to test, without the risk of it acting autonomously and making the tests inconsistent. Listing 7-2 shows the barebone structure of this system.

Listing 7-2. *Example of barebone structure of an AI system capable of customizing the bot's behavior based on different skill levels*

```csharp
using UnityEngine;
public class AIBrain : MonoBehavior
{
    System.Action behave;
    public AILevel Level;
    public enum AILevel : byte
    {
        Test,
        Easy,
        Medium,
        Hard
    }
    //Called from other classes at setup time
    public void SetLevel(AILevel level)
    {
        Level = level;
        switch (level)
        {
            case AILevel.Test:
                behave = DoTestAI;
                break;
            case AILevel.Easy:
                behave = DoEasyAI;
                break;
            case AILevel.Medium:
                behave = DoMediumAI;
                break;
            case AILevel.Hard:
                behave = DoHardAI;
                break;
            default:
                behave = DoTestAI;
                break;
```

```
        }
    }
    void OnServerBehave()
    {
        behave?.Invoke();
    }
    void DoTestAI() { /* Do nothing */ }
    void DoEasyAI() { /* Play as a noob */ }
    void DoMediumAI() { /* Play as a normal player */ }
    void DoHardAI() { / Play as a professional */}
}
```

As you can imagine, the actual implementation of each skill level is game-specific: making bots for Chess is not the same as making bots for Call of Duty, or Ariokan. Bots nowadays are usually made in three ways:

1. Machine learning: Which consists of training a statistical model based on realtime simulations (i.e., matches) that create a large amount of data ("dataset") that is then processed by a neural network, which causes the AI to autonomously learn how to behave in the context of the game. This approach suits better games whose content and rules do not change often (i.e., shooters), as every core change causes the AI to become instantly obsolete unless it is retrained to learn the new rules.

2. Heuristics: A hardcoded algorithm where the developer decides which action to perform based on "generally good rules of thumb." For example, a heuristic in a shooter game is to always move towards the enemy so, at some point, you can engage in a fight with them. Another one is to retreat when your health is low. Note that these are assumptions that don't consider the other factors that might have an important impact when making gameplay choices: for example, if the enemy ran out of ammo and is reloading, shouldn't we attack instead of retreating, even if our health is low?

3. Utility AI: Works by assigning numerical values (called "utilities") to different outcomes or actions, allowing the bot to evaluate and choose the best course of action based on multiple factors.

CHAPTER 7   COMMON MULTIPLAYER FEATURES

Utility AI requires some manual work as every action or outcome in the system needs to be assigned a numerical value (as you can see in Figure 7-1) and a formula to calculate the utility, but it is very flexible even across game modes, and lets you customize several difficulty levels with overrides (see Figure 7-2). It's an ideal solution for games where the rules can be customized, and where new content comes out frequently (i.e., Card Games)

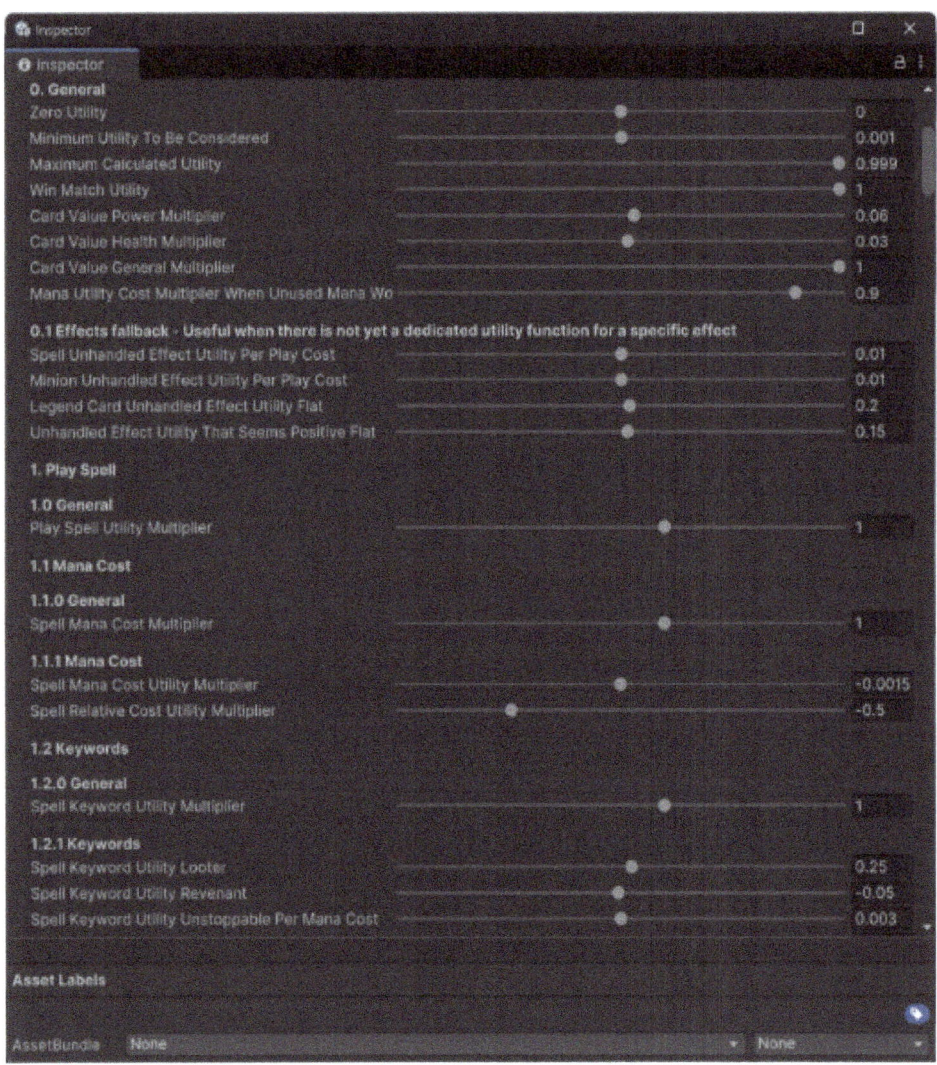

Figure 7-1. *Example of Utility AI configuration from Ariokan. You can see a mix of flat values and multipliers, which are then taken into account in formulas at runtime to establish the best outcome (i.e., what card to play)*

CHAPTER 7 COMMON MULTIPLAYER FEATURES

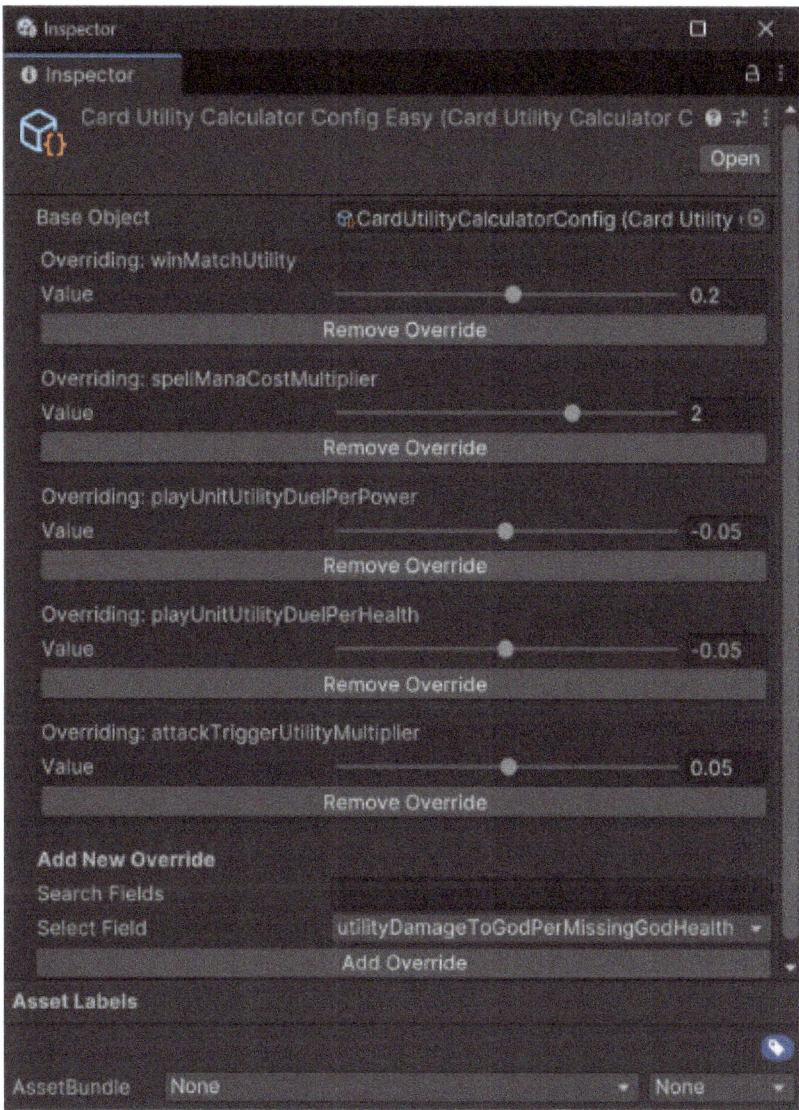

Figure 7-2. *Example of skill override for the Utility AI configuration from Ariokan to create an "Easy" AI. Note that the value of winMatchUtility at the top is just "0.2" compared to the "1" in section "General" of Figure 7-1, meaning that this AI will not give a lot of value to actions that lead to victory, simulating a newbie's ability to make mistakes*

Treat Bots as Remote Players

Even though they act like players and run on the local machine when playing in host mode, it's important to remember that bots are not local players. Bots always need to be treated as if they were remote players, especially when updating their UI, to avoid messing with the local player's UI.

Be sure to have a flag in our system that lets you easily recognize the bot as a bot, so you can add custom logic to prevent issues.

Bots Need to Be Credible

Especially during your game, bots will be the main opponents and companions of your players. For this reason, it's important to invest a bit of development time into making them credible

- **Give them usernames:** From a randomly generated list, or using the names of players who haven't been active for a long time.

- **Ensure they have personalities:** Let them play emotes when a specific situation happens. You can also let them write messages in the chat based on what a human would say in the current situation.

- **Let them be useful:** Use their deep knowledge of the game state to point out things that are helpful to humans. For example, if an enemy is close to an important objective that all players can see, let that point flag the potential dangers to other players through the communication system (chat, pings, voice-guided system).

The more credible a bot is, the less it will break the immersion for players, and the more players will be engaged and happy to play with it.

Reconnection

Power and connection outages are very frequent, especially in mobile gaming, where roaming players continuously move between telephone cells and receivers, and cause players to suddenly leave a match they were enjoying. In the context of casual games this is usually not a problem, but in the context of competitive ones, it can have a negative impact on the player's ELO and progression, causing frustration and churn.

Reconnection is a feature that lets players resume an online game from which they disconnected, so they can continue playing as if they never disconnected.

Implementing reconnection requires careful planning, because your game needs to be able to do three things: accept players connecting after the game started ("late joiners"), synchronize data in a way that lets players "get it back" when they reconnect, and keep track of disconnected player characters so they can be restored.

Accepting Late Joiners and Reconnecting

Netcode frameworks and matchmaking systems usually provide options that let you decide whether you want to accept late joiners after a match starts. This is usually a checkbox in the settings of the NetworkManager, or in your matchmaker's configuration.

In order for a player to reconnect, it's important that you store some information about the specific match they were connected to, when the connection happens for the first time: specifically, you need to store the IP address and port of the server the player connected to, and you need to store this information in a persistent storage that survives across sessions (i.e., a file on the client device), so that, when a non-voluntary disconnection happens (i.e., the client crashes), the client can read this information at startup and try to reconnect to the server through direct connection.

When the game ends "naturally," this information can be cleared up so it doesn't interfere with the startup logic.

> **Tip** You can use Unity's PlayerPrefs API to store and retrieve the IP and port of the server easily, across platforms.

Synchronizing for Reconnection

In order to support reconnection, late joiners need to be able to retrieve the latest information about the game. Luckily, this is mostly automatically done out of the box by synchronized data structures like SyncVariables (in *Mirror/FishNet* netcode frameworks) and NetworkVariables (in *Netcode For GameObjects*).

As long as you're able to store all relevant data into variables using these data structures, late joiners will receive the latest value of these variables. At that point, the networked callbacks (i.e., OnNetworkSpawn/OnValueChanged) of these variables/networked classes will give you the opportunity to update the UI to match the state of the simulation, as you can see in Listing 7-3.

Listing 7-3. Example of a ColorManager that properly synchronizes information for late-joining clients

```
using UnityEngine;
public class ColorManager : NetworkBehavior
{
    NetworkVariable<Color32> m_NetworkedColor = new
    NetworkVariable<Color32>();
    [SerializeField]
    Material m_Material;
    public override void OnNetworkSpawn()
    {
        base.OnNetworkSpawn();
        if (IsClient)
        {
            //Manually load the initial Color to catch up with the state of
            the network variable.
            //Useful when re-connecting or hot/late-joining a session
            OnClientColorChanged(m_Material.color, m_NetworkedColor.Value);
            m_NetworkedColor.OnValueChanged += OnClientColorChanged;
        }
    }
    public override void OnNetworkDespawn()
    {
        base.OnNetworkDespawn();
        if (IsClient)
        {
            m_NetworkedColor.OnValueChanged -= OnClientColorChanged;
        }
    }
```

```
    void OnClientColorChanged(Color32 previousColor, Color32 newColor)
    {
        m_Material.color = newColor;
    }
}
```

As a consequence, it's very important that you do not synchronize data through RPCs, because they are, by definition, "fire and forget" method calls that will not be received by those devices that are not connected when the RPC is invoked.

Restoring Player Characters

What do you do to the player character when the player disconnects, destroying their connection to the server?

Normally, you'd destroy it, but if the player can reconnect, you need to keep it around as a "zombie," store its data, and reapply it when they reconnect, reassigning the ownership of the networked object to the new connection of the player.

To do this, you need to be able to identify the player with some information that never changes between sessions (i.e., the player's profile ID). Otherwise, if your game logic assumes that a player session or client ID will always be the same, which is not the case when a player disconnects and reconnects, it'll break.

To recognize what "zombie" player object belonged to a specific player, you can use a `Dictionary<string,GameObject>` where the `string` is the immutable player ID, and `GameObject` is the object that represents the player. When a player disconnects, you store this association in the dictionary, moving the ownership of that zombie object to the server (which might even start an AI to make the zombie player "do something" in the meantime).

When a player reconnects, you can check the dictionary to retrieve their object and re-assign ownership of the object to the new connection that represents the late-joining player, so they can continue playing as if they never left the game.

Tip Reconnection is very important for competitive team games and games with long sessions (i.e., League of Legends), but is a negligible feature in casual, short-session games or games in which disconnecting for one minute is going to have an irreversible impact (i.e., card games)

CHAPTER 7   COMMON MULTIPLAYER FEATURES

Replays

In their most basic form, "Replays" are a feature that allows players to rewatch how a match unfolded. They're an important feature for competitive games as they let players study their own actions to improve, but also for content creators as they allow them to calmly create video clips of content that can be posted on social media.

There are two ways to implement replays: through recordings and through simulation.

Recorded Replays

Recorded replays consist of recording the match in realtime from the local player's perspective.

This form of replay is the most straightforward to implement and can be implemented in any game, but comes at a huge performance (and storage) cost as the game needs to constantly record during the Game, which is a performance-sensitive section of the application's lifetime.

This makes it impractical to use it on mobile and handheld devices, while on desktop and console platforms, it can cause serious performance issues. Another disadvantage is that the recording only captures the local player's screen, making it impossible to experience and examine what happened from the perspective of other players. Storing these recordings on the cloud, so players can access them from multiple devices, is also problematic as they take up a lot of space, which can quickly fill up the allowance of the service provider.

Simulated Replays

Simulated replays consist of recording all players' inputs in realtime from the server's perspective, storing them into a file that is sent to clients at the end of the match, and that clients can then read to re-simulate what happened during the match.

As you can imagine, a game can support simulated replays only if its gameplay is deterministic, as even a little divergence in the output when replaying an input will make the rest of the replay simulate an alternative reality that never happened.

Simulated replays are often implemented using the *Command Pattern*, a design pattern that lets you "encapsulate" methods and parameters, that you'd normally invoke directly, into a sequence of "commands" that can then be stored in a queue or stack and played forward (= "executed"), backward (= "reverted"), or delayed, as you can see in Figure 7-3.

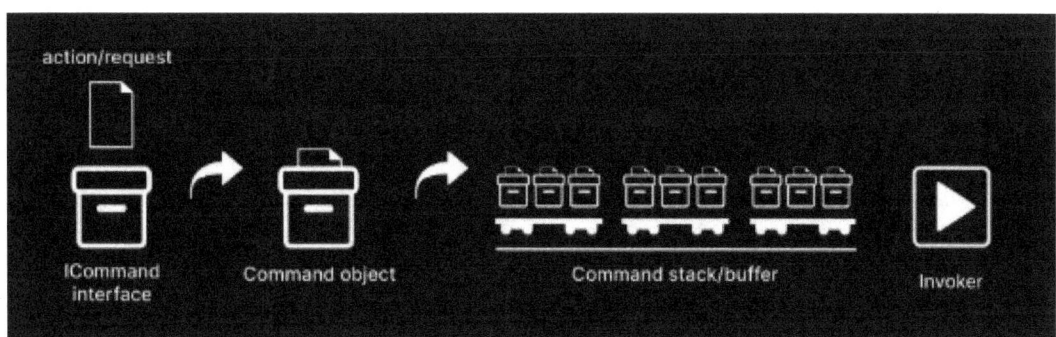

Figure 7-3. *Command pattern overview. Source:* `https://unity-connect-prd. storage.googleapis.com/20240301/learn/images/a69a1b76-127a-42ea-9225- 1bfcfce00444_Copy_of_6-1_CommandDiagram.png`

To implement the command pattern, you need to be able to encapsulate gameplay actions into objects that contain the logic to perform and undo the action. Listing 7-4 shows an ICommand interface that you can use to achieve this:

Listing 7-4. Interface that defines a Command Object in the command pattern. This could also be an abstract class.

```
public public interface ICommand
{
    void Execute();
    void Undo();
}
```

At this point, you can encapsulate gameplay actions by implementing the ICommand interface like in Listing 7-5:

Listing 7-5. Example of a gameplay action ("Play Card") encapsulated in a Command Object

```
//Command object
public class PlayCardCommand : ICommand
{
    Player player;
    Card card;
    public PlayCardCommand(Player player, Card card)
    {
        this.player = player;
        this.card = card;
    }
    public void Execute()
    {
        player.PlayCard(card);
    }
    public void Undo()
    {
        player.UndoPlayCard(card);
    }
}
//Gameplay action
public class Player : MonoBehavior
{
    List<Card> cardsInHand;
    List<Card> cardsOnField;

    public void PlayCard(Card card)
    {
        cardsInHand.Remove(card);
        cardsOnField.Add(card);
    }

    public void UndoPlayCard(Card card)
    {
```

```
        cardsOnField.Remove(card);
        cardsInHand.Add(card);
    }
    public bool CanPlayCard(Card card)
    {
        return cardsInHand.Contains(card);
    }
}
```

Now, whenever a player wants to play a card, we'll call a method that runs the appropriate checks and creates a Command if needed, like in Listing 7-6:

Listing 7-6. Example of a method that creates the Command Object

```
void TryToPlayCard(Player player, Card card)
{
    if (player == null
    || !player.CanPlayCard(card))
    {
        return;
    }
    ICommand command = new PlayCardCommand(player, card);
    CommandInvoker.ExecuteCommand(command);
}
```

The CommandInvoker in Listing 7-7 is the component that actually executes commands, and keeps track of them in case we want to undo them. You can see a visual representation of it in Figure 7-4:

Listing 7-7. Example of a CommandInvoker responsible for executing and undoing commands

```
public class CommandInvoker
{
    static Stack<ICommand> undoStack = new Stack<ICommand>();
    static Stack<ICommand> redoStack = new Stack<ICommand>();

    // executes a command and saves it in the undo stack
```

```csharp
    public static void ExecuteCommand(ICommand command)
    {
        command.Execute();
        undoStack.Push(command);

        // clear out the redo stack if we make a new move
        redoStack.Clear();
    }

    public static void UndoCommand()
    {
        if (undoStack.Count > 0)
        {
            ICommand activeCommand = undoStack.Pop();
            redoStack.Push(activeCommand);
            activeCommand.Undo();
        }
    }

    public static void RedoCommand()
    {
        if (redoStack.Count > 0)
        {
            ICommand activeCommand = redoStack.Pop();
            undoStack.Push(activeCommand);
            activeCommand.Execute();
        }
    }
}
```

CHAPTER 7 COMMON MULTIPLAYER FEATURES

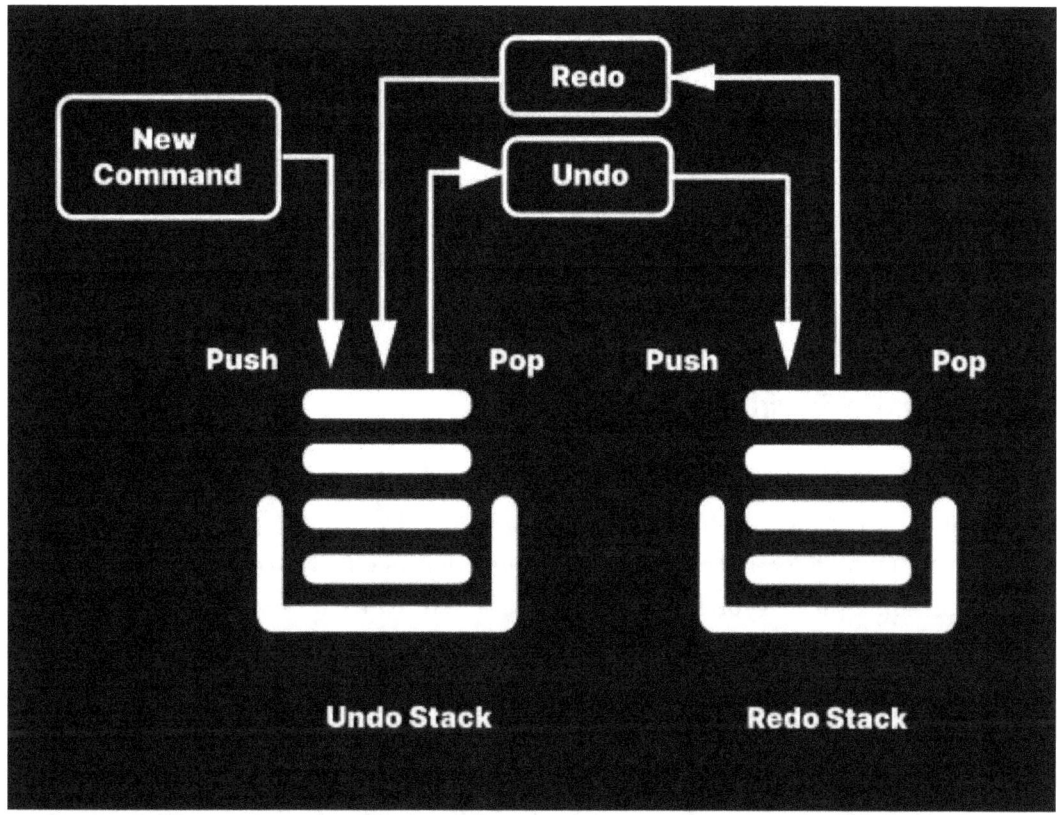

Figure 7-4. *CommandInvoker behavior overview. Source:* `https://
unity-connect-prd.storage.googleapis.com/20240301/learn/images/
b651c92b-96b4-4a68-ba35-02f32753fbf0_Copy_of_6-4_UndoRedoStacks.png`

Implementing replays with this pattern requires additional coding efforts but comes with many advantages:

- If all players know what commands were executed, replays can be viewed from any player's perspective.

- Replays can be stored as a series of commands (i.e., as a JSON in a text file), which takes way less storage space.

- Recording commands does not require high processing power, so there's no impact on the gameplay.

- The pace of the replay can be dynamically adjusted.

And some disadvantages:

- The game needs to be fully deterministic, which is not trivial for gameplay elements that rely on randomness.

- No retro-compatibility: if a game mechanic changes, the replay will use the new behavior of the mechanic when replaying. As a consequence, replays recorded before the change will show a different course of events than the one originally "recorded."[21]

Deterministic Randomness

Randomness is the natural nemesis of determinism, but we game developers learned how to tame it to produce deterministic replays: even if your gameplay has randomized parts (i.e., you have a "deal damage to a random enemy" effect), you can still achieve determinism in replays if you know how randomness works in the computer world.

Most algorithms that produce "random" results are in fact pseudo-random: they can create sequences of numbers or data that seem random but are generated by a deterministic algorithm.

Given that definition, it might sound like a generator of random numbers always gives the same results. So how is it possible that we actually get different results every time? The answer is: "seeding."

A "seed" is a piece of information used to initialize a pseudo-random generator. It's usually a number, and very often it's the current date and time (down to milliseconds) of the device: that's how running a generator always gives different results!

Knowing this, it's easy to figure out that if we always use the same seed, we can always generate numbers in the exact same order, achieving determinism.

As a consequence, storing the seed at the beginning of the match and saving it into the replay will ensure that our generator initializes in the same way as in the original match.

The next step is to ensure that the deterministic generator produces the same results across platforms, and is used by code that is exclusively under our control and uninfluenced by external systems: for example, Unity's built-in Random class can't be the core of your deterministic random numbers generator as it does not guarantee the same results, even given the same seed, across platforms, and as it is shared between multiple systems (i.e., the Particle System). Listing 7-8 provides the CrossPlatformRandom generator I use for Ariokan's replays.

Listing 7-8. CrossPlatformRandom C# implementation, based on the version published in 2014 by user Sean Colombo on Stackoverflow, which uses a Linear Congruential Generator. Source: **https://stackoverflow.com/a/23378151**

```
using System;
public class CrossPlatformRandom : Random
{
    //Use the same values as Borland Delphi, Visual Pascal, etc: http://
    en.wikipedia.org/wiki/Linear_congruential_generator#Parameters_in_
    common_use
    const int LCG_MULTIPLIER = 134775813; // 0x08088405 const int LCG_
    INCREMENT = 1;
    int _seed; public int Seed => _seed;

    /// <summary>
    /// Initializes a new instance of the CrossPlatformRandom class, using
    a time-dependent
    /// default seed value.
    /// Please note that values generated from this are NOT guaranteed to
    be the same
    /// cross-platform because there is no seed value. In cases where the
    caller requires
    /// predictable or repeatable results, they MUST specify the seed.
    /// </summary>
    public CrossPlatformRandom()
    {
        // System.Random is time-dependent, so we will just use its first
        number to generate
        // the seed.
        Random rand = new Random();
        this._seed = rand.Next();
    }

    /// <summary>
    /// Initializes a new instance of the System.Random class, using the
    specified seed value.
    /// </summary>
```

```csharp
/// <param name="seed">A number used to calculate a starting value for
the pseudo-random number sequence. If a negative number is specified,
the absolute value of the number is used.</param>
public CrossPlatformRandom(int seed)
{
    _seed = seed;
}

int GetNext() // note: returns negative numbers too
{
    _seed = (_seed * LCG_MULTIPLIER) + LCG_INCREMENT;
    return _seed;
}

/// <summary>
/// Returns a nonnegative random number.
/// </summary>
/// <returns>A 32-bit signed integer greater than or equal to zero and
less than System.Int32.MaxValue.</returns>
public override int Next()
{
    return this.Next(int.MaxValue);
}
```

```csharp
/// <summary>
/// Returns a nonnegative random number less than the specified
maximum.
/// </summary>
/// <param name="maxValue">The exclusive upper bound of the random
number to be generated. maxValue must be greater than or equal to
zero.</param>
/// <returns> A 32-bit signed integer greater than or equal to zero,
and less than maxValue; that is, the range of return values ordinarily
includes zero but not maxValue. However, if maxValue equals zero,
maxValue is returned.</returns>
/// <exception cref="System.ArgumentOutOfRangeException">maxValue is
less than zero.</exception>
```

```
public override int Next(int maxValue)
{
    if (maxValue < 0)
    {
        throw new System.ArgumentOutOfRangeException("maxValue is less
        than zero.");
    }

    ulong result = (ulong)(uint)GetNext() * (ulong)(uint)maxValue;
    return (int)(result >> 32);
}

/// <summary>
/// Returns a random number within a specified range.
/// </summary>
/// <param name="minValue">The inclusive lower bound of the random
number returned.</param>
/// <param name="maxValue">The exclusive upper bound of the
random number returned. maxValue must be greater than or equal to
minValue.</param>
/// <returns>A 32-bit signed integer greater than or equal to minValue
and less than maxValue; that is, the range of return values includes
minValue but not maxValue. If minValue equals maxValue, minValue is
returned.</returns>
/// <exception cref="System.ArgumentOutOfRangeException">minValue is
greater than maxValue.</exception>
public override int Next(int minValue, int maxValue)
{
    if (minValue > maxValue)
    {
        throw new System.ArgumentOutOfRangeException("minValue is
        greater than maxValue.");
    }

    return minValue + this.Next(maxValue - minValue);
}
```

```csharp
/// <summary>
/// Fills the elements of a specified array of bytes with random
numbers.
/// </summary>
/// <param name="buffer">An array of bytes to contain random
numbers.</param>
/// <exception cref="System.ArgumentNullException">buffer is null.</
exception>
public override void NextBytes(byte[] buffer)
{
    if (buffer == null)
    {
        throw new System.ArgumentNullException("buffer is null.");
    }

    for (int index = 0; index < buffer.Length; index++)
    {
        buffer[index] = (byte)this.Next((int)byte.MaxValue);
    }
}

/// <summary>
/// Returns a random number between 0.0 and 1.0.
/// </summary>
/// <returns>A double-precision floating point number greater than or
equal to 0.0, and less than 1.0.</returns>
public override double NextDouble()
{
    return this.Sample();
}

/// <summary>
/// Returns a random number between 0.0 and 1.0.
///
/// Since System.Random no longer uses this as the basis for all of the
other random methods,
```

```
/// this method isn't used widely by this class. It's here for
completeness, primarily in case Random
/// adds new entry points and we are lucky enough that they base them
on .Sample() or one of the other existing methods.
/// </summary>
/// <returns>A double-precision floating point number greater than or
equal to 0.0, and less than 1.0.</returns>
protected override double Sample()
{
    return ((double)this.Next() / (double)int.MaxValue);
}
}
```

Finally, it's important that you store the "min" and "max" values used as a range for the calculation of each random generation (i.e., lowest card id, highest card id), so that replays stay consistent even if these values are different in the current version of the game that is playing the replay. Once you have a file that contains all this information, all you need to do to rewatch a match is to start a "replayed" match, read the replay, set the seed, and execute each command, using the deterministic random generator when needed.

Spectator Mode

"Spectator mode" is a feature that allows players to watch somebody else's game, in realtime or with a delay, directly from the game.

Due to its nature, it's rare for casual games to implement a spectator mode. In competitive games, spectator mode can be implemented mainly in two ways: through direct connection, or delayed streaming.

Spectating Through Direct Connection

Spectating through direct connection allows players to watch a game in realtime by connecting as a special late joiner that doesn't have any gameplay influence, but receives network updates in realtime.

For example, you could connect as a third player to an in-progress 1v1 fighter game to watch what's happening in realtime, without being able to send any inputs over the network that would interfere with the game.

This technique is easy to implement (just put the late joiners in a "Spectator" team that is unable to send inputs and trigger gameplay actions) but comes with several issues:

- Scalability: spectators connect to the server where the match is running, so the server has to waste CPU power to maintain the connection and send updates to it. This limits the number of potential simultaneous spectators.

- Cheating: as you have access to the match, you can gather information about what is happening to provide an unfair advantage to yourself or one of the players, especially in games where "fog of war" exists (i.e., League of Legends). This is also called "stream sniping."

For these reasons, spectator mode is rarely implemented this way unless the game wants to support realtime coaching, and is instead implemented in the form of delayed streaming.

Spectating Through Delayed Streaming

Spectator mode through delayed streaming allows players to watch a game through a delayed replay, without connecting to the actual game server in realtime.

The way it works is that the game server sends the replay, in realtime, to a "streaming server" that relays it, with a delay, to whoever is spectating a specific match. Players then use the replay to simulate the match on their local device, without tampering with or influencing the actual match.

With this approach, the game server only has to maintain one extra connection (the one to the "streaming server"), as the streaming server is the one spectators connect to. Moreover, since the "streaming server" can send the replay data with a delay (usually a few minutes), it's much harder for spectators to cheat as what they see is outdated information.

The main problem of this approach lies in its requirements: your game needs to support replays, and therefore needs to be fully deterministic, and you need to be able to spin up a streaming server whenever someone wants to spectate a match.

Party Matchmaking

Many games let you join games with a party of friends, against random strangers. How is that possible? The answer is: "party matchmaking."

Party matchmaking is a feature that lets you matchmake as a group instead of individuals, giving all members of your group the information needed to connect to the same server, and in the right team. It can also be used to create custom 1v1 matches where you play against your friends.

To implement party matchmaking you need three core elements: a lobby, a matchmaker, and a party leader.

As explained in Chapter 4, a lobby is a system that allows players to form groups by inviting each other or by advertising the lobby itself so that players can join, and allows its members to share information. In the context of party matchmaking, the lobby lets the party leader:

1. Collect information about the party (i.e., what characters every person in the party is going to play, what game mode is going to be played).

2. Share information about the server the party needs to connect to.

As you can see in Figure 7-5, the party leader is just one of the players, and is the one responsible for creating the matchmaking ticket as a representative of the entire party, including information from other players.

Chapter 7 Common Multiplayer Features

Figure 7-5. *screenshot of League of Legends lobby. The party leader is identified by a crown icon (see green arrow), the game mode is circled in red, and characters selected by party members are circled in yellow*

Once the matchmaker finds a suitable match, the party can join on a specific server (identified by port and ip address), and the party leader receives this information and shares it with the rest of the party through the lobby.

At this point, all players know the ip address and port of the server they need to connect to, and can use direct connection to join the match.

A similar logic can be applied when creating custom games between friends such as in a 1v1 scenario: in that case, since the players are competing and need to end up in different teams without strangers, the party leader can queue up in a special 1-player queue which will immediately start a server for that player, and then they can share the server info through the lobby so the other player can join.

This ensures that no strangers are involved in the matchmaking process, so friends can play only with each other.

Conclusion

In this chapter, you learnt about the implementation details of advanced multiplayer-related features that many popular games implement nowadays. Now you know when it's worth investing in those features, and what the main challenges and considerations are to take into account before adding them to the roadmap of your project.

In the next chapter, you'll learn about user-generated content: a powerful, and game-changing, mechanic.

CHAPTER 8

User-Generated Content

"User-generated content" (a.k.a. "UGC") is a powerful feature that lets players autonomously add new content to your game, in order to increase the number of viable gameplay options, features and the longevity of the game.

In this chapter, you'll learn about the main advantages and challenges of implementing UGC in your game.

Why Is UGC Important?

The depth and longevity of most games are limited by the skillset and budget of the team behind the game: if a team can allocate only a certain amount of resources to the development and maintenance of a specific game, players will, eventually, exhaust the content of the game, and move on to play something else.

This is usually fine for single-player games (and small projects in general), as selling the game using a Premium model can be enough to turn it into a successful commercial project. However, for multiplayer games (especially LiveOps ones), having additional content that players can never get enough of is basically a requirement to sustain themselves, retain players, and increase their lifetime value. The problem with making gameplay content is that it is expensive: new game modes, items, and characters need to be designed, balanced, implemented, polished, and marketed.

UGC solves this problem by offloading most of that work to players, letting them create new content that others can have fun with, with little-to-no supervision from the development team.

CHAPTER 8   USER-GENERATED CONTENT

Empowering Players

Players are the greatest resource of a game developer, not only because they sustain the industry with their wallets, but also because they provide free feedback and are a great source of ideas (good and bad).

Even without technical knowledge, they can feel whether what they're playing is fun or not, and that feeling is usually way less biased compared to what the development team feels about a specific feature.

This gives them the ability to think outside the box, and try crazy ideas when given the chance. Games without UGC usually give this chance in the form of "builds," that is, in RPGs, that's a specific combination of weapons, stats, and abilities that makes players' characters specialized in "something." In card games, the build is the deck of cards you choose to play with.

This might give us the illusion that a build is UGC, but reality is that since we live in the age of the internet, when one player finds a particularly efficient/competitive build, they post it online and everybody else just copy-pastes it, effectively reducing the amount of "interesting" content to play as everybody sticks to what is the current "Meta" (= strongest build of the current patch). That's why even in games like *Clair Obscur: Expedition 33*, that allow deep build customization, most people end up playing the same overpowered builds that let you one-shot anything that dares to cross your character's path, or why competitive games like *League Of Legends* have dedicated websites where you can browse the builds of each champion, as you can see in Figure 8-1.

CHAPTER 8   USER-GENERATED CONTENT

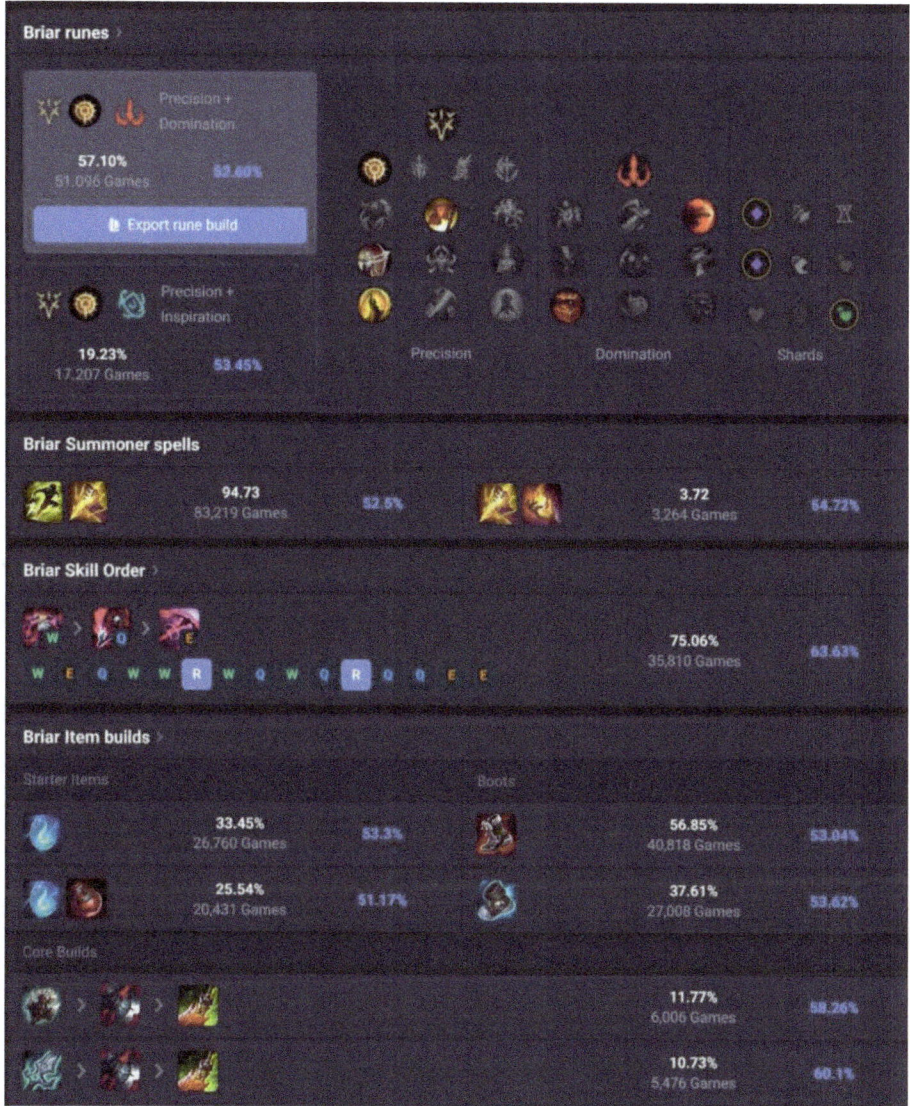

Figure 8-1. Screenshot of the recommended League of Legends build for the character "Briar," on "op.gg," as of patch 15.15

To unlock the true power of UGC, a game must have some feature that lets players autonomously invent and implement new gameplay and/or cosmetic content that doesn't already exist officially in the game.

Here are a few examples of how different games approach this in different ways:

CHAPTER 8   USER-GENERATED CONTENT

In *Minecraft*, players can invent new blocks by adding Java classes and textures to the game's code. These new files usually come as mods that can be added to the game client through a mod loader (i.e., *Forge*, *NeoForge,* and *Fabric*), as you can see in Figure 8-2. Once installed, these mods enhance or change core mechanics in a way that was not intended by the original developers.

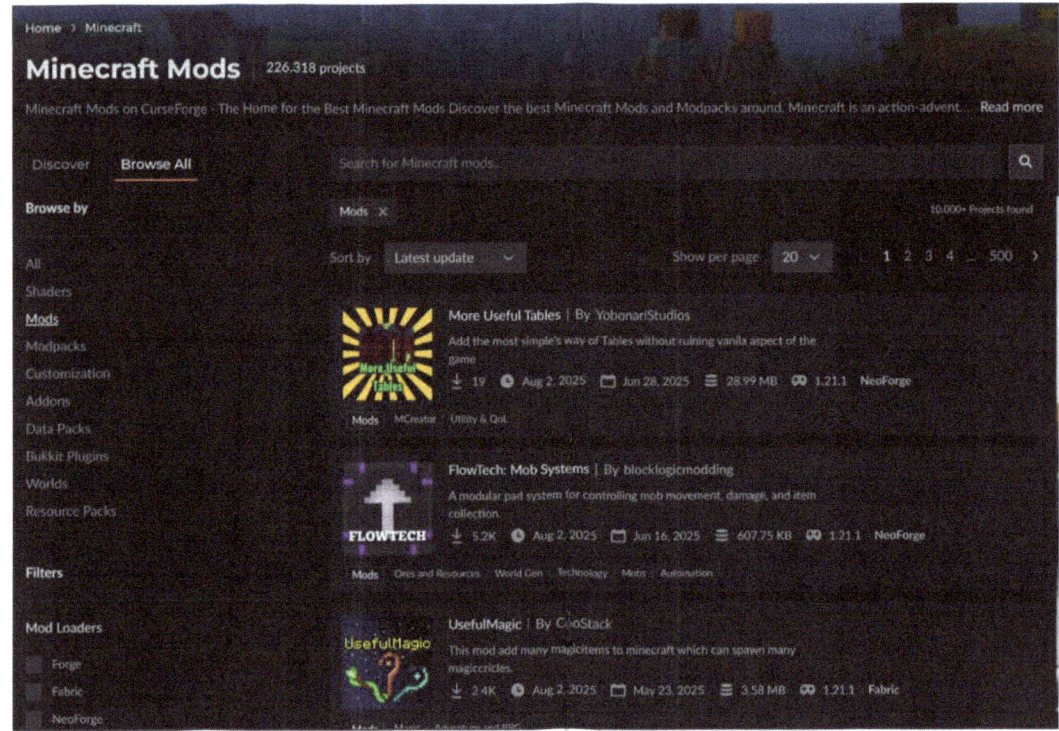

Figure 8-2. *Minecraft mods available on CurseForge.com, compatible with different mod loaders*

The game *Roblox* uses a different approach: there players can create and trade cosmetic items, and invent new game modes by using the official tool "Roblox Studio," which acts almost as a game engine, as you can see in Figure 8-3.

CHAPTER 8 USER-GENERATED CONTENT

Figure 8-3. *Roblox Studio, an official tool made by Roblox that lets you create new content for the game*

Even though both Minecraft and Roblox approaches require coding skills that the average player doesn't have, this didn't stop many from creating UGC on those games/platforms. However, there's one more approach that makes the creation of UGC accessible to anyone: in-game editors.

For example, in *Ariokan*™, players can use the in-game cards editor to invent new cards by combining stats, keywords, and effects, and by adding flavor content such as name, lore, and artwork, as you can see in Figure 8-4. This makes it way easier for the average user to contribute to the ever-growing library of cards that everyone can play, heavily increasing the amount of content players can generate.

195

Chapter 8　User-Generated Content

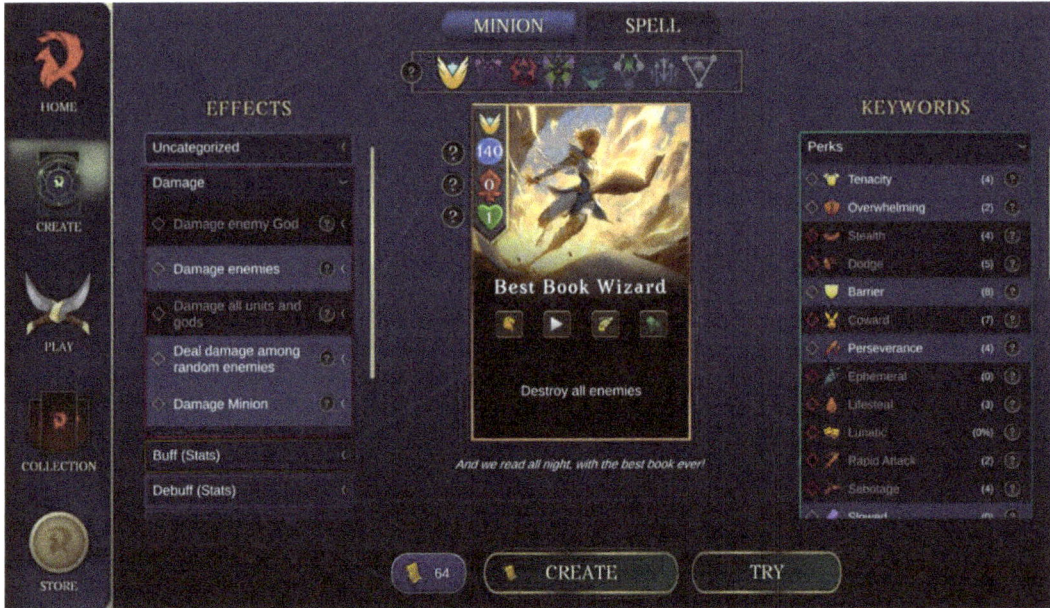

Figure 8-4. Ariokan's in-game cards editor, where players can create new unique cards at any time

Balancing UGC

A core component of every competitive multiplayer game is balancing. In a standard game with limited content, balancing is handled by the design team by looking at the interactions between the existing elements of the core game loop. When it comes to UGC, balancing needs to be taken to another level: as players create new content all the time, designers must create systems that keep both existing and future content balanced.

This might sound like an impossible task, but *Ariokan* proved it's possible to do that if you add:

1. Automatically enforced rules that limit what players can create

2. Mathematical formulas that determine the "value" of each combinable piece, in both simple and complex situations (i.e., when they're part of specific combinations)

This is easier said than done: it took our team several years of refinement to get to a point where players can make strong but fair decks that other players can deal with. For example, in the early versions of Ariokan players could add up to five effects and keywords to cards, and cards could cost 0. Since in Ariokan the play cost ("Mana") of a card is driven by the "positivity" of its combinable pieces, this allowed players to add multiple "negative" effects on a card (i.e., "sacrifice X points") to lower its play cost down to 0. With a deck full of 0-cost cards, you could play infinite cards in a turn as soon as your opponent ran out of Mana.

Eventually, we raised the minimum mana cost of each card to 15 (in a 100-base system), limited the number of effects a card can have, and ensured that every "negative" effect you put on a card to discount its cost will actually trigger when you play that card.

Assigning a mathematical formula to every piece of the equation is not difficult as long as you keep the assumptions consistent and avoid hardcoded values: if you decide that the value of "one card in hand" is "X Mana," then drawing three cards should cost at least "3X."

I say "at least" because there are multiple factors to consider, such as the fact that "drawing 3 cards" with a single card is way stronger than "drawing one card" three times using three different cards, because the former only require you to play one card instead of three to achieve the same result, as you can see in Figure 8-5.

CHAPTER 8   USER-GENERATED CONTENT

Figure 8-5. *Example of Mana cost curve in Ariokan. Notice how the Mana cost of the "Draw X cards" effect changes non-linearly depending on the amount of cards the player will draw. Drawing more cards with a single instance of this effect costs way more than drawing less cards with multiple instances*

If your game is complex, you might also want some pieces of the build to have a cost that scales based on another piece of the build, like in Figure 8-6. Keep in mind that every game is different; therefore, you need to adjust the values and calculations according to the specific mechanics of your core game loop.

CHAPTER 8   USER-GENERATED CONTENT

Figure 8-6. Example of Mana cost curve in Ariokan that scales on another part of the build. Notice how the Mana cost of the "Overwhelming" keyword changes depending on an external factor, such as the Power of the minion

Testing UGC

Another one of the main challenges when it comes to UGC, is testing. When content is limited, interactions between build elements, or even between entire builds, are predictable. However, when content is practically infinite, ensuring that existing and future content work as they should is very hard to predict.

That's why UGC-centric games rely heavily on automated tests to ensure that the several pieces of combinable content work both "in a vacuum" and in real gameplay scenarios. The least you can (and should) do to sleep better at night is to automatically check that the core game loop mechanics work as they should, and that the rules that define what content can be generated are enforced properly. If you're working in Unity, you can do this through the Unity Test Runner and its related package.

199

CHAPTER 8   USER-GENERATED CONTENT

As you can see in Figure 8-7, in Ariokan, we have 530+ automated tests that run in Host mode, and yet sometimes bugs show up. If we had to test features only manually, we'd waste an incredible amount of time.

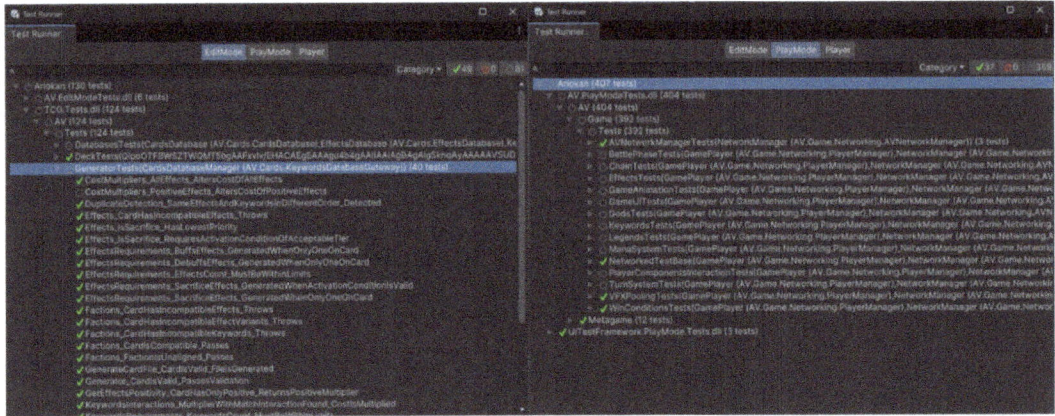

Figure 8-7. *Ariokan's automated tests for both Edit mode and Play mode. Edit mode tests validate the project's integrity and UGC creation rules; Play mode tests validate the core game loop*

Moderation

If your game lets players create content, you can be 100% sure that some of them will end up creating offensive, not safe for work ("NSFW"), and illegal content, either on purpose or by mistake. That's why every UGC game that wants to create and maintain a safe space for its players must have proper moderation mechanisms, both manual and automatic, that keep the UGC in line with the community guidelines.

This section guides you through the most common use cases of UGC moderation and gives you practical tips on how to detect and deal with the different types of unwanted content that might appear in your UGC-based game.

Not Safe for Work ("NSFW")

At the Game Developers Conference ("GDC") of 2009, the talk "Spore's Wake: What Seriously Happened?" introduced a now industry-wide metric called "time to penis" ("TTP"), which measures how much time it takes for a player to create a penis using in-game tools.

CHAPTER 8 USER-GENERATED CONTENT

This might sound like a joke metric, but it's actually one of the most important metrics to keep track of if you're making a UGC game. Unless your game supports NSFW content, you should aim for a TTP = infinite time (= not possible).

Some players like to have sexually explicit content in their game: genitals and nudes are one of the first pieces of content that show up and proliferate in unmoderated UGC-based games. And it's not only about pornographic material: it's also about extremely gore images, like the ones that depict heavily injured people or organs.

This is not a problem if your game targets the NSFW market, but it becomes one if you're targeting a standard consumer market where people don't want to see this type of material.

Luckily, nowadays there are tools that can detect this type of content and will help you reject it when they detect it.

For example, you can use Google's Vision API to detect, on a cloud function running server-side, if an image is pornographic or medical, using the snippet in Listing 8-1.

Listing 8-1. Example of C# cloud function that uses Google Cloud Vision API to moderate images uploaded by players

```
using Google.Cloud.Vision.V1;
async Task<bool> ImageContentIsSafe(Stream bytes)
{
    Image image = Image.FromStream(bytes);
    var clientBuilder = new ImageAnnotatorClientBuilder();
    //some metod to get your API credentials
    clientBuilder.JsonCredentials = await Helpers.
    GetGoogleVisionCredentialsAsync();
    ImageAnnotatorClient client = clientBuilder.Build();
    SafeSearchAnnotation annotation = client.DetectSafeSearch(image);

    // Each category is classified as Very Unlikely, Unlikely, Possible,
    Likely or Very Likely.
    return annotation.Adult != Likelihood.VeryLikely //porn?
    && annotation.Medical < Likelihood.Likely; //surgery,etc?
}
```

CHAPTER 8   USER-GENERATED CONTENT

Offensive Content

Apart from colorful images, some players tend to create racist, offensive, or political UGC content that might hurt other player's feelings or push a political agenda, breaking the suspension of disbelief that makes players happy while they're focused on the game.

Since most of this offensive content comes in the form of text (i.e., the name or lore of a card), it can be easily detected by dedicated tools and plugins that can be integrated in your project (i.e., *Bad Word Filter PRO*, if you're using Unity). These tools use a combination of regular expressions and pre-compiled databases of swear words to detect most "offensive expressions," even when they're written in the most creative ways. Since these tools automatically check words across multiple languages, it's possible to come across "false positives" (words detected as "offensive," which are not), but it's better to be safe first and add exceptions later through manual intervention, than allowing offensive content by default in the first place. Adding such plugins directly to your game client will help you provide immediate feedback whenever players mistakenly add offensive text to the content they're making, as you can see in Figure 8-8. Whether you add the checks on the client-side or not, always remember to add them on the server-side too if you want to be 100% sure to block offensive content.

CHAPTER 8 USER-GENERATED CONTENT

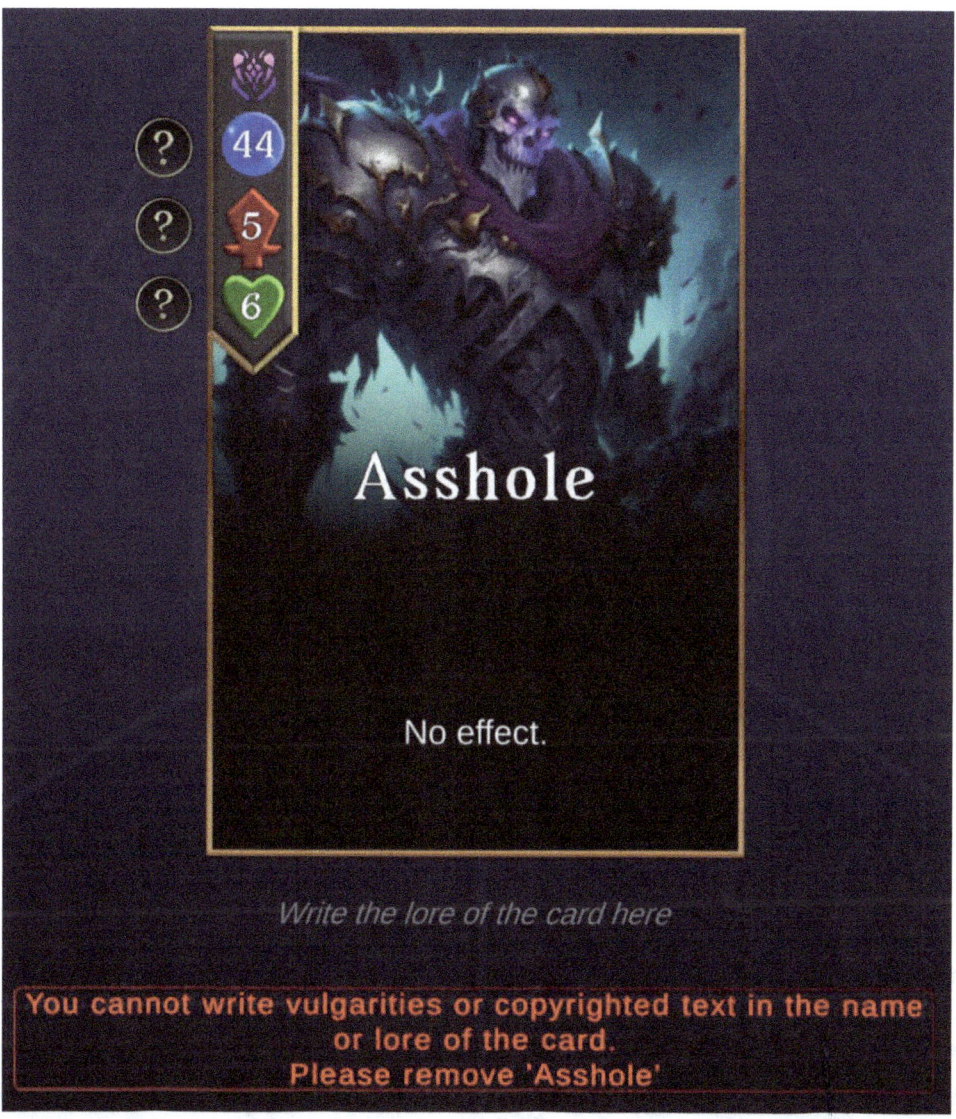

Figure 8-8. *Client-sided offensive content detection system that notifies the player. The error message helps avoid confusion about what term might be the offensive one in long sentences*

Political content is harder to track and usually requires some manual checking from the content moderators. To help your players flag political content they would not like to see in the game, you should implement an in-game reporting system that lets players flag individual pieces of content.

203

CHAPTER 8   USER-GENERATED CONTENT

Copyrighted Content

Pretty much all UGC platforms and games face the problem of players uploading copyrighted content, either as a form of unauthorized advertising or because they want to "import" their favorite characters from other games and intellectual properties.

Unfortunately, this can put your game (and entire business) at risk, since in most countries the platform holder (you) is responsible for the content that players upload. Luckily, you can protect yourself from a legal standpoint in at least two ways:

1. By making players accept Terms of Service ("ToS") in which they take responsibility for the content they upload.[22]

2. By promptly removing or altering copyrighted material as soon as you detect it or it is flagged to you.

To prevent players from uploading copyrighted content, you can limit their possibility to add "unpredictable" content. For example, you can remove the possibility to upload images from their device, and let them pre-select images from a list of curated and safe artworks instead. However, this will heavily limit the variety of the content.

Nowadays, a good compromise is to allow players to upload content from their device, warning them about the risks of uploading copyrighted material, and offering the option to dynamically generate content within the game through artificial intelligence, as you can see in Figure 8-9, as at the time of writing, the output of generative artificial intelligence is not copyrightable.

Figure 8-9. Example of artwork generation/upload popup

UGC Content at Scale

A major challenge related to UGC is the need to retrieve and distribute the content in realtime at a global scale, and at the right time.

Not doing that can cause several issues, such as players stumbling upon somebody else's content that their game instance does not know about.

Storage and Delivery

When you install a non-UGC-centric and non-LiveOps game, you get all the content of the application directly on your device: there's no need to download new content, because all the content is already there. LiveOps games break this paradigm a bit with frequent "over the air" updates: new events, external links, and daily quests are not pre-installed and are retrieved dynamically from some remote server owned by the gaming studio. UGC-centric games bring this to another level entirely: as players continuously create new content, most of the content is not pre-installed, and needs to be downloaded while the game is running.

That's why two core components of UGC-centric games are the cloud storage and the delivery mechanism.

The cloud storage is usually made up of three parts:

1. An indexed database that stores the non-binary data of the UGC (i.e., names, keywords, effects, stats, author, ID)

2. A storage server that stores the binary data of the UGC (i.e., images), which databases usually do not handle in a performant way

3. (Optional) a Content Delivery Network service capable of caching and distributing the content fast regardless of the end user's location

As concerns the delivery mechanism, whenever a client wants to retrieve data from the storage, they can either do it with a direct request or through a cloud function running in the game's backend services. Once the client retrieves the information, usually in the form of JSON + binary files, if the UGC data is immutable (= cannot be changed after creation), the client can cache it so it doesn't have to ask the same info again the next time.

CHAPTER 8   USER-GENERATED CONTENT

Note   for moderation purposes, only the game's backend services should be able to write data into the cloud storage, while all game clients should be able to read from it directly.

Services like *Epic Title Storage, Unity Cloud Content Delivery, Unity Cloud Code* and *Unity Cloud Save, Steam Workshop* (Figure 8-10) let you implement both the cloud storage and the delivery mechanism without having to worry about scalability.

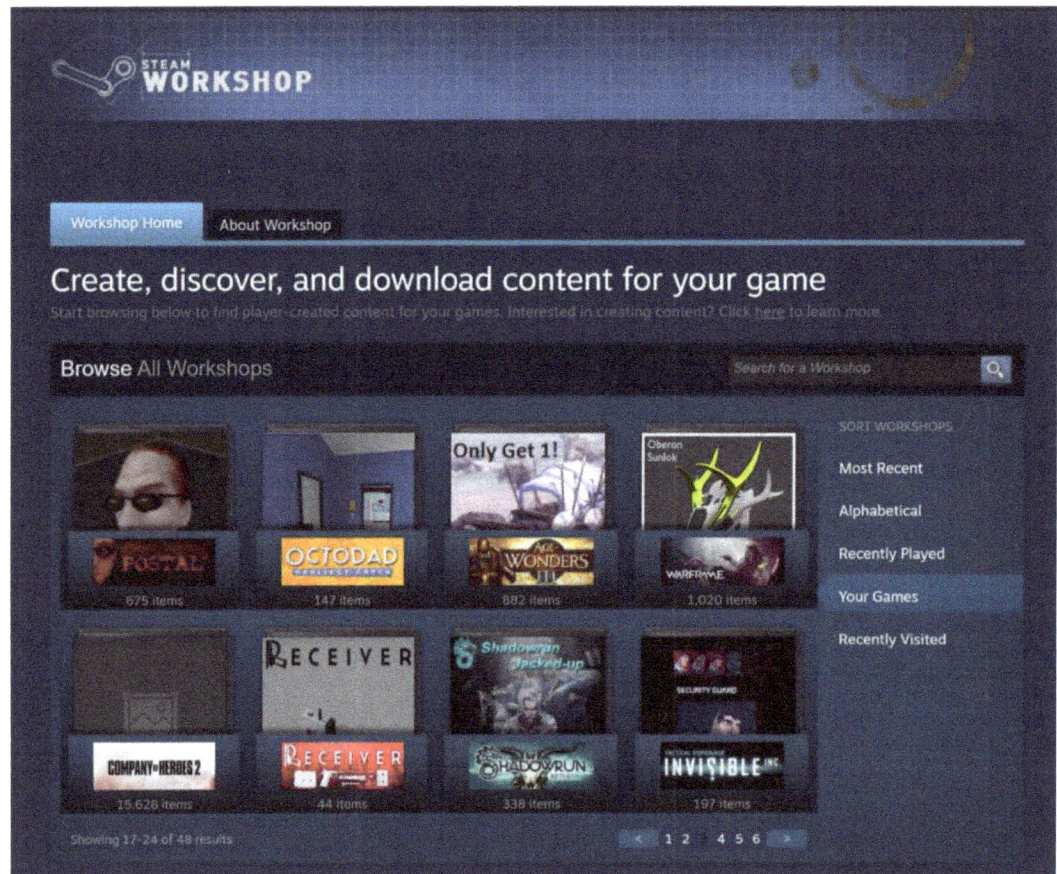

Figure 8-10. The Steam workshop, which lets players publish and download UGC through Steam

Tip   Bundling UGC directly in the game's build whenever you make a new patch will lower the amount of requests needed to the services.

Synchronizing Local and Global Content

What happens if in a UGC-based card game like Ariokan, player "A" gets matched with player "B," who is playing a new card they just created and that player A's client knows nothing about?

As you can imagine, the answer is "probably something bad": crashes or unintended behaviors that will ruin the involved players' experience.

That's why every UGC-based game needs to identify some moments in which to synchronize the content they "know about" with the new content available online and with which they might stumble upon. These "content synchronization moments" don't need to happen all the time: a game client that is not actively interacting with content doesn't need to waste their own and the server's resources to download new content that might have been released. A good rule of thumb is to download new content in these situations:

- At login time
- When creating new content, so you can check for duplicates
- When interacting with content, that is, when making a new character build/deck, or when navigating screens that let you search/filter content
- When starting a match against other players, since they might have new content in their build

Note Remember that if you have dedicated servers, they'll also need to download new content when initializing a match between players.

Conclusion

User-generated content is a powerful feature that can hugely expand the longevity of a game and player engagement, but comes with a few, non-trivial, and often game-specific challenges you need to think of ahead of time. However, when done right, it can make the difference between a limited experience and an endless world of possibilities.

Epilogue

Wow, you finished the book! Now it's a good time to think about your next steps: What are you going to change or integrate into your current project, based on what you read? If you came across something that made you say "maybe I should do this", now it's probably the time to go and do it (or at least discuss it with your teammates and business partners).

It could also be that you realized that going multiplayer is not as easy as it may sound, and you might be tempted to do another type of game instead.

And you know what? That'd be ok too. As Pokémon's Professor Oak always used to say: *"There's a time and place for everything."*

Regardless of what you decide to do, I hope that this book helped you understand what it takes to design, make, ship, and maintain multiplayer games and that you can use this knowledge to plan your next (or current) project a bit better.

And while this book ends here, your journey starts now. If you need help along the way, or simply want to have a chat, feel free to reach out to me ("Paolo Abela") on whatever social media exists nowadays (is LinkedIn still a thing?).

Index

A

Analytics frameworks, 117
ARPDU, *see* Average revenue per daily active user (ARPDU)
Authority models
    client-authoritative model, 44, 45
    distributed authority, 45, 46
    selection, 47
    server-authoritative model, 42, 43
    types, 42
    use cases, 47
Average revenue per daily active user (ARPDU), 124

B

Backend services, 4, 7–9, 14, 15, 48, 205, 206
Bots, 163
    credible, 170
    latency, 163
    players' actions, 164, 165
    remote players, 170
    skill levels, 165
        barebone structure, 165–167
        easy/hard, 165
        ELO score, 165
        heuristics, 167
        machine learning, 167
        test, 165
        Utility AI, 167–169

C

CAC, *see* Customer acquisition cost (CAC)
CAC recovery time (CACRT), 124, 137, 138
CACRT, *see* CAC recovery time (CACRT)
CIDR, *see* Classless Inter-Domain Routing (CIDR)
Classless Inter-Domain Routing (CIDR), 22, 24
Client, 34–37, 42, 43, 45, 46, 51–55, 58, 59, 62, 65–68, 75, 76, 83, 85–88, 94–96, 99–101, 104, 105, 108, 114, 152, 157, 158, 171, 174, 205, 207
Client-authoritative model, 44–47
Client authority, 67
Client–server architecture, 36, 37
Client-side prediction (CSP), 65–67
Code caves, 111, 112
Code obfuscation, 112, 113
Code patching, 110, 111
Communication
    definition, 15
    elements, 15, 16
    encoding, 17
    human, 16
    machines, 18
    protocol, 17
    symbols/words, 17
Communication frameworks, 18
    OSI model, 18, 19
    TCP/IP, 20, 21
Compiler, 110

INDEX

Connecting players
    LAN multiplayer, 81, 82
        direct connection, 82–84
        network discovery, 84, 85
    local multiplayer, 79–81
    online multiplayer, 85
        dedicated servers, 85
        latency, 85
        NAT, 87, 88
        port forwarding, 85
        relay servers, 86, 87
    remote players
        lobby, 90, 91
        matchmaker, 88–90
Cost to serve (C2S), 124, 125, 128, 147, 161
CSP, *see* Client-side prediction (CSP)
C2S, *see* Cost to serve (C2S)
Customer acquisition cost (CAC), 121, 124

D, E

Demo, 137, 140, 141
Deterministic lockstep, 67
    advantage, 68
    considerations, 72
    delay-based lockstep, 68, 69
    issue, 68
    limitations, 72
    rollback-based lockstep, 69, 70
        prediction, 70, 71
    wombo-combo, 71, 72
DHCP, *see* Dynamic Host Configuration Protocol (DHCP)
Digital marketplaces, 142–145, 147
Direct to consumer (D2C), 141, 144
Distribution, 141
    D2C, 144
    digital, 142, 143
    physical, 142
DLC, *see* Downloadable content (DLC)
Downloadable content (DLC), 11, 125, 126, 147
D2C, *see* Direct to consumer (D2C)
Dynamic Host Configuration Protocol (DHCP), 26

F

Fear of missing out (FOMO), 115, 137, 146
FIFO, *see* First In, First Out (FIFO)
First In, First Out (FIFO), 57
FOMO, *see* Fear of missing out (FOMO)

G

GaaS, *see* Games as a Service (GaaS)
Game Developers Conference (GDC), 200
Games
    Ariokan, 55, 95, 195–197
    core game loop, 1
    developers, 19, 30
    development, 39
    digital, 91
    F2P, 121
    League Of Legends, 192, 193
    lifecycle, 9, 10
    Minecraft, 194
    physics-based, 3
    Player *vs.* Players (PvP) modes, 40
    post-apocalyptic
        survival game, 40
    publisher/team, 40
    Roblox, 194, 195
    single-player games (*see* Single-player games)

Games as a Service (GaaS), 11, 115
Game state and events,
    synchronization, 51
    networked variables (*see* Networked
        variables)
    network messages, 61, 62
    network tick rate, 51, 52
    object, 51
    RPCs, 58, 59, 61
GDC, *see* Game Developers
    Conference (GDC)

H

Hackers, 86, 95, 108, 109, 111, 113
Hole punching, 87
Hosts, 18, 19, 22–27, 29, 30, 34–36, 38
HTTPS, *see* Hypertext Transfer Protocol
    Secure (HTTPS)
Hypertext Transfer Protocol Secure
    (HTTPS), 21, 28, 29

I, J, K

IETF, *see* Internet Engineering Task
    Force (IETF)
Internet Engineering Task Force (IETF), 25
Internet Protocol Address (IP Address)
    definition, 22, 38
    ipconfig command, 23, 24
    IPv6, 24
    NAT, 25, 26
    network interface, 24
    network *vs.* host, 22
    private, 25
    public, 24
    reserved, 26
    troubleshooting, 23
    versions, 22
Internet Service Provider (ISPs), 24
IP Address, *see* Internet Protocol Address
    (IP Address)
ISPs, *see* Internet Service Provider (ISPs)

L

Lag compensation techniques
    client authority, 67
    CSP, 65–67
    deterministic lockstep (*see*
        Deterministic lockstep)
LANs, *see* Local area networks (LANs)
Last In, First Out (LIFO), 57
Lifetime value (LTV), 124, 125, 128
LIFO, *see* Last In, First Out (LIFO)
Live service games, 115
    game analytics
        F2P, 121
        matchEnded event, 117, 118
        Onboarding flow analytics funnel,
            Ariokan, 120, 121
        profitability, 121
        questions, 118–120
    mobile, 115
    monetization, 115
    player, 115
    remote configuration, 116
        dashboard, 116
        feature flag, 116, 117
        implementation, 116
        OTA update, 117
Lobby, 77, 90, 91, 187, 188
Local area networks (LANs), 27, 28, 52,
    81–83, 85, 86
LTV, *see* Lifetime value (LTV)

M

Machine learning, 167
Man-In-The-Middle (MITM), 104, 105
Massively Multiplayer Online (MMO), 2, 137
Matchmaker, 88–91, 187, 188
Matchmaking systems, 171
Memory scrambling technique, 108
Meta-configuration files, 76–78
Metagame, 4, 6–8, 14, 120
MITM, *see* Man-In-The-Middle (MITM)
MMO, *see* Massively Multiplayer Online (MMO)
MOBA, *see* Multiplayer online battle arena (MOBA)
Mobile games, 116, 136
Moderation
    copyrighted content, 204
    NSFW, 201
    offensive contenet, 202, 203
    political content, 203
Monetization, 115, 123–147
Multiplayer-centric, 40
Multiplayer codebases
    prefixes, 62, 63
    role-specific code, 63, 64
Multiplayer games, 114
    add-on, 39
    async, 41
    backend services, 7–9
    chess, 1
    client-server architecture, 36
    core game loop, 4, 5
    definition, 1
    developers, 115
    lifecycle, 11, 12
    limitations
        fast-paced player movement, 2
        physics-based interactions, 3
        time manipulation, 3
    metagame, 6
    playtesting, 13, 14
    vs. single-player games, 1, 2
    sync multiplayer, 41
Multiplayer online battle arena (MOBA), 4, 42

N

NAT, *see* Network address translation (NAT)
Netcode frameworks, 48, 157, 171
    documentation, 48
    existing *vs.* custom netcode frameworks, 51
    factors, picking, 49, 50
    first-person shooter, 48, 49
    game state and events, synchronization (*see* Game state and events, synchronization)
    local multiplayer, 81
    network discovery, 85
    selection, 48
Netcode rollback, 69, 72, 73
Network address translation (NAT), 24–27, 29, 45, 85, 87, 88
Network architecture
    client, 35
    client–server architecture, 36
    P2P architecture, 37
    server, 35
Network discovery, 82, 84, 85
Networked variables, 53
    authority mechanism, 53
    callback mechanism, 53, 54

custom serializers, 55–57
data types, 55
join mechanism, auto-sync, 54
and RPCs, 59
Network messages, 51, 61, 62
Network tick rate, 51, 52, 65, 154
Non-playing characters (NPCs), 2, 4, 50, 51, 68
NPCs, *see* Non-playing characters (NPCs)

O

Open Systems Interconnection (OSI) model, 18, 19, 38
Optimization, 48, 149, 150, 152, 157, 161
Optimizing servers
client-only scene objects, 153
data type, 156
delta updates, 161
framerate, 154
headless mode, 155
media files, 151, 152
operating system, 150, 151
store data, 159, 160
synchronization, 157
chess, 157, 158
particle systems, 157
standard approach, 158, 159
UI, 158
user experience, 158
VFX and media, 157

P

Party matchmaking, 91, 187, 188
Peer-to-peer architecture (P2P), 37
Playtesting
definition, 12

host mode, 76
meta-configuration files, 76–78
multiplayer games, 13, 14
multiple instances of game, 73, 75
single-player games, 12, 13
Ports, 28
forwarding, 85
numbers, 28, 29
Pricing
discounts, 146, 147
factors, 144
regional, 145, 146
studio's track record, 144
P2P, *see* Peer-to-peer architecture (P2P)

Q

Quality-of-Service (QoS), 19

R

RAM, *see* Random access memory (RAM)
Random access memory (RAM), 35, 72, 105, 106, 149–153, 156, 157, 159
Reconnection, 171
implementation, 171
late joiners, 171
player characters, restoring, 173
synchronization, 171–173
Remote procedure calls (RPCs), 51, 58–61, 66, 67, 76, 104, 113, 163, 164, 173
Replays, 174
recorded, 174
simulated, 174
advantages, 179
CommandInvoker, 177, 178
command object, 177
command pattern, 175

INDEX

Replays (*cont.*)
    CrossPlatformRandom generator, 180–183, 185
    deterministic randomness, 180, 185
    disadvantages, 180
    ICommand interface, 175–177
Request for Comments (RFC), 24, 25
Revenue models, 123
    differences between models, 140
    Freemium, 136
    free-to-play (F2P), 128
        advantages, 126
        disadvantages, 126
        Overknights, 127
        PC/Console, 128
        UA, 127
        videogames, 127
    in-app purchases (IAP), 128
        advertising network, 136
        boosters, 130–132
        cosmetics, 129, 130
        Gacha games, 134, 135
        loot boxes, 134
        partial drop rate table, *Morimens*, 135
        premium currency, 128, 129
        seasonal passes, 133
    licensing, 138
    monetization-related terms, 123, 124
    premium, 124, 125
        DLC, 125, 126
    secondary markets, 139
    subscription, 137
RFC, *see* Request for Comments (RFC)
Role-playing game (RPG), 1, 4, 5, 192
Round-Trip Time (RTT), 27, 65, 68, 69, 87
Routing, 26, 27, 85

RPCs, *see* Remote procedure calls (RPCs)
RPG, *see* Role-playing game (RPG)
RTT, *see* Round-Trip Time (RTT)

S

Securing network communications, 104, 105
Security and anti-cheating strategies
    black-hat hacker, 92
    cheaters, 92
        categories, 92
        competitive games, 92
        detection, 114
        game development, 93
        local cheats, 94, 95
        state-changing cheats, 95
        vulnerable games, 93
    memory locations
        calculation, 107, 108
        client-authoritative, 108
        health manager, 108
        memory layout, 108
        memory scrambling, 108
        projected properties, 109
        scan, 106, 107
        techniques, 109
        tools, 106
    network communications, 104, 105
    protecting code
        code caves, 111, 112
        code obfuscation, 112, 113
        code patching, 110, 111
        secrets, 113, 114
        separating assemblies, 113
    RAM, 105
    server-authoritative gameplay
        competitive setting, 104

data, 100
elements, 99
environment, 96
HealthManager, 99, 101, 102, 104
implementation, 96–99
interaction, 100, 101
OnTriggerEnter method, 101
rule, 96
server, 104
Server, 35
dedicated, 85
density, 150
relay, 86, 87
Server-authoritative model, 42, 43
Simple Network Management Protocol (SNMP), 84
Single-player games
backend services, 7
core game loop, 5
definition, 1
lifecycle, 10, 11
vs. multiplayer games, 1, 2
playtesting, 12, 13
Premium revenue model, 10, 11
Solitaire, 1
studio, 39
SNMP, *see* Simple Network Management Protocol (SNMP)
Socket, 29–31
Spectator mode, 185
delayed streaming, 186
direct connection, 185, 186
SYN, *see* Synchronization message (SYN)
SYN-ACK, *see* SYN message with an acknowledgement (SYN-ACK)
Synchronization, 38, 48, 51, 52, 65, 75, 76, 78, 82, 157
Synchronization message (SYN), 30, 32
SYN message with an acknowledgement (SYN-ACK), 30

T

TCP, *see* Transmission Control Protocol (TCP)
Time to live (TTL), 27
Time to penis (TTP), 200, 201
TLS, *see* Transport Layer Security (TLS)
Transmission Control Protocol/Internet Protocol (TCP/IP) model, 18, 20, 21, 26, 38
Transmission Control Protocol (TCP), 29–33
Transport Layer Security (TLS), 21
Transport protocols
TCP, 30–33
UDP, 30, 33, 34
TTL, *see* Time to live (TTL)
TTP, *see* Time to penis (TTP)

U

UA, *see* User acquisition (UA)
UDP, *see* User Datagram Protocol (UDP)
UGC, *see* User-generated content (UGC)
User acquisition (UA), 124
User Datagram Protocol (UDP), 29, 30, 33, 34
User-generated content (UGC), 191, 207
balancing, 196–198
content at scale, 205
delivery, 205, 206
local/global content, synchronization, 207
storage, 205, 206
games, 192

INDEX

User-generated content (UGC) (*cont.*)
    importance, 191
    moderation (*see* Moderation)
    players, 192
        Ariokan, 195, 196
        League Of Legends, 192, 193
    Minecraft, 194, 195
    Roblox, 194, 195
    testing, 199, 200

V, W, X, Y, Z

Videogames, 127

GPSR Compliance

The European Union's (EU) General Product Safety Regulation (GPSR) is a set of rules that requires consumer products to be safe and our obligations to ensure this.

If you have any concerns about our products, you can contact us on

ProductSafety@springernature.com

In case Publisher is established outside the EU, the EU authorized representative is:

Springer Nature Customer Service Center GmbH
Europaplatz 3
69115 Heidelberg, Germany

www.ingramcontent.com/pod-product-compliance
Lightning Source LLC
LaVergne TN
LVHW081450060526
838201LV00050BA/1753